The Political Economy of Desire

In this thought-provoking analysis of the genealogy of western capitalist 'development', *The Political Economy of Desire* departs from the common position that development and underdevelopment are conceptual outcomes of the Imperialist era. Instead, it positions the genealogy of development within early Christian writings in which the western theological concepts of sin, salvation, and redemption are expounded. Linking the writings of early theologians, such as Augustine and Anselm, to the processes of modern identity formation – of which phenomena such as the West, the First World, the Rule of Law and the individual subject and his or her freedoms are but a part – the concept of development is thus traced to a particularly Christian dynamic. As such, the promise of development is considered as analogous to the way in which the Word of God was used to call Christianity into being, with the promise of salvation. *The Political Economy of Desire* then goes on to consider how this promise continues to influence western ontology: as the capacity of development discourse to maintain the identity of the West – in generating 'knowledge' of the underdeveloped world as a fixed reality which is at once an 'Other' and yet entirely predictable and observable – is traced to a spiritual and doctrinal adaptability according to which it is able to remain an effective conqueror of souls and minds.

Drawing upon legal theory, anthropology, economics, historiography, philosophy of science, theology, feminism, cultural studies and development studies, this book contains the best of interdisciplinary work in international law.

Jennifer Beard, BA (Hons), LLB (Hons), LLM, PhD, is a senior lecturer in the Law School of the University of Melbourne. She is Co-Director of the Law and Development Programme for the Institute for International Law and the Humanities, as well as a barrister of the Victorian Bar, Victoria.

The Political Economy of Desire

International law, development and the nation state

Jennifer L. Beard

With a Foreword by Anne Orford

Routledge·Cavendish
Taylor & Francis Group

a GlassHouse book

First published 2007 by Routledge-Cavendish
2 Park Square, Milton Park, Abingdon, Oxon OX14 4RN

Simultaneously published in the USA and Canada
by Routledge
270 Madison Ave, New York, NY 10016

A Glasshouse book

*Routledge-Cavendish is an imprint of the Taylor & Francis Group, an
informa business*

© 2007 Jennifer L. Beard

Typeset in Times New Roman by
RefineCatch Limited, Bungay, Suffolk
Printed and bound in Great Britain by
MPG Books Ltd, Bodmin, Cornwall

British Library Cataloguing in Publication Data
A catalogue record for this book is available from the British Library

Library of Congress Cataloging in Publication Data
Beard, Jennifer.
    The political economy of desire : international law, development
and the nation state / Jennifer Beard.
       p. cm.
    ISBN 1–904385–35–4 (hardback) — ISBN 0–415–42000–8
(pbk.)   1. International law—Philosophy.   2. Postcolonialism.
3. Law and economic development.   I. Title.
KZ3410.B42 2006
341—dc22
                                                    2006021367

ISBN10: 0–415–42000–8 (pbk)
ISBN10: 1–904385–35–4 (hbk)

ISBN13: 978–0–415–42000–6 (pbk)
ISBN13: 978–1–904385–35–6 (hbk)

For Roberta Evelyn Beard, whose courage and non-judgemental generosity have enabled me to live a life of security and possibility

Contents

Foreword

This exciting and innovative book challenges conventional ways of engaging with the concept, practice and institutions of development. The discourses that international professionals have produced in this field have tended to be sociological, economic, functional and instrumental. In conventional terms, underdevelopment is seen as a problem to be solved, with more or less attention paid along the way to those who lose out in the resulting distribution of costs and benefits, and with more or less attention paid to questions of human rights, sustainability or the protection of biodiversity. Critics of the central premises of this field of international legal practice have argued that development professionals do not act upon an already existing world divided into developed and developing countries, but instead that 'development, the problem' is produced in and through these professional practices. This tradition of critical scholarship has argued that the roots of the modern development enterprise lie in the challenges posed to classical imperialism in the twentieth century. In an era of decolonisation characterised by the commitment to formal independence of colonised states in Asia, Africa and Latin America, the institutions and doctrines of development emerged to guarantee continued foreign management and control over the inhabitants of newly independent territories, and access to their labour and resources.

In *The Political Economy of Desire*, Jennifer Beard separates us from these ways of knowing, thinking and writing about development. Dr Beard rejects the notion that the division of the world into developed and underdeveloped is an outcome of the Imperial era. She offers instead a genealogy of development discourse commencing with the early Christian history of the West. For Dr Beard, the forms of discipline and subjectification found in contemporary development discourse have their precursors in the emergence of a particular form of Christian subjectivity during the early centuries of Christian practice. In the early chapters of the book, she traces the emergence of a distinctively Christian form of subjectivity based on concepts of sin, debt, faith and salvation, and determined by disciplinary practices of public penance (the marking out of the outsider) and private confession (training in self-discipline). Dr Beard shows that these practices, shaped by events such as the discovery of the New World and the Reformation in Europe, continue to constitute and discipline the subjects of development. She develops this argument through a close reading of texts written during the period of discovery of the New World, such as those of the Christian explorers Christopher Columbus and the scholars Jean Bodin and Hugo Grotius, and through an analysis of the works of those such as Francis Bacon and John Locke who fantasised about the construction of the sovereign state out of the savage origins of the New World. Her reading of the Peace of Westphalia and of the work of later nineteenth century scholars shows that a division of the world into civilised, barbaric and savage realms worked to maintain the sense of self of those who imagined themselves within the 'good and faithful Neighbourhood' of Europe. In the final chapter, Dr Beard traces the contours of this relationship between the saved and the damned through to the modern period in the literature of law and development and the practice of economic, political and legal restructuring of nations named as underdeveloped.

In addition to its substantive contribution, the book also represents an important methodological innovation in legal engagement with the development enterprise. Dr Beard resists the contemporary consensus that positivist social science method represents the appropriate mode of analysis in this field. Instead, this book successfully integrates international legal scholarship with contemporary developments in social and political theory. In particular, while there has been much recent attention in law and the humanities given to the notion of political theology, Beard here provides a compelling history of ideas in support of the notion that contemporary juridical and political concepts have a theological origin.

The result is a genealogy of development which journeys exuberantly through time and across disciplines, providing meticulous and careful readings of the most significant materials in the legal archive of the relevant periods along the way. In doing so, *The Political Economy of Desire* opens up new possibilities and avenues for further research into the relationship between human rights, development, economic restructuring and the rule of law.

Anne Orford
Melbourne

Preface

This book contains a genealogy of the concept of development. The writing of it was inspired principally by my work as a lawyer, who found herself representing the British Commonwealth one day at an international conference in Addis Ababa in Ethiopia. The conference had been designed to assist the Ethiopian Parliament to fulfil its constitutional mandate to establish a national human rights commission and ombudsman. Upon my arrival I had explained to a rather flustered European that I was not actually a representative of the Commonwealth but, on the contrary, a representative of a non-governmental organisation (NGO) set up to *lobby* the Commonwealth Heads of Government Meeting. It did not matter, I would do. The important thing was that all regions were *represented*. I asked then to have the cost of my travel reimbursed. The man called across the large hall of the convention centre that the 'woman from the Commonwealth' had arrived and he asked what account my expenses should be charged to. A female English voice shouted back, 'Put it on the Lomé account'.[1] Less than three years out of law school I had arrived in a land that had maintained, against all odds, its independence from European imperialism, to represent the Commonwealth at the expense of the European Union. During the conference I met a lovely man, from a university in Ireland, who had doubted the necessity of his participation but had thought the offer to attend too good to refuse. I listened to an Italian speak for three-quarters of an hour on his attempts to restore to Ethiopia an obelisk that had been taken to Italy during its invasion of what

---

1 In 1975 the nine-nation European Economic Community (EEC) concluded an agreement, called Lomé I, with 46 African, Caribbean, and Pacific (ACP) nations that exempted most ACP exports from tariffs. On 23 June 2000 the European Union and 77 African, Pacific and Caribbean nations met in Cotonou, Benin to sign a 20-year trade and aid accord, known as the Cotonou Agreement, to replace the fourth of the Lomé conventions, which had expired on 29 February 2000. The Cotonou Agreement is aimed at combating poverty, promoting sustainable development and the gradual integration of ACP nations into the world economy and the World Trade Organization.

was then Abyssinia. The organisers had mistakenly thought he was an expert on *ombudsmen*. I was embarrassed to be so warmly welcomed by the few Ethiopian delegates I spoke to. I returned to the NGO where I was working in New Delhi, India, to find media reports criticising the predominance of racism in Australia and the rise of a political party called One Nation. I resigned from my position as programme officer for the Human Rights Commission Project shortly thereafter, and not long after that began to write the thesis, which has become this book. The journey of writing has been personal but I hope there are parts of it that might be of interest to others.

Acknowledgments

There are many people to whom I owe thanks because without them my journey along a Rousseauian path of writing and hiding myself, and all that it has taught me, would not have been possible. I am sincerely grateful to Abha Singhal Joshi, Adrian Howe, Andrew Robertson, Ann Davis, Belinda Fehlberg, Bill Lyon, Camille Cameron, Chaloka Beyani, Christine Chinken, Claire Young, Hashim Tewfik, Helen Rhoades, Hilary Charlesworth, Ian Duncanson, Ian Malkin, Janine Larson, Jeff Bennett, Jenny Morgan, John Howe, John Waugh, Judy Grbich, Jyoti Larke, Malavika Vartak, Maree Ringland, Maureen Tehan, Maya Daruwala, Michelle Groves, Ray Finkelstein, Robyn Sheen, Ross Campbell, Ruth Buchanan, Sharad Puri, Sundhya Pahuja, Om, Asha and Monica Pahuja, Susan Boyd, Tina Takagaki, and Vicky Priskich, each of whom in their own way gave me great comfort during my research. For their helpful comments on various drafts of the book, in part or whole, I would also like to thank Anne Orford, Adrian Howe, Costas Douzinas, David Kennedy, Ian Duncanson, John Howe, Judy Grbich, Peter Rush and Susan Boyd. For editing assistance I am grateful to Ian Malkin, Vicky Priskich, Fiona Ring and Maureen Tehan. I also wish to thank the Law School at the University of British Columbia for providing me with an inviting space to rewrite my thesis into this book. Extraordinary thanks must go to my doctoral supervisor, interlocutor and friend, Dr Anne Orford, whose faith in my merit as a legal scholar was critical in initiating, encouraging and sustaining my otherwise faltering belief in my own designs. Finally, to my mother Roberta Beard, I leave my deepest thanks.

Chapter 1

Introduction

Development as a political economy of desire

Public international law and socio-economic development both rest on the belief that individuals, and more belatedly, peoples, are meant to live in circumstances that grant them certain rights and freedoms fundamental to their humanity. To this end, international law seeks to provide peace and security, mechanisms of good governance and the protection of human rights and freedoms. Likewise, the United Nations General Assembly has defined 'development' as the 'multi-dimensional undertaking to achieve a higher quality of life for all people' in the contexts of peace, the economy, environmental protection, social justice and democracy.[1] The nation state, another modern concept, has established itself as an instrumental conduit of both international law and development.

Yet, while international law, development and the nation state may be understood as instrumental to the *process* of improving human life, the concept of development is also used to describe the end state of that process. In this sense, the concept of development provides modernity with a space of transcendence in these 'godless' times as well as a certain objectivity to international law and the nation state. The concept of development sets out the objectives of international law and the nation state by signifying the kind of world development practitioners are working to achieve. In consequence, whatever 'development' means will determine the ends of international law and the nation state and thus define the roles of law and the state at the national or international level, as well as the regulation of other subjects (usually defined by law) such as organisations, corporations or individuals.

The concept of development can be understood as transcendental in so far as its meaning extends beyond the limits of ordinary experience. The transcendental element within the meaning of development concerns both a

---

1 *An Agenda for Development* (Ad hoc Open-Ended Working Group of the General Assembly on An Agenda For Development, 1997, para 1).

material yearning for a higher quality of life by means of technical and economic progress as well as a non-material and arguably numinous yearning for the fulfilment of an historical end. The transcendental element of development is infinitely distant from the reality of the so-called 'developed' world, yet is essential to it. It is essential because the transcendental element of development is the central idea around which an entire discourse of development takes place – a discourse that identifies and gives meaning to the 'developed' world as such. In this respect, one might say that development is represented only in its absence but functions as the origin of an entire discourse and its effects.[2] One might argue that development as transcendence is the beginning and the end of a development discourse but it is never present, or conceivable except as an infinite series of continuous interpretations of, and effects on, human becoming that ultimately elusive definition. Development as *process*, therefore, is neither natural nor self-fulfilling except perhaps as an industry of professionals: the lawyers, economists, politicians, bankers, activists, missionaries and the bureaucrats of international economic institutions, who act as conveyors of its discourse.

With these thoughts in mind, this book is written not in an attempt to find the meaning of development but to find out how the discourse of development came to be, to find out why development is necessary as a concept and what logic is implicit in the act of dividing the world into one part said to be complete and authoritative and another said to be incomplete and flawed. In doing so, the book does not examine development as a particular set of economic and social practices but rather as a metaphysical concept that produces these practices within a particularly Christian dynamic dating back to early and medieval times.

It is suggested in this book that development is not only a metaphysical concept but also a proper name. Development names the peoples of 'the West' and thereby separates them from 'most of the world'.[3] To assign the concept of development to history – that is, to abandon or renounce the concept and what it represents – would strip the West of its current identity qua development and cause a break in a long chain of binary differences to which it is linked: namely Christian/pagan, modern/primitive, civilised/barbaric, First World/Third World, North/South and western/oriental. These binary differences are each invested with the meanings of all the others in the chain. As a consequence, this book is as much concerned with the notion of 'western' identity as it is with the concept of development itself.

---

2   See Derrida, 1994, p 138.

3   Chatterjee, 2004, 3. One might argue that the developed world does not recognise itself in this way. In response, I say that it does not need to, because, as Catharine Mackinnon says of male dominance, this naming, 'is the standard for point-of-viewlessness, its particularity the meaning of universality' (MacKinnon, p 638).

The abandonment of concepts or identity is always taking place, and although abandonment can be a mutual operation in the sense that a new identity must always emerge from any confrontation with another identity (the Other), the abandonment of an identity is nonetheless an extremely threatening and emotionally and/or physically violent process of change. Think, for example, of the transformation taking place within nation states as their 'national identity' takes up the multicultural immigration of people who challenge and eventually change that identity as well as the identity of its 'nationals'. These changes are extremely complex and strike at the heart of ethical debates about what is right and wrong in human society.

Since this book suggests that the definition of development (everything that gives it distinctness, delineation, meaning) ought to be opened to the point that it can no longer be identified – to the extent that the West ought no longer call itself 'developed' – many readers will find this book confrontational. It is important to keep in mind that the confrontation comes from understanding the arguments being made about development; it does not come from the style in which the arguments are being put although readers not familiar with critical philosophies will find some of the terminology new, unfamiliar or out of context. Those readers who are able to acknowledge and consider what is being said, however, may rest assured in the knowledge that confrontation is an invitation to transformation and, in that sense, development remains comprehensible.

In this book, it is argued that western identity is a relation of binaries that are 'thought and lived as if they expressed the true order of things'.[4] If, indeed, western identity has its own discursive expression of power, knowledge and meaning that is constituted around these binaries, then one must pursue this space as its own discourse in order to understand how the discourse of development erupted onto modernity's centre stage.[5] Development discourse exists, arguably, as a frame that makes possible a resilient continuation of a western identity that trips along as 'a god who is dead [but] continues to resonate'.[6] The developed nations merely stand in for an infinitely distant reality that will always exceed 'men's imprisonment to the earth'.[7] The point, put simply, is that western identity reverberates, is symbolised by, and made manifest in, the more powerful element of particular binaries – 'Christianity', 'civilisation', 'the West' – to which the binary of 'development' has been recently admitted. As each binary is threatened or faces deconstruction, so too is western identity threatened with the symbolic disintegration and fear-inducing meaninglessness that has been discussed in relation to the abandonment of identity. This book is a study of these crises.

The argument made in this book is that the developed world that calls itself

4   Connolly, 2002, p 64.   5   Foucault, 1984, p 84.   6   Debray, 2004, p 276.
7   Arendt, 1998, p 1.

the West has positioned itself into a space of transcendence at the global level since the discovery of the New World in the fifteenth century. Yet, the developed world, like any idol, is an inadequate representation of transcendence itself. Once named, the developed world merely reduces the concept of development to predicative discourse in such a way that the idea remains always infinitely active and unattainable; at once imaginable and yet unfathomable. The discourses of development that emerge from development's predication are, at worst, a false eschatology, and at best, they offer humanity an instance of the inadequacy of representation.

Here lies the paradox. The idea of development as 'a bereaved apprehension' does not threaten the identity of the developed world – it creates the identity.[8] The incommensurability of development's transcendence plays an essential function by introducing the very element of loss. This sense of loss, namely the inability to properly know and represent what development is, is transferred from the concept of development itself into its 'weaker' opposition: underdevelopment. Underdevelopment thus fills the lack, appearing at development's very origin. In other words, we cannot represent development without the binary of underdevelopment – both concepts emerge from the other. The people with faith in the discourses of development are thus allowed both to represent and dream of a potential state of fulfilment, which is being kept from them by the incompetence of, and lack (of prudence, technology, industry, law, etc.) in the peoples of the underdeveloped world. Whatever the binary nature of development discourse chooses to locate in its 'weaker' side of underdevelopment is thus possessed of the causes of poverty, exploitation and unequal redistribution of resources. The developed world, on the other hand, possesses elements of global fulfilment, which is due to all people when the lack of the underdeveloped world is fulfilled.

In short, humanity is left with faith in development, and, *ipso facto*, faith in the developed world. The term 'faith' here is used deliberately to evoke the sense of a people seeking to erase the torture of crisis brought on by the loss of, and alienation from, 'mere being' with a 'certain community of meaning'.[9] Development discourse assigns the unfathomable a name, and puts an end to angst-inducing uncertainty.[10] This then is what is gained by placing the quality of life of all people into a developmental framework that exceeds and resists language: the capacity of the developed world to imagine itself and its place in human history through its continued encounter with an underdeveloped world from which it has, figuratively speaking, emerged.

It should be clear to the reader that the argument here is not merely that development is used as a convenient name for a particular socio-economic status. Rather, the concern is with how development makes sense of the lives

---

8   The term 'bereaved apprehension' is taken from Derrida, 1993, p 61.
9   Stavrakakis, 1999, p 32.   10   Fink, 1995, pp 60–61.

of 'most of the world',[11] and thus erases other explanations that are perhaps not based on current conceptions of progress, temporality, geography, space, religion, gender or race, etc. Needless to say, development discourse represents a very real and effective form of imperial power that is concerned with the maintenance of a particular (western) version of subjectivity through its appropriation of history by means of a continuous and 'hazardous play of dominations' that have hardened the discourse of development into 'an unalterable form in the long baking process of history'.[12]

It is not being suggested that the reality of the present as it is would cease to be if development were not to exist as a concept. And yet, if the concept of development were to be taken from our lexicon, our conception and use of terms such as 'the North', 'the First World', 'the industrialised nations' or 'the West' might be fundamentally different. All of these terms are closely associated with particular social and economic divisions in and of the world. Importantly, it is the developed world that claims for itself that space, which exists only as transcendence but functions as meaning. In other words, countries claim to be 'developed' even if the concept is beyond definition (that is transcendent) because it is a concept that is relied upon by international society in order to regulate and legitimise (that is, give meaning to) social actions.

In order to explore the premise that there exists such a thing as western identity, and here 'identity' means the conversion of difference into a belittled Otherness through the construction of binaries, the book relies on a wide range of sources from different cultures, historical periods and disciplines. In doing so, this book cannot assume the scholarship of many critical post-colonial theorists working in the area of law and development, or in development studies more generally, who think of the 'underdeveloped' and/ or the 'developed' worlds as an outcome of the Imperial era.[13] The story of development is part of a much older struggle by Christian peoples of western Europe that has any one of many possible origins – 'numberless beginnings, whose faint traces and hints of colour are readily seen by the historical eye'.[14]

This book does not recite a history of a 'western' identity or its 'development', which tells the reader about the improvement of human life through technical and economic progress that begins in a heart of darkness and ends in some Hegelian civil society. That kind of history is merely a narrative told within development discourse, an 'error we call truth'.[15] The chapters of this book are to be read as representative of what Ernesto Laclau refers to as theoretical 'interventions', 'which shed mutual light on each other, not in

---

11 Chatterjee, 2004, p 3.   12 Foucault, 1984, p 80.

13 See e.g., Ahluwalia, 2001; Bhabha, 1986, p 148; Chakrabarty, 1992; Doty, 1996; Fanon, 1967; Gandhi, 1998, p 125; or Nandy, 1983.

14 Foucault, 1984, p 81.   15 Ibid, p 80.

terms of the *progression* of an argument, but of what we could call the *reiteration* of the latter in different discursive contexts'.[16] In this book, each chapter is a reiteration of a discontinuity in the history of 'the West' that has significance for the emergence of a development discourse in the twentieth century. The purpose of identifying these discontinuities is to articulate certain contingent social constructions that attempt to fill the loss of meaning created when there is a loss of faith in the symbolic reality of a particular identification of the West 'as it was' so to speak, and the effect this has on emergent western identities. These identities include both the 'West' as a body and the individuals within it. Both bodies are 'totally imprinted by history'.[17]

The bodies of particular interest are national and individual in nature. The national is interesting in so far as the nation state is the subject of development's discourse as well as the instrument meant to bring development to the individual. The individual, in turn, is interesting because it has emerged in the West in formation with nation and national development.

The subjects of development

It is argued that development calls western society into being at the subjective level. Etienne Balibar has already begun researching the question of subjectivity in western philosophy by undertaking an historical analysis of '*Man as* (a, the) *subject*' through representations of 'Man', the 'subject' and the 'citizen'.[18] One of Balibar's theses is that in the 'history of the "problem of Man", as "citizen" and as "subject", at least two great breaks have taken place, which . . . marked irreversible thresholds'.[19]

The first occurs with the 'decline of the ancient world' and the interpretation of subjection or *subjectus* as 'the subject's subjection as (willing) *obedience*, coming from inside, coming from the soul'.[20] Balibar describes this form of subjectivation as an 'interiorized voice',[21] or arguably what Adam Smith referred to as 'the invisible hand':[22]

> . . . that of a transcendent authority which everyone is bound to obey, or which always already compels everyone to obey, including the rebels . . . because the foundation of authority is not located *outside* the individual in some natural inequality or dependency, but *within* him, in his very being as creature of the verb, and as faithful to it.[23]

As Balibar explains, the *inner* subject is one, 'who confronts transcendental

---

16 Emphasis in the original. Laclau, 1989, p xii.   17 Foucault, 1984, p 83.
18 Balibar, 1994, p 4.   19 Ibid, p 9.   20 Emphasis added. Ibid.
21 Emphasis in the original. Ibid, p 10.   22 Smith, 1993, p 292.
23 Emphasis in the original. Balibar, 1994, p 10.

law, both theological and political, religious (therefore also moral) or imperial (monarchical) – because he hears it, because in order to be able to hear it, he has to be able to be called by it'.[24] An element of hierarchical compulsion of the subject by the transcendental Other is still present here but the subjection is nonetheless reciprocal, relational.[25] The inner subject is thus:

> a *responsible*, or an *accountable*, subject, which means he has to respond to give an account (*rationem reddere*) of himself, i.e. of his actions and intentions, before another person, who righteously interpellates him. Not a Big Brother, but a Big Other . . . always already shifting in an ambivalent manner between the visible and the invisible, between individuality and universality.[26]

This book offers an engagement with Balibar's 'interiorized voice' using Michel Foucault's research of technologies of the self in early Christianity.[27]

Christians and pagans

The early Christian Church was indeed a body that shifted between individuality and universality. During the early centuries of Christian practice, the individual Christian subject was constantly willing itself into the universal body of Christ – the Church – in readiness for a greater unification with God. This practice can be read in terms of the Christian yearning for humanity's salvation when 'the flesh will once again be made whole and in which space will be subsumed by time'.[28] This book is about how the promise of development might be conceived in the same way that the Word of God was used to call Christian subjectivity into being with a promise.

By constituting itself as the body of Christ on earth, the early Roman-Christian church restructured traditional bonds of family and kinship, which Regis Debray sees as the moment from when the West would be able to think of the social bond as 'something decided, not preserved', where 'nature would no longer dictate the law'.[29] According to Debray, the destiny of the Church became by nature a project with 'an unlimited capacity for recruitment, since the eternal father could henceforth have foreign sons who were not registered with the local authorities, all by virtue of an adoption ritual called baptism, which was valid anywhere . . . Thus a Christian always had something to busy himself with – outside'.[30]

The constitution of Christ's body on earth was obtained by the deployment of certain disciplinary techniques, which were in turn supported by

---

24 Emphasis in the original. Ibid, p 9.   25 Emphasis in the original. Ibid, p 10.
26 Balibar, 1994, p 9.   27 See Foucault, 1999b.   28 Spence, 1996, p 24.
29 Debray, 2004, p 178.   30 Ibid, p 181.

the promise of salvation that the body of the Church represented. Any unredeemed part of that body, the pagan and the unbaptised soul, remained fallen from God's mercy. It is argued here that this fallen state was translated by Christianity into a debt – a manifestation of sin – that prevented the Christian body from accrediting itself with totality and thus completion. The idea of humanity as a body of unredeemed debt required a particular conception of humanity's bond to God based on concepts of sin, repentance, mercy, faith and salvation, which are introduced in Chapter Two and analysed through the interpretation of certain early and medieval Christian texts. The analysis highlights the effects that the Christian notions of mercy and justice had on a Christian will to power, which constituted, informed and disciplined a body of people and produced an extremely resilient 'Christian' identity. The will to power underlying that identity continues to influence western ontology, since its doctrinal and spiritual adaptability make it an effective conqueror of souls and minds.

God and man

Chapter Two, developing Foucault's research, traces the emergence of a particular form of subjectivity determined by disciplinary practices of early and medieval Christian repentance. It is argued that early Christians were interpellated by an interior voice that willed their turn to God and His mercy. This turn to God was expressed in practices of *exomologesis,* a form of repentance that was eventually transformed into spectacular forms of public penance. The subjectivation of Christians in this way accords, it is postulated, with the subjectivation Balibar refers to as an 'interiorized voice', referred to above. The displacement of these early penitential practices by subsequent forms of repentance that emerged from a practice of *exagoreusis* (the opening of one's heart to another) is then traced into a system of private, auricular confession. Foucault's thesis is then taken up, that from this practice of *exagoreusis* emerged the western European concept of the self – what is referred to here as the 'confessional subject'.[31]

The purpose of exploring the effects of these practices of subjectivation is to explore whether they might still be found in contemporary relations of power at both the individual and international level, particularly in discourses of development. The current author's belief is that these Christian forms of discipline and subjectivation still play a role in the conceptual construction of development and its effects. Particular interest is shown as to how these practices were adapted by events such as the discovery of the New World and the religious reformation in western Europe, when the

31 Foucault, 1988.

confessional subject began to abandon the Church as the 'Big Other' and learnt instead to make its own laws of becoming.

Three principle forms of subjectivation can be discerned from the abandonment of the Church as the Big Other (and the displacement of the interiorised voice). The first is what has been referred to above as the 'confessional subject'. In Chapters Two and Three of this book, it is argued that the practice of private penance, which was regulated by the Roman Catholic Church, was transformed into monarchical power and the divine right to rule the subjective forces of the body politic as a means to constrain and stabilise the subject emerging from the destabilising forces of religious reformation. Although the confessional subject of the Middle Ages recognised what it meant to make the law, without democracy there was no ground upon which to legitimate that authority.

The second form of subjectivation is similar to what Balibar has referred to as the construction of the citizen and what is argued here to be the successor to the confessional subject. Balibar argues that this construction of the 'citizen' occurred when a 'secular and democratic social organisation was declared' during the revolutions at the end of the eighteenth and nineteenth centuries. During that period, the individual is:

> no longer called before the Law, or to whom an inner voice dictates the law, or tells him that he should recognise and obey the Law; he is rather the man who, at least virtually, 'makes the Law', i.e. constitutes it, or declares it to be valid. The subject is someone who is responsible or accountable because he is (a) legislator, accountable for the consequences, the implementation and non-implementation of the Law he has himself made.[32]

Although the citizen as lawmaker requires notions of democracy to acquire the political sense of an inherent right to 'make the law', in order for this notion to have emerged, political authority first needed to be removed from God 'on high' and located instead in humanity itself, first in the Roman Catholic Church, then in the divine monarch and/or the democratic citizen. All of these forms of governance depend upon the soul of the confessional subject (and later the citizen) for their power.

The citizen thus came to be determined by 'the inalienable character of their "rights" ', which were 'attributed individually' but 'achieved and won collectively'.[33] Since the practice of ascertaining these rights had to be conducted 'by means of a collective and universal access to politics' this practice of citizenship at the collective or universal level was intertwined with the emergence of imperialism, sovereign states and international law.

---

32 Balibar, 1994, pp 10–11.   33 Ibid, p 12.

As Balibar notes, 'that a *new* form of power emerges does not imply that the ancient one disappears'.[34] Despite the appearance of the citizen as subject, the interiorised voice that had been compelled to obedience by God still lurked in the shadowy uncertainty of the right of the citizen to make the law. This ghostly subjectivity was ideally suited to the nascent market economy materialising during the Middle Ages. Arguably, the subjectivity of the citizen was split between the interiorised voice of a willed obedience, 'always already shifting between individuality and universality' and its constitution as a responsible and accountable subject of rights. In so far as the subject was unable to determine its own interpellation – to speak the Word and call itself into being – it remained a subject of exchange that makes no law. This subject of exchange exists in a state of instability, subjected only to the laws of consumption. It has lost the power to perform its own subjection – to determine itself by 'the inalienable character of [its] rights'[35] – overcome by the flow of subjective and objective reciprocity.

Whereas the confessional subject and the citizen find freedom in a negotiated obedience to an external sovereign (God, reason, nation, the constitution, human rights, etc.), the subject of exchange finds freedom through the sacrifice of a determined self to an unlimited exchange. This subject of exchange is rarely mentioned perhaps because it is a creature of capitalism always hiding on the other side of the coin from its ostensible authority, the sovereign monarch. And yet, the revolution of capitalism is all around us still, shaping the end of history as already having happened. These changes in the relationship between the individual and society are explored in Chapter Three along with how a nascent capitalism began to circulate the body (both social and individual) with transformative effects.[36] Chapter Three also discusses the subject split between its citizenship and its commoditisation.

The Old World and the New World

Chapters Three and Four shed light on the resilience of the Christian body through an analysis of texts written during the period of discovery and the Enlightenment. The discovery of the New World, itself a consequence of the 'westernisation' of Christian Europe since the fall of Constantinople to the Muslim Ottoman Empire in 1453, not only strengthened the western outlook of Christianity (and literally, its western identity) by closing the trade route from Europe to the east and forcing Christian powers to 'go west', but also gave meaning to 'the West' on a global scale in the following way.

The newly discovered world, as it turned out, was not more of the same but a whole 'New World' as it came to be called that required interpretation. If

---

34 Emphasis in the original. Balibar, 1994, p 13.   35 Balibar, 1994, p 12.
36 See Derrida, 1976, p 266.

the Roman Christian Church represented the redeemed body of Christ on earth, this New World could not. And yet the discovery of a world beyond knowledge, beyond description, seemed to mark the very essence of God. The ensuing search for a Golden Age or Eldorado are evidence of a belief that the New World held the origin of man where a return to the mystery of wholeness might be discovered. In fact, all that was discovered was gold, spice, territory, and, importantly, unredeemed souls.

By interpreting the New World as a world of unredeemed souls, the Roman Christian Church discovered the possibility of its own transcendence. What seemed a crisis of interpretation became an opportunity to strengthen the representation of the Roman Church as the embodiment of Christ's body on earth. The riches of the New World were erased – appropriated and myth-ologised – and instead the unredeemed souls of New World peoples were used as the mark of a world with nothing of value to offer a god-fearing Europe. The leaders of the Church, having assumed the authority to discharge the sins of individual Christians, now also assumed the authority to discharge the debt of humanity as a whole. It did so by positing Christian people as the divine body of a future-perfect present, while casting the New World into the fallen state of unredeemed sin. This representation became possi-ble because of a temporal element emerging within Christian identity that enabled Christians to identify themselves in relation to a 'younger', more primitive world. The New World was thus represented as having lapsed into a space of irrationality, femininity, primitivism and physicality.

The quality of a previously unknown world and its topographies attracted and astonished, intimidated and unsettled the Christian world as a whole. The identity of the New World literally and fundamentally transgressed the borders of Christian identity. In Christian discourses, the New World was thus marked out as a transgressive subject as it was invaded and colonised like any other Christian subject by being subjected (made subject) to practices of Christian repentance. The peoples of the New World were thus brought to justice under an enforced confessional relationship that traded subject recog-nition in return for the repression of other ways of being and knowing. This relationship, it is argued, remains a form of willed obedience in the sense that 'non-western', 'underdeveloped' peoples have been attributed with an inter-iorised voice, which means they have 'to respond to give an account' of their actions and intentions, before another person, who righteously interpellated them as subjects of history.[37]

Enlightenment narratives of New World primitivism and savagery further strengthened this constitution of the New World since the Old World was able to imagine itself into a time that is both within and outside the bounds of subjectivation. This is how the West makes its claim to transcendence.

37 Balibar, 1994, p 9.

From the moment of the discovery of the New World, the Christian religion enabled the Old World to take up Christ's promise anew, in order to represent *itself* in an historic dimension (since ideas of history were also changing) as the broker of (the New World's) salvation. By marking out the New World in this way, prior to entering into mutual negotiations of recognition, the Old World created an object of desire more real than God. The western subject no longer looked to God to find out who it was, since it could seek the answer in the reply of the New World Other by positioning itself in the place of God – the Big Other.

It is argued that the peoples of the New World could free themselves from this space of belittled otherness only by disappearing under the Word of Old World law, such that the identifying marks of sinfulness were removed as they became unified with the other world. In so far as this was possible, New World peoples had to incorporate themselves into the Old World by accepting the framework of justice imposed on them by the international laws of the family of civilised nations (the Old World), thus becoming confessional subjects that negotiated a space of becoming in accordance with the law. At the international level, this involved a mapping of the concept of the confessional subject onto the concept of the nation state and its citizens. As a consequence, both worlds became haunted by a sense of loss as well as driven by the desire to address that loss by holding the New World (and its underdevelopment) accountable to what has emerged as the promise of development. The texts of Christian explorers such as Christopher Columbus and scholars such as Jean Bodin and Hugo Grotius are relied upon to explore these suggested outcomes of the discovery of the New World and its Fall (through conquest).

The barbaric and the civilised

Christian belief and practice can also be said to have influenced the emergence of the national body politic as a subject of international law and development. Chapters Four and Five explore the repercussions of the new binary relationship between the New World and the Old World in relation to the emergence of a Westphalian system of nation states. In particular, Chapter Four examines the construction of the sovereign state from fantasies about savage origins represented 'empirically' by the New World. Francis Bacon's *New Atlantis* is a remarkable example of this kind of fantasy. A reading of this fictional account of the perfect body politic provides ways in which to understand how the sovereign nation was constructed from a variety of Christian-scientific narratives derived from the salvation discourses of the Christian church. The subsequent work of John Locke is used to support these findings in addition to examining in more detail the transformation of Christian disciplinary practices into bio-political techniques used by the state to regulate the conduct of individuals in accordance with the conception and desires of nation.

Chapter Five then approaches the subject of nation from an international perspective, questioning the motives behind the proclaimed peace of the Westphalian state system during a period of 'High Imperialism'. This chapter analyses the barbarism and savagery of the so-called 'civilised' Old World as it strives to maintain its identity by purging from its boundaries all that is impure and therefore unlawful, in addition to revoking the 'universal' laws of nature from the peoples of the New World by proclaiming itself to be the source of civilisation and therefore of (positive) law.

The developed and the underdeveloped

By the sixth and final chapter, it will have been made clear that this book differs from other critical analyses of development discourse, which limit their historical analyses to the post-colonial, post-world-war era, describing the origin of the concept as particularly modern. *The Development Dictionary*, for instance, refers to 'the age of development as that particular historical period which began on 20 January 1949.[38] That date marks the declaration by Harry S. Truman in his inauguration speech, that the Southern hemisphere comprised 'underdeveloped areas'.[39] According to *The Development Dictionary*, Truman's speech also marks the cognitive base for 'both arrogant interventionism from the North and pathetic self-pity in the South'.[40] While it is true that Truman was one of the first people to coin the term 'development' and apply it to over half the world's population, this book will reveal that the genealogical origin of development discourse is not so easily located. Indeed, even the commencement of this genealogy in the early-Christian history of 'the West' is an irresolvable arbitrary beginning.[41]

In recognising the arbitrariness of origins, Chapter Six begins by focusing on Truman's inaugural address, not in order to reinforce its appeal to origins, but to deconstruct that appeal. On the basis of the preceding four chapters, Truman's address can be understood as an almost inevitable 'Freudian slip' made on behalf of the Old World, by its leading spokesperson, as it struggled to maintain its identity through its continued encounter with an unredeemed world from which it had saved itself. Chapter Six explores the suggestion that Truman's address is chosen as the origin of the post-world-war era because Truman championed the free world of capitalism, which is now led by the United States of America, but threatened by the 'false philosophy' of Communism. Indeed, America had been prophesised as the saviour of the Old World since its discovery, as the preceding chapters will have explained.

---

38 Sachs, 1992, p 2.   39 Ibid.   40 See also Escobar, 1995 and Crush, 1995.
41 As Arjun Appadurai has noted of modernity, 'all major social forces have precursors, precedents, analogs, and sources in the past. It is these deep and multiple genealogies that have frustrated the aspirations of modernizers in very different societies to synchronize their historical watches' (1996, p 2).

Chapter Six will conclude with a consideration of the ways in which development discourse continues to allow the West to maintain its identity as such by 'knowing' the underdeveloped world as subject; as a 'fixed reality which is at once an "Other" and yet entirely knowable and visible'.[42] Since development's chosen moment of a post-world-war origin, *The Development Dictionary* states that:

> a large part of the world's peoples ceased being what they were, in all their diversity, and were transmogrified into an inverted mirror of others' reality: a mirror that belittles them and sends them off to the end of the queue, a mirror that defines their identity, which is really that of a hetero-geneous and diverse majority, simply in the terms of a homogenizing and narrow minority.[43]

As a scholar of post-colonial literary theory, Homi Bhabha argues it is 'precisely this function of the stereotype as phobia and fetish that ... threatens the closure of the racial/epidermal schema for the colonial subject and opens the royal road to colonial fantasy'.[44] A fantasy based on an entire discourse around the role of international law, the nation state and the governance of individual lives. Take, for example, the following story of development told by Robert Calderisi, the World Bank's country director for Central Africa:

> A few years ago our President, Mr Wolfensohn, visited a squatter settle-ment outside the Brazilian city of Sao Paulo where the World Bank had helped finance a water and sanitation project. While the vice governor of the state showed him around, a large group of women followed them at a short distance and waved papers in the air rather proudly. 'Do you know why they are so happy?' the vice governor asked. 'Because they now have running water and no longer have to drag it in buckets on their shoulders up these steep hills, I presume', said Mr Wolfensohn. 'Yes, that's true', the vice governor replied, 'But that's not the reason they're showing you those papers'. 'Is it because they are proud to have contributed to some of the costs of the project?' 'Yes', the vice-governor said, 'That's true, too. But what they are waving at you are their first bills for water service. It is the first time they have seen their names and addresses on an official document and the first time they feel included in government programs they have only heard about in the past on radio'.[45]

Calderisi tells this story to extol the promises made good by development.

---

42 Bhabha, 1986, pp 148, 158.   43 Sachs, 1992, p 2.   44 Bhabha, 1986, p 158.
45 Calderisi, 2001, p 57.

The irony of wanting one's name to appear on a bill for payment of a basic need is joined by the presumption of the women's desire to be acknowledged as a particular kind of global and 'developed' subject. Calderisi's story indicates that development is a story of joy upon becoming a paying subject of the developmental economy, which in turn enables individuals to be called forth from that mass of nameless, starving faces used to represent the underdeveloped world. What Calderisi's story is attempting to tell us is that the discourse of development can protect the undeveloped subject from global insignificance. Only those who respond to the christening force of development will be answered; only the subject that allows itself to be inscribed by development discourse can necessarily confess its allegiance to it and thereby obtain recognition as a 'true subject'. Within development discourse, the subject exists in so far as the word has wrought him or her from nothingness. Those who cannot confess will not be redeemed and must remain a manifestation of sin, cast out as false truth.

This is the process of development. Development is transcendence; the place that everyone is trying to get to, to complete themselves. Development is desire – the desire to become that which language promises but never achieves. Development is western imperialism: a never-ending lack, and it is what holds together the global economy. Only those who are willing to reaffirm in words and action the goals of development will be chosen to read their names on the bill for water service and take part in an economy of desire that promises salvation and development. The 'West', as the narrator of development, takes the place of meaning and promises fulfilment instead of the primordial estrangement of being otherwise. Based on this and other experiences, Calderisi states, 'our President has stressed how important it is that development include everyone'.[46]

46 Ibid.

Chapter 2

Faith through understanding

Despite the fact that many 'non-western' peoples are members of what one would consider the 'developed' world, the concept of development remains closely associated with western identity and its claims to capitalist prosperity and liberal democracy. Western identity, as argued in Chapter One, is also very much dependent on its Christian origins for the ways in which it constitutes, informs and conducts its presence in the world. For this reason, the book covers Christian practices that might be said to exist in ideas of subjectivity today. In particular, the reader should think of how the promise of development might be conceived in the same way that the Word of God has been used to call subjectivity into being with a promise.

Since the promises of both the Christian God and development are eschatological in nature, one way to conceive them or perhaps any promise, is as a bond. The term 'bond' is rich in meaning. Generally, it represents a relationship that binds or restrains. Legally and financially, the bond represents in general terms an obligation and acknowledgement of indebtedness. Perhaps not coincidently, this is essentially how early Christians also understood God's promise of salvation – as an acknowledgement of indebtedness and obligation to God. One might also perceive the promise of development in this way since the concept of development promises a future that is open to those people who carry out particular practices of obedience. For example, nations are asked to liberalise trade barriers to goods and services as a kind of willed obedience to the promise of development. Development in this sense is most often understood in terms of economic growth and material prosperity obtained following willed obedience to market forces. The subject of development is required to defer to market forces that are unknown yet able to make promises. Anne Orford has demonstrated how trade liberalisation is thus able to require the sacrifice of those values that are espoused 'publicly and collectively – democracy, civility, politics, the family of nation – for the global market, and as the price of inclusion in the community of believers'.[1]

---

1 Orford, 2005, p 197.

Orford states that this 'economy of sacrifice [is] accompanied by the promise of the reward of the righteous in the future by the Father (God/Market) who sees in secret' and suggests further that the sacrifice required is that of the feminine.[2]

A second way of approaching the promise is through the lens of law and/or justice where development's promise is no less than an assurance of what may be expected from the future. Thus, one must approach the promise from the converse perspective – not as an acknowledgement of indebtedness but as a guarantee of what it to come. As Grotius, one of the so-called 'fathers of international law' has written:

> A noteworthy proof of what I am saying is furnished by the Scriptures, which teach us that God Himself, who cannot be bound by any estab- lished law, would act contrary to His nature if He did not make good His promises (*Nehemiah* ix 8; *Hebrews* vi 18, x 23; *First Corinthians* i 19 [i 9], x 13; *First Thessalonians*, v 24; *Second Thessalonians* iii 3; *Second Timothy* ii 13). From this it follows that the obligation to perform prom- ises arises from the nature of immutable justice, which in its own fashion is common to God and to all beings possessed of reason.[3]

Here, God's immutable justice underlies 'His promises', which He is obliged to keep lest He betray His own reason. God's reason is, of course, no less than salvation itself. The modern notion of fundamental human rights and freedoms are perhaps the most essential example of the immutable terms of development's promise. From this perspective, in Christianity as in law, just- ice is the obligation that God (the legal system) has toward the Christian (legal) subject and society as a whole. This notion of the promise as justice erases the uncertainty of God's mercy. Here the Christian (legal) subject does not will their obedience through an acknowledgement of indebtedness in order to seek merciful forgiveness. Instead God (justice in law) simply is; justice is the promise, determined by reason of its essential nature as such. The promise is framed by its own immanence. Grotius speaks not of faith in God's mercy but of God's immutable justice. The possibility of God's betrayal is thus understood as the betrayal of justice itself. God is located here within a justice system, which requires the promised promise.

In order to give to the promise the nature of justice, mercy must be expelled from its definition. Approaching the promise from the perspective of justice, therefore, is not a cry for mercy. Yet, the very fact that God makes promises means also that God could forsake humanity by not keeping these promises. Faced with this threat, one can only have faith in God's mercy and believe that God is (as good as) His promise. This sort of faith described the belief of

2 Ibid, p 182.   3 Grotius, 1814, Book II, Ch. XI(IV).

Christians in the early centuries of their religion, who understood God's promise from the point of their indebtedness to Him (and His mercy). This was not, however, the belief of Grotius described in the passage above, which perceives the promise as justice. The discourse of development could therefore be said to take account of two conceptions of the promise: that of the bond, which is subject to mercy, as well as of justice, which is ostensibly immutable.

The Christian bond

In the first centuries of Christian practice, Christian life was understood as an act of faith not in God's justice but in His mercy. Early Christians knew 'neither *who* nor *what* awaits whom or what'.[4] Christians lived within God's promise, gathered together by 'the promised or threatened language' of His Word, which, promising all the way to the point of threatening and vice versa, gathers Christians 'together in its very dissemination'.[5]

The Word of God – His promise – was given to humanity through His son, Jesus Christ, who became man in order to acknowledge the state of indebtedness in which humanity existed and to redeem humanity of that debt by sacrificing His own life. Following Christ's resurrection and ascension, early Christians were able to acknowledge their indebtedness to God by entering His (son's) body – the Church – through baptism. The purity conferred by baptism was to be kept without blemish so that following baptism, 'if a man were to quit this present life . . . there would be nothing at all left to hold him liable, inasmuch as all which held him is released'.[6]

Christian life was thus an act of faith. Christ's coming did not restore perfect completion to humanity but only provided it with the means to redemption through baptism into the immortal Word. The space of creation would eventually be subsumed by this immortal concept of time, corrected by the Second Coming in which the flesh will once again be made whole.[7] Thus, the Christian theologian Augustine of Hippo (354–430) argued in both *The Literal Meaning of Genesis*[8] and the final books of the *Confessions*,[9] that creation occurred in a time outside of space. Time, for Augustine, was

---

4   Derrida's analysis of the promise of language is here being used somewhat out of context. See Derrida for context, 1998 pp 21–22.
5   See Derrida, 1998 pp 21–22.   6   Augustine, 1887, 2.28.46.
7   Spence, 1996, p 24.
8   Augustine, 1990a. St Augustine served as Bishop of Hippo from 396 until his death in 430.
9   Augustine, 1955, Book X. The *Confessions*, written in 397, is a single work in 13 books in the form of a long prayer addressed directly to God. The first nine books contain an autobiographical description of Augustine's conversion to Christianity; the last three books contain an allegorical explanation of the first chapter of Genesis. Book X contains a discussion on memory and Book XI a discussion of time.

'the model of wholeness, of fulfilment, or pure presence; space by contrast [was] the imperfect fragmentation of such a whole'.[10] Faith in the Word was figurative of a desire to represent a presence that was constantly deferred.[11] In this sense, time was comparable to unfathomable transcendence, like that element of development described in Chapter One, which cannot be named.[12]

Until the Day of Judgement, the truth of the Word of God and those asked to receive it could not be guaranteed. Instead, 'in the ordeal of a threatening and threatened promise', humanity had been cast out since Adam and Eve, cut off from their origin, always already destined to be forsaken by either or both God and themselves.[13] Early Christians could 'testify only to the unbelievable':[14]

> To what can, at any rate, only be believed; to what appeals only to belief and hence to the given word, since it lies beyond the limits of proof, indication, certified acknowledgement [*le constat*] and knowledge. . . . It is always a matter of what is offered to faith and of appealing to faith, a matter of what is only 'believable' and hence as unbelievable as a miracle. Unbelievable because *merely* credible.[15]

Knowledge of God's Word, like the market today, lay beyond the bounds of His subjects. The turn to God was therefore not an affirmation of a particular way of living but, rather, an active denial of their life, which was, after all, a creation of sin. There was nothing true of the self except that which was in God.[16] Those who desired the truth had to perform the truth as best they could in order 'to come to the light'.[17] This 'presence of oneself in the conscious intention as such, belong[s] without doubt to the essence of the promise'.[18]

The turn to God was essential to one's salvation because early Christians believed that all of creation was a manifestation of sin. Sin was not an act or misdeed but the actual bond that arose between God and humanity at the moment of creation. This same promise can be found in discourses of development that will be discussed in Chapter Six.

According to Augustine, the desire to return to unity with God – to an original state of completeness – resulted in the predication of a 'boundlessly free' Christian subject:

---

10 Spence, 1996, p 24.   11 Derrida, 1976; 1995.
12 See Jacques Derrida's work on the sensitivity of textuality to a deferred future and the concomitant promise of an (impossible) presence and stable identity. See Derrida, 1976; 1995.
13 Derrida, 1998 p 22.   14 Ibid, p 20.   15 Emphasis in the original. Ibid.
16 Tellenbach, 1940, p 55.   17 Augustine, 1955, Book X, Chapter 1.1.
18 Derrida, 1995, 41.

> From love man returns back to God, seeking *to bring himself* into subjection to God, not to make himself equal with Him. . . . The more *he directs his utmost efforts* towards this end, the more blessed and the more exalted will he become, and he will be boundlessly free (*Liberrimus*) under the sole domination of God.[19]

In Augustine's time, freedom was thus secured by subjecting oneself completely to God so as to live within His promise: 'He who has My commandments and keeps them, it is he who loves Me. And he who loves Me will be loved by My Father, and I will love him and manifest Myself to him'[20] The aim was to find freedom in obedience to divine will.[21] The early Christian was, in effect, an inscription of God's Word so that each Christian became the Word of God. This sacrifice of the self to the Word was to be achieved by living a life of faith in obedience to the teachings of Christ, the New Testament and the Acts of the Apostles. 'What manner of subjection is this?' asks Origen (182–251), 'I believe it is that state in which we should *desire* to be subject to Him, even as the Apostles are, and all the saints who have followed Christ'.[22]

Recognising in the pure person an implicit desire of baptism, those with a perfect contrition of heart, who acted with perfect charity or pure love of God, were granted the 'Baptism of Desire' (*baptismus flaminis*), which is still accepted by the Roman Catholic Church today. The subject of Christianity (or of the market today) was always already compelled to obey the will of God.

> All of them [the saints] therefore were all renowned and magnified, not through themselves or their own works or the righteous actions which they had wrought, but through his will; and therefore we who by his will have been called in Christ Jesus, *are not made righteous by ourselves, or by our wisdom or understanding or piety or the deeds which we have wrought in holiness of heart, but through faith*, by which Almighty God has justified all men from the beginning of the world; to him be glory for ever and ever. Amen.[23]

19 Emphasis added. Augustine, 1966, Book I, Chapter 12.21.   20 *John* 14:21.

21 See Lea, 1896, p 31.

22 Emphasis added. This quote from Origen is taken from Tellenbach, 1940, p 3. Origen, one of the fathers of the early Christian Church, was born, probably at Alexandria, about 182 and died at Caesarea not later than 251. On living in obedience according to the Word of God, see also, Augustine, 1955, Book XIV, Chapter 4. Tellenbach notes that Origen and Augustine differed in opinion concerning creation, Origen believing that the world was not created as something good in itself, but only as punishment for sin; Augustine believing that 'the whole creation is good, including the sinners, just as a painting has dark colours in the right places' (Tellenbach, 1940, p 8)

23 Emphasis added. St Clement, 'The Epistle of St Clement to the Corinthians' in Harmer, 1893, pp 49, 32.

A similar religious faith is to be found in the work of Adam Smith in his defence of free trade, or more particularly international free trade. In Book IV of *The Wealth of Nations*, Smith offers a theology of the global market, which is guided by an 'invisible hand'. Here, in Smith's work, God begets providence and providence begets the market:

> As every individual, therefore, endeavours as much as he can both to employ his capital in the support of domestick industry, and so to direct that industry that its produce may be of the greatest value; every individual necessarily labours to render the annual revenue of the society as great he can. He generally, indeed, neither intends to promote the publick interest, nor knows how much he is promoting it. By preferring the support of the domestick to that of foreign industry, he intends only his own security; and by directing that industry in such a manner as its produce may be of the greatest value, he intends only his own gain, and he is in this, as in many other cases, led by *an invisible hand* to promote an end which was no part of his intention. Nor is it always the worse for society that it was no part of if. By pursuing his own interest he frequently promotes that of the society *more effectually than when he really intends to promote it.*[24]

In Smith's market, the individual has been subsumed by the will of God. Unlike the relationship between citizen and sovereign, where the public good is regulated by political exchange, within the market it is the individual who can 'judge much better than any stateman or lawgiver' what his capital can best produce.[25] This is because the invisible hand leads the individual into freedom, 'not through themselves or their own works or the righteous actions which they had wrought, but through his [God's] will'.[26]

Smith's individual was not the citizen-subject become lawmaker referred to in Chapter One. The subject described here is one who cannot 'acquire the religious knowledge necessary for salvation without the assistance of God'. Similarly today, salvation is only due to those who submit themselves obediently to the guiding hand of invisible market forces.[27] Human behaviour and its predestination are understood as a form of (economic) scripture, representative of divine truth.[28] With this in mind, in the early centuries of Christianity, Augustine was able to understand his life figuratively as 'a story, not only of his own sin but also of God's charity'.[29]

Once true being was obtained so too would the subject have found its complete identification in God. Both God and self were thus understood as

---

24 Smith, 1993, pp 291–92.   25 Ibid, p 292.
26 See quote of St Clement above in Harmer, 1893, p 32.   27 Colish, 1968, p ix.
28 Root, 1997, p 28; Burke, 1970.   29 Root, 1997, p 28.

'elements of an intimate personal relationship destined for permanent and indissoluble union'.[30] As Balibar writes, this kind of subjection was based on that:

> transcendental origin, which makes those who obey into the members of a single body . . . the subjects *will* their own obedience. And if they will it, it is because it is inscribed in an economy of creation (their creation) and salvation (their salvation, that of each taken individually and of all taken collectively). Thus the loyal subject . . . (he who 'voluntarily', 'loyally', that is, actively and willingly obeys the law and executes the orders of a legitimate sovereign) is necessarily a *faithful subject*. He is a Christian, who knows that all power comes from God.[31]

Clement of Alexandria writes, 'We have learned to call freedom the freedom with which the Lord alone endows us, delivering us from pleasures, lusts and the other passions'.[32] This relationship was the bond – the acknowledgement of indebtedness received and believed by the early Christian subject as well as today's capitalist. The obedient subject does not seek understanding but rather lets the self slide under the signifying power of God or the market, as the case may be, in order to achieve at least some semblance of totality, to reach a point beyond desire where one might rest in a time beyond space.

Exomologesis

This desire to submit oneself to God's will was given expression in the concept of repentance – a desire to be Christian. Repentance was a continuous search for the divine by nourishing the soul and deploring earthly sinfulness. This desire of Christians to subject themselves to God's will is best understood in relation to the early Christian practice of *exomologesis*. *Exomologesis* was based on the belief that human salvation could be achieved only by a change of mind and heart towards Christ and away from the sinfulness of the world.[33] Accordingly, a Christian whose desire to follow the Word of God had lapsed back into sin was required to turn back to God with an even greater desire for mercy and reconciliation or be banished from their congregation.

The way of *exomologesis* was to seek counsel from the Church, and to recognise publicly one's Christian faith and to humbly acknowledge one's

---

30 O'Donnell, www.ccat.sas.upenn.edu/jod/augustine.html (on file with author).
31 Emphasis in the original. Balibar, 1991, p 41.
32 Clement of Alexandria, 1991, Book III, Chapter 44.4, p 283.
33 The term 'to repent' used in the New Testament stems from the Greek term *metanoia*, meaning a change of mind.

existence as sinner.[34] The penitent was thus not in a relationship of negotiation with God but rather acknowledged and performed their state of indebtedness to Him. This is evident in the following passage from Cyprian:

> That for brethren who have lapsed, and after saving Baptism have been wounded by the devil, a remedy may by penance be sought: not as if they obtained remission of sins from us, but that through us they may be brought to a knowledge of their offences, and be compelled to give fuller satisfaction to the Lord.[35]

By performing their sinfulness, both the penitent and the congregation were made witness to faith as well as sinfulness. 'It was not a way for the sinner to *explain* his sins but a way to *present* himself as a sinner' in order to seek God's mercy.[36] As Foucault notes:

> To carry out the *exomologesis* of one's belief is not simply to affirm that one believes but also the fact of this belief; it is to make the act of affirmation an object of affirmation, and thus to authenticate it either for oneself or before others. *Exomologesis* is an emphatic affirmation, whose emphasis bears above all on the fact that the subject ties himself to this affirmation and accepts the consequences of it.[37]

The practice involved an explanation by the penitent of why he or she wanted the status as well as a description of their faults, and formed the principal means of discipline by the early Church.[38] Here is how Tertullian describes the practice in the latter half of the second century:

> *Exomologesis* requires that . . . you prostrate yourself at the feet of the priests and kneel before the beloved of God, making all the brethren commissioned ambassadors of your prayer of pardon.[39]

Exomologesis eventually developed into the practice of public penance, and included the whole act of confession and the obligation of the sinner to seek from the bishop the imposition of the status of a penitent, which could take years to perform. Moreover, sinners had only one chance of redemption because public penance of this kind could not be repeated. As a result, public penance was normally deferred until as close to death as possible.[40] Public

---

34 Foucault, 1988, p 41; Paden, 1988, pp 64–65.   35 Cyprian, 1844, Vol. 75.4.
36 Emphasis added. Foucault, 1988, p 42.   37 Foucault, 1999b, p 155.
38 See Lea, 1896.   39 Tertullian, 1959, p 9.
40 Over time there was a gradual change in this practice so that an individual could seek penance more than once through the presbyter. See Lea, 1896.

penance became a means by which the Christian Church was able to maintain an identity of internal purity, which in turn reinforced the reconciliation that the Church offered between God and His subjects. It is important to note, however, that in the early centuries of Christian practice, banishment from the Church could destroy a person's *means* to a Christian life and so salvation, but the Church did not itself claim the power to forgive sins and save souls.[41] The Church sought only to make life easier for the act of repentance – of becoming one with Christ's body through *exomologesis*. Christian life was thus a continuous form of willed obedience to the bond; a task for each Christian, who could seek no more than guidance from their fellow constituents. The individual was not an agent in this process. The subject could only perform and acknowledge their subjection to God's mercy because they did not possess the knowledge of deliverance. This knowledge is discovered later and with it, God's immutable justice is also conceived. Until justice supplants mercy, Christian subjects were never able to properly repent or express the true definition of obedience and so define their subjectivity in terms of their own justice.

Exomologesis and public penance

Both the eastern and Roman systems of penance remained focused on the concept of the Church as the embodiment of Christ and the exclusion of the penitent from communion and the Mass. In the eastern system the penitents were gradually admitted to the different penitential 'stations' before complete reunification. The stations were designed gradually to re-admit the sinner back into the Church that had expelled them and were modelled on those through which converts advanced to baptism.[42] The codes were at the discretion of the bishops who administered them. This discipline was first mitigated and eventually ceased to be observed by the close of the fourth century. The Roman penitential discipline did not recognise the various stations, but was otherwise similar in practice to that of the East. The penitential exercises were not settled in detail and the 'punishment' properly so-called, consisted of exclusion from communion for a longer or shorter period. Those performing public penance did so for sins of a particularly serious nature, such as

41 Lea, 1896, p 10. Episcopal courts developed in each diocese to determine the cases between sinner and the congregation. These were in no sense courts of spiritual conscience. Their jurisdiction was solely in the *forum externum*; any influence, which they might exert over the *forum internum*, over the sinners relation with God, was indirect and incidental. The Church could grant the penitents the means to reconciliation and the opportunity of being judged by God but it did not pretend to absolve them.
42 Writing in the middle of the 4th century, Basil the Great, the Bishop of Caesarea, states that the confession of sin is public and those at different stages of the *exomologesis* are described as weepers, hearers, kneelers and standers (Lea, 1896).

unchastity, homicide or heresy. Over time the discipline became applicable to crimes that the civil law punished with death, exile, or grave corporal penalties.

Although the penitent willed their repentance, the process also required practices of spectacular public subjection that marked the penitent with physical punishment and humiliation in order to inscribe onto the subject with greater force the dissonance between that subject and the Word of God.[43] The subject would, for example, have their head shaved, be covered in ashes, fast, pray, weep, and wear sackcloth.[44] The greater the turn away from God the more 'performative', long, demanding and humiliating the act of repentance and the disciplining effects of subjectivation:

> For the sake of all sins was Baptism provided; for the sake of light sins, without which we cannot be, was prayer provided. What hath the Prayer? 'Forgive us our debts, as we also forgive our debtors. Once for all we have washing in Baptism, every day we have washing in prayer. Only, do not commit those things for which ye must needs be separated from Christ's body: which be far from you! For those whom ye have seen doing penance, have committed heinous things, either adulteries or some enormous crimes: for these they do penance. Because if theirs had been light sins, to blot out these daily prayer would suffice. In three ways then are sins remitted in the Church; by Baptism, by prayer, by the greater humility of penance . . .[45]

Unlike baptism and prayer, the purpose of the greater humility of penance was to abash one's own sense of self as unique through harsh treatment of the body and mind; a performance aimed at portraying the effects of a sinner who had denied the self unity with God through disobedience to His honour. Public penance thus creates what Gilles Deleuze and Felix Guattari have referred to as a 'collective memory' that codes the flow of desire to accord with that of the collective whole:[46] 'to *breed* man, to mark him in his flesh, to render him capable of alliance, to form him within the debtor-creditor relation, which on both sides turns out to be a matter of memory – a memory straining toward the future'.[47] The very performance of willing obedience served to mark out a community of Christians using 'the cruellest mnemontechnics' of spectacle and performance, violent exclusion and inclusion, martyrdom and reform.

---

43 The Latin etymology of 'transgression', namely, *transgressus*, past participle of *transgredi* to step beyond or across.

44 Lea, 1896, p 22.

45 Augustine, www.ccel.org/fathers2/NPNF1-03/npnf1-03-30.htm Paras 15 and 16 (on file with author).

46 Deleuze and Guattari, 1983, p 191.

47 Emphasis in the original. Deleuze and Guattari, 1983, p 190 referring to Nietzsche, 1989.

As argued throughout this book, the practice of identification and sub-jective embodiment of a community produced through the practice of *exo-mologesis* remains present both in the manner in which individual subjects will their own commoditisation and how the developed world constitutes itself in relation to the underdeveloped world by marking out the latter as transgressive but nonetheless within the bounds of development's promise.

In terms of the first trace of *exomologesis*, economic man is perhaps the best example of the modern performance of obedience to indebtedness. Judith Grbich has in her own writings made a number of suggestions about the theoretical formations of the self as a productive or economic subject in later modernity.[48] Grbich's interest lies in how women's bodies are consti-tuted as the proof of the modern model of economic man by a devaluation of their labour as unproductive or unresponsive to market forces. In pursuing her interest, Grbich discusses how the taxpayer's body is calibrated by the state 'upon the price of other commodities, including the commodities of capital, the new financial products of modern economics'.[49] Here, we examine traces of how the individual of capitalist society experiences a particular form of exchangeable subjectivity that is recognised in the active and willing commoditisation of self.

A second trace of *exomologesis* that emerged in the violent relationship forged between the Old World and the New World during the period of discovery, which is analysed in Chapter Three, can be explained briefly here. In Chapter Three, it will be argued that the discovery by the Old World of the New World and its fall (through conquest) was rationalised by the Old World as a catalytic act of redemption that positioned the Old World beyond that fall into a time redeemed. The Old World does not in fact reach a state of transcendence, which is unfathomable. Rather, it constructs a rational space, through language, but one that cannot provide the sense of fulfilment that can only be found in transcendence. From this space of assumed transcend-ence the Old World marked, in phenomenological terms, the New World as the unredeemed manifestation of sin. As a consequence both worlds are haunted by a sense of loss and driven by the desire to address that loss. In developmental terms this is done by holding the Third World and its underdevelopment accountable to the promise of development.

The peoples of the New World could free themselves from this publicised and spectacularised lapsarian space only by disappearing under the Word of Old World law, such that the identifying marks of sinfulness might be removed as they became unified with the other world. In so far as this was possible, New World peoples had to accept the framework of justice imposed on them by the imperialism of the Old World, thus becoming confessional subjects (see below) that negotiated a space of becoming in accordance with

48 See Grbich, 1996a and Grbich, 1996b.   49 Grbich, 1996a, p 138.

the development manuals of the Old World. At the international level, this involved a mapping of what is referred to here as the 'confessional subject' onto the concept of the nation state and its citizens.

Such practices have governed the relationship between the Old and the New Worlds since their first encounter, in order to secure for the Old World an identity of purity and revelation set within its own fantasy of a time redeemed. This fantasy continues to exist because the New World/the Third World remains marked as a body that reminds the Old World of a past life when it was unredeemed, without credit, and bonded to God's covenant by its own primitive unworthiness. In this way, I suggest that the practice of *exomologesis* has not been entirely displaced but continues to form the basis of any relation between western imperial power and another subject that refuses to negotiate at a confessional level (for a discussion of what is meant by 'the confessional level' see below). This suggestion presumes that all subjects entering the global stage are made to recognise at some level an international society of states, which is discussed in Chapter Five.

It is suggested that this society of states is determined by a western imperial schema,[50] which is still influenced by Christian disciplinary techniques. In particular, it is suggested that colonised subjects are required both materially and politically to bring themselves into subjection to Empire, 'not to make themselves equal' to use the words of Augustine,[51] but rather to maintain recognition by an international audience that promises salvation. Racism and narratives of civilisation have been burned on to the identity of the West so that it is unable to conceive of the colonial subject in any way but as an indebted Other. Nonetheless, discourses of development do attempt to bring the subject into alliance as an equal but only so that the colonial subject might confess the truth of development as it is understood by western confessors. 'Underdeveloped' countries are not the only subjects to undergo these processes of humiliation. Those so-called 'rogue' states, such as Iraq or Cuba, who deny the West their obedience are also marked as penitents for harsh sanctions and violence to render them 'capable of alliance'. Here the colonial subject is not a 'lawmaker' – freedom can be secured only by subjection to a higher power. There is no negotiation between subject and law, only a spectacular public form of punishment.

To further explore these imperial relationships, we turn now to a discussion of the emergence of the 'confessional subject' in the Middle Ages.

Defining the word

As the Church began to fill with the peoples of western Europe throughout the Middle Ages, a system of private, auricular confession based on a practice

---

50 See Pahuja, 2005.   51 Augustine 1966, Book I, Chapter 12.21.

known as *exagoreusis* was introduced, which eventually replaced public penance. In this displacement the very condition of Christianity was transformed; ordained with the potential to absolve itself of sin within mortal life and thereby obtain eternal salvation. This movement can be seen as the replacement of mercy by justice. As part of the same process, through the institutionalisation of private penance, the Church transformed its power to destroy by expulsion into a correlative power to save by positioning itself in the space of God. As a result, the task of salvation fell into human hands.

The difference between *exomologesis* and the latter practice of *exagoreusis* hinges on a particular reading of redemption – the former signifying humanity as marked by indebtedness, the latter constituting each Christian as an exchangeable (redeemable) form operating within a system of justice as determined by the Church. Neither practice entirely displaced the other. As argued above, both practices leave mimetic traces in subsequent western discourses of development. Both practices are forms of disciplinary power predicated by an economy of desire produced out of humanity's attempts to achieve a sense of completion understood as promised.

Exagoreusis

Exagoreusis was based on an oral form of repentance whereby the penitent sought to model the self as closely as possible on the image of Christ by negotiating their redemption with another person acting as their spiritual guide. The idea was to confess one's transgressions so that one might learn to avoid behaviour that was spiritually harmful and be instructed instead on a more true form of being. The return to God was acted out most significantly in the ascetic practices of the 'desert fathers'. The 'desert was an ideal site for *ascesis*, short of martyrdom, and the man who went there placed himself under a virtual obligation to reinvent himself'.[52] Although the 'desert fathers' isolated themselves in order to transform the self, they continued to maintain contact with spiritual counsellors with whom they would engage in the practice of *exagoreusis*, that is, the opening of one's heart to another in order to attain inner peace.[53] *Exagoreusis* may be defined as 'spiritual direction' since it is 'founded on the capacity of the master to lead the disciple to a happy and autonomous life through good advice'.[54] In this respect, *exagoreusis* performed the same purpose as *exomologesis*, namely the sacrifice of the autonomous self by obedience of the individual to the Word of God. It differed from *exomologesis* in so far as the task of ensuring obedience was not

---

52 Harpham, 1987, p 24.
53 Connolly, 1995, p 14. See the discussion of the works of John Cassian by Griffiths, 1964, p 25 i.
54 Foucault, 1988, p 44.

by a complete turn to God (or the Church) but through negotiation with the master (man) as representative of God.[55] The master, and later, the self – not God – was expected to have complete control over the will of the subject. It is this philosophy that Foucault argues is the source of the western European concept of the self.[56] This confessional practice is also arguably a source of a particularly western notion of justice. Where the previous chapter argued that economic man's relation to capitalist development contain traces of a promise based on a bond of indebtedness, here we explore traces of an 'immutable justice' in the promise of development. Both approaches to development's promise are intertwined in so far as the market makes possible the immanence of development's justice at its limit.[57]

Confessing privately

The practice of *exagoreusis* was adopted and developed by Celtic Christians in place of the public penitential system of continental Europe around the late fifth and early sixth centuries. It became incorporated into the system of penance and was useful as a disciplinary technique because it did not require public and prolonged completion of penitential works and it allowed the act of penance for grave and venial sins to be integrated into one ritual. The technique was based on the belief that by gaining a greater awareness of the elements of one's own sinfulness, one could remedy oneself accordingly.[58]

Thus the practice arose, particularly amongst Celtic monks, to make full and regular confession throughout one's life for all one's faults. Lay people were also in regular contact with the monasteries and they, too, would have had recourse to a particular monk for help and advice. The practice was subsequently adopted by monastic communities on the European continent, particularly as the Church expanded and the maintenance of a community of saints seemed to many an impossible means of dying to the world. This is the form of *exagoreusis* adopted and adapted by St Benedict in the sixth century.[59] Benedict's Rule declared that a monk must reveal everything to the figure of authority, the abbot:

55 Ibid.   56 Ibid.

57 See for example, Orford, 2005, for a discussion of how human rights law supplements the economic laws of international trade.

58 Connolly, 1995, p 20.

59 The Rules of St Benedict were written between 530 and 560. They rely on the rules and traditions of Christian monasticism that existed from the 4th century to the time of its writing such as those of St Pachomius (4th century Egypt), St Basil (4th century Asia Minor), St Augustine (4th and 5th century North Africa), Cassian (5th century Southern Gaul) and, most evidently, the Rule of the Master, an anonymous rule written two or three decades before Benedict's Rule.

> The fifth degree of humility is that he [the monk] hide from his abbot none of the evil thoughts that enter his heart or the sins committed in secret, but that he humbly confess them.[60]

In correcting oneself the aim of the sinner was to divest one's self of its own mortal ingenuity and thereby reduce the risk posed by one's own free will. The result sought was unity with Christ, and one's space of emergence was limited to this ideal.[61] As Janet Coleman writes:

> One's own sense of self as unique would be humbled through daily focusing on one's own faults, ... Gradually the habit of selflessness would develop and with wilful behaviour and consciousness behind one, the monk would be, as Augustine and Plotinus sought to encourage, a man without a personal memory. ... the creation of a man whose personal past was relegated to oblivion, and he lived only for the future. ... His memory faculty was now only a storehouse of divine texts, completely given over to the *verbum mentis* which could take him, if only momentarily, to unity with God.[62]

Here the subject no longer gave their body and mind outright but rather negotiated a subject space within which to receive God – a kind of earthly, verbal self-inscription.

From the Carolingian period (750–1000) onward, auricular confession gradually began to displace the practice of public penance in western Europe.[63] The practice of *exagoreusis* took the redeemable soul as an object of knowledge connecting the political power of the Church to the individual souls of the Christian population. The human soul became the source of justice connecting power on high with the power from within. In doing so, the confessor and the person confessing their sins negotiated, calculated, programmed, anticipated, provided, predicated and foresaw a framework of Christian justice. This is what justice is made of, the Christian rule of law that is described below in an analysis of the texts of Anselm, Archbishop of Canterbury. It is the same providential power, a calculation not a promise that will be accorded

---

60 *Saint Benedic's Rule for Monasteries*, 1948, p 27.   61 Braswell, 1983, p 22.
62 Coleman, 1992, pp 135–36.
63 The bishop still performed the functions of public penance on Holy Thursday, but it was becoming an insignificant means by which the Church dealt with sinners. This led to public penance being assigned to the commission of public sins and non-public penance for sins that had remained secret. This new orthodoxy found in the capitularies of various bishops was incorporated into official Carolingian legislation by the reform councils of 813. In practice the two forms of penance remained mixed depending on the knowledge of the priests and their access to texts (Meens, 1998, p 35). For a history of the displacement of public penance by private auricular confession, see Lea, 1896, p 191 and Tentler, 1977. See also Foucault, 1979 for a history of criminal punishment in the Middle Ages and its links to public spectacle.

the sovereign monarch and the nation state as the western subject continues to negotiate for itself an exchange of meaning that promises fulfilment.

God's promise became that which had already happened – the confessional subject was known in advance – determined beforehand.[64] As Sundhya Pahuja and the current author have observed in an examination of the origins of law, by founding authority, 'the narrative of origin erases the possibility of being – of arriving – otherwise. Moreover, it prevents the subject of narration from being more than the origin allows'.[65] The subject is always already that which is born of its origin. This 'confessional subject' was an individual, who had learnt to understand the self as a form of sovereignty over one's own being – the precursor to Balibar's citizen.

The manual to salvation

To facilitate the process of confession, the Church generated a plethora of prescriptive writings, which were divided generally into penitentials for parish priests (practical in nature, focusing on the administration of the sacrament), the summae (focusing on theological subtleties and the practical aspects of confession), and evangelical manuals, sermons, and anonymous treatises in the vernacular.[66] These manuals were based on earlier penitential guides through which St Columbanus and his followers had transmitted the practices of Celtic penance to Britain and western Europe.[67] Written by Celtic monks in the sixth, seventh and eighth centuries, they were designed to help the spiritual counsellor guide individual Christians away from behaviour which was spiritually harmful, to heal them from the effects of sin and to instruct them in virtue.[68] The manuals would often contain the words to be used by the priest and included ways in which the penitent might be expected to respond. Subsequent manuals resembled the older Celtic manuals but became increasingly thorough. Minute and suggestive lists were drawn up and all sins were investigated in their finest particulars to determine the exact amount of guilt involved in every possible case. It was a mortal sin for the priest to fail in this duty. All possible lapses from rectitude in every sphere

---

64 See Derrida, 1998, p 20.   65 Beard and Pahuja, 2003.   66 Root, 1997, p 59.

67 Recent work disputes the Celtic origins of private practice and argues instead that Frankish aristocrats supported the Celtic practice only because it had already been accepted practice on the continent during the 6th century (Dooley, 1982, pp xliii, 390; Wood, 1982, pp 72–74).

68 *The Pennitential of Cummean*, for example, a Celtic manual written in or around 650, is divided into two parts. The first comprises a prologue in the form of a homily on the remission of sins. Reference is made here to the healing power of penance as a remedy for the salvation of souls. This is followed by eight chapters in which penance is set out according to the eight capital sins of gluttony, fornication, avarice, anger, dejection, languor, vainglory and pride. Part two then deals with lesser offences, the misdemeanour of boys and questions concerning the sacred host. See Meens, 1998, pp 35, 47.

of human life were investigated and estimated and catalogued and defined. The priests were to be discreet,

> so that like a skilful leach he may bathe with wine and oil the wounds of the wounded, diligently enquiring into the circumstances of the sinner and of the sin, whereby he may understand what counsel to give and what remedy to exhibit, using various experiments to cure the sick.[69]

Both verbal and bodily signs were surveyed. For example, Alain de Lille (c.1128–1203), in his directions to the confessor, endeavoured to instruct him about the conclusions to be drawn from the face of his penitent.[70]

Sin and punishment

As a result of the detailed lists of prescribed behaviour in the penitential manuals, a change took place in the meaning of sin. The meaning changed from sin being the alienation of humanity from God into an abstract concept and object of human knowledge – distinct acts, desires or thoughts for which the guilty individual must pay a penalty in temporal suffering in either this life or the next. As a consequence, the concept of repentance as a turning toward God was fully reconceptualised into a concept of penal justice or punishment. That which was then marked out was the sin within a person, not the person as such. Although the confessional practice that developed from *exagoreusis* was still referred to as 'penance' (*poenitentia*), the penitential works were no longer a performed attempt at identification by making a spectacle of those who strayed from the Word. Repentance was thus transformed from a status to a process of reform dictated by just forms of punishment. Thus, penance became expressly identified with 'punishment' (*poena*) for previous sinful acts identified through the technique of *exagoreusis*.[71] The popular eleventh century text on the subject, *Concerning True and False Penance*, thus refers to *poenam tenere*, 'to undergo punishment'.[72] The author states

> Properly speaking, punishment (*poena*) is a hurt (*laesio*) which punishes and avenges (*vindicat*) what one commits ... Penance (*poenitentia*) is therefore an avenging (*vindicatio*) always punishing in oneself what he is sorry to have done.[73]

---

69 Lea, 1896, Vol. I, p 229.   70 Alan of Lille, 1981.
71 Grafton, Shelford and Siraisi, 1992, p 32.   72 Berman, 1983, p 172.
73 This interpretation of the sacrament of penance was posited in the canon by means of its Latin translations, which were used by medieval scholars as the authoritative representations of the original. Humanist scholars of the late Middle Ages and early Renaissance later challenged these errant translations. Erasmus, for example, in his translation of the New Testament into Greek, Hebrew and Latin, pointed out that the sacrament of penance underpinning the entire

The idea of penance as a status was thus slowly replaced by a process whereby the individual penitent was able to undertake the task of their own punishment upon themself for the commission of particular acts in order to avoid greater punishment in the afterlife. God's mercy was thus undermined by a more earthly framework of penal justice.

The confession provided the Church with the means to inject into Christian practice and belief an objective 'Christian' system of justice that sought to credit rather than liberate the interior self.[74] Christians were in a relationship of negotiation with God, freed from the inscription of debt brought about by their alienation. Sin had become an object of exchange – an eye for an eye; the confession of sin is returned in exchange for a pure, Christian self. The Christian subject had become, like Christ, a broker of the Word in the constant deferral of meaning. The self was no longer mysterious. The penitent could mark out their own identity in 'a methodical way and subject the forces of sin and worldliness to his purity of will and achievement'.[75] The result: a split subject that sacrifices a part of itself for the promise of true representation. The relationship of the individual to God was therefore no longer based on a bond of indebtedness to be redeemed at the Last Judgement but rather a progressive journey of recognition.

It is no surprise that the practice of buying and selling indulgences also gained ground during this time,[76] nor, as Asad notes, was it surprising that judicial torture and inquisitorial procedure replaced the early medieval accusatorial procedures of duel, ordeal and sacred oath in the detection of truth. The divine was no longer directly involved in questions of guilt or innocence.[77] By 1215 the Lateran Council would forbid priests to take part in trial by ordeal so that human agencies would be used to determine guilt. Asad claims that it was 'changes in the practices defining the truth and not the other way around', 'which lead to the "recognition" of "superstition" '. This process, in turn, defined what was meant by 'rationality'.[78] It is with this rationality that humanity is able to set itself 'free' – a rationality that begins to be discursively produced as the modern phenomenon of the Reasonable Man and God's immutable justice.

framework of confession and absolution, the incarnation and the practice of indulgences were all based on the false interpretation, 'to do penance' (*poenitentiam agite*). Erasmus argued, in contrast, that the text had commanded Christians to 'repent' (*metanoeite*), that is, to come back internally to their true senses (Grafton, Shelford and Siraisi, 1992, p 32).

74 Murray, 1981, p 275.   75 Paden, 1988, p 64.

76 Indulgences were a remission of the temporal punishment by the Church in exchange for payment.

77 Asad, 1983, p 289.   78 Ibid, p 291.

Truly individual

The confessional subject was to be christened into a sovereign space of its own making, its boundaries given 'absolute' dimensions like space and time.[79] In the same way that the medieval artists used set schemata, such as the triangle or the circle, to represent the human form, the penitential manuals provided schemata for the confessional self to draw upon.[80] Yet, as the manuals became more and more detailed, they also became further adapted to the individuality of each penitent, such that the original schema would be sketched upon until the imperfections had been erased. In this way the idea of 'seizing and holding the idea of human perfection', sought later by Renaissance artists, arguably emerged here first in the formation of subjective space by the practice of *exagoreusis*. Here also, perhaps, we see man inherit his fundamental rights as a human being.

By the fifteenth century, Bartholomaeus de Chaimis, after exhausting all the generalities of sins, gives specific instructions for the examination of children and married people, princes and magistrates, lawyers, physicians, surgeons, courtiers, citizens, merchants, traders, bankers, business partners, brokers, artisans, apothecaries/druggists, goldsmiths, tavern keepers, butchers, tailors, shoemakers, money lenders and borrowers, bakers, actors, musicians, farmers, peasants, tax- and toll-collectors, rectors and administrators of hospitals and religious houses, clerics, simple priests, canons and incumbents of benefices, bishops and secular prelates, abbots and regular prelates and, finally, monks and friars.[81] Here, the individual self is linked to the identity of the group. As Ullman notes, it was the office 'which absorbed the individual, but the office and power it contained were not of human origin or making, but of allegedly divine provenance'.[82] This is important to note because it was the divine origin of these discursive offices that secured their boundaries protecting them from the deferral of meaning while, at the same time, keeping these offices within the authority of the Church and the promised promise. The penitential manuals constituted, 'in solitary omnipotence' a truth with which the confessing subject was invested.[83]

79 Haraway, 2000, pp 111, 114.
80 'To the Middle Ages, the schema is the image; to the post-medieval artist, it is the starting point for corrections, adjustments, adaptations, the means to probe reality and to wrestle with the particular. The hallmark of the medieval artist is the firm line that testifies to the mastery of their craft. That of the post-medieval artist is not facility, which they avoid, but constant alertness. Its symptom is the sketch, or rather the many sketches, which precede the finished work and, for all the skill of hand and eyes that marked the master, a constant readiness to learn, to make and match and remake till the portrayal ceases to be a second-hand formula and reflects the unique and unrepeatable experience the artist wishes to seize and hold. It is this constant search, this sacred discontent, which constitutes the leaven of the Western mind since the renaissance and pervades our art no less than our science' (Ullmann, 1967, p 44).
81 Bartholomaeus de Chaimis, in Lea, 1896, Vol. I, p 371.   82 Ullmann, 1967, p 44.
83 See Foucault, 1979, p 35.

The investment of man with truth meant that the practice of *exagoreusis* had fundamentally different effects on the individual than did the process of public penance, and the performance of *exomologesis* from which it was derived. *Exagoreusis* was based on a discursive exchange of truth about oneself that involved a 'character reconstruction', which corrected special personal defects in order to reintegrate one's personality into the divine, rather than a physical inscription onto the body of the subject, in order to render them more receptive to unification.[84] *Exagoreusis* brought the divine into the self whereas the practice of *exomologesis* had sought the submission of self to the will of God 'on high'. In this process a new deployment of power is released. It is a system of justice that determines the Word of God.

Here the Word, like in the earlier works of Augustine, is sacred and must not be used 'falsely'. Indeed, the Church made lying in confession a sin. The Church also reinforced the private and secretive nature of confession in order to promote a complete and honest confession, and thus a complete and honest Christian subject. In order to save the confessional subject, the confessors needed to know what they could otherwise not know. It was therefore important that the Church created conditions in which that knowledge was brought within the authority and safekeeping of the Church. This seal of confession bound both the priest and the penitent to silence after confession by forbidding the writing out of a confession or even thinking about the sins once confessed. This practice served to encourage speaking within the confessional but to limit it otherwise.[85] As Jerry Root, a scholar of comparative literature notes, 'individual penitents must especially scrutinize the contents of their own confession to avoid falling into sin in the very act of attempting to remit it'.[86] Root argues that confession was not only a personal outpouring of words but also 'a craft, a skill that can and must be learned' – a 'technique of self-production' confined by the dictates of rectitude.[87] The task of the confessor was acknowledged to be fraught with risk, and the suggestiveness of their interrogations led the Church to warn priests against suggesting too much such that the attention of the flock is given to sins previously unknown to them.[88]

The confessional self

The penitential manuals formed the basis of a Christian system of justice within which each Christian was given the means to make good their

---

84 McNeil, 1938, p 46.   85 See Lea, 1896, Vol. I, p 432; and Root, 1997, p 74.

86 Root, 1997, p 69.   87 Ibid, p 3.

88 For example, The Roman Ritual of Paul V recognised the use of interrogation but warned against wasting time on meaningless and curious inquiries, or teaching sin to the innocent or young through imprudence. See Lea, 1896, Vol. I, pp 74, 369–70.

indebtedness to God in return for their salvation. The Christian subject was no longer at God's mercy but located within a system of lawmaking that could determine salvation in advance. The concept of individual agency, inherent in the latter Roman Catholic constructions of the self, arose from the perception that individuals had the potential to direct themselves rather than subjecting themselves to the divine promise.

Humanity had usurped the medium of language for itself. It is this usurpation that arguably produces the predication of subjectivity in the discursive spaces of the 'confessional subject'. As Warren points out, this technology of revealing one's self in total obedience can lead paradoxically to the self(-)constituting self. As Foucault remarks, 'By telling himself not only his thoughts but also the smallest movement of consciousness, his intentions, the monk stands in a hermeneutic relation not only to the master but to himself'.[89] In this way, the confessional subject became 'the creator of his own progress' – a discursive body in a relationship of (verbal) exchange.[90]

As Asad notes, the need for verbalisation, of signifying in human terms that which would otherwise remain unknown of the truth about oneself makes possible 'the putting into practice of certain types of knowledge-based expertise, the exercise of distinctive forms of authority, and the characteristic justifications for applying – or threatening – pain in the confrontation of guilt, sickness, error'.[91] In this sense the penitent always keeps within themselves the potential to become their own authority/author, thereby weakening the certainty of meaning possessed by former authorities/authors.

In fact, the manuals were no more able to determine the truth about Christian subjectivity and its ultimate salvation, than the interiorised voice that willed a turn to God and His mercy. God and the truth about salvation continued to be subject to the ambiguity surrounding their interpretation. As McVeigh, Rush and Young have written, 'the recognition of the work of language at the source of law is a reminder both of the impermanence and contingency of legal form and of its mutability in use and transmission'.[92] The law waits to be spoken, to be exchanged and negotiated into being. Hence the need to describe in minute details the characteristics of the true Christian subject, to legislate the inherent rights of the individual at the subjective level of the person. Language, and the human mastery of it, had to assume the power of inscription and bondage. The confessional subject thus stands paradoxically both as a founder of the 'fundamental indeterminacy' of the modern citizen-subject in western society, as well as the source of inherent and inviolable human rights and freedoms.

89 Foucault, 1988, p 45.
90 Warren, www.orb.rhodes.edu/encyclop/culture/lit/griselda.html (on file with author).
91 Asad, 1983, p 306. See also, Asad, 1993.   92 McVeigh, Rush and Young, 2002.

In so far as the process of confession was one of translation and inter-pretation, it was a relational process dependent on sharing meaning with an Other. In this respect, the relation remains promissory in nature: a rela-tion that promises fulfilment by offering the promisee an assurance of what may be expected from the future by claiming to act within a system of justice. This is the immutable justice that binds the subject into a particular chain of signification where the Word remains the model of wholeness, of pure presence, against which the Christian subjects must redeem them-selves in exchange for meaning. As Lacan notes in the context of subject formation:

> What I seek in speech is the response of the other. What constitutes me as subject is my question. . . . I call him by a name that he must assume or refuse in order to reply to me.[93]

This is the christening force of naming discussed in Chapter One in the analysis of Calderisi's story about the inscription of subjectivity onto the women who had sought recognition as 'true subjects' of development. In so far as the self is a negotiated subject, it is determined by the signification of its space of becoming – whoever or whatever has sovereignty over that space has control over the identity of the subject. In western medieval Christian practice this meant that subjects were given to constructing themselves according to the desire of the Church – a desire made possible through faith in the redemptive power of the Word. The practice of *exagoreusis* did not, could not, however, achieve God's promise of salvation. Instead, *exagoreusis* produced a human condition that is a permanent deferral of truth; one that could never redeem the sinner in this world.

The conflict between the respective desires of the Church and the subject is well illustrated by the autobiographical work of the theologian Peter Abelard (1079–1142). The *Historia Calamitatum* is supposedly written by Abelard to a friend as a exegetical work 'of a well defined rhetorical type known as *consolatoria*', which seeks to comfort the recipient with the message that the writer's troubles have been much worse than those of the recipient.[94] Abelard uses his *Historia* to expose his life as a person who has used reason to overcome the depths of carnal sin and insult to God in order to rise through 'philosophy and bodily mutation to the stature of a spiritual man'.[95] Amongst other issues, Abelard's *Historia* deals with his trial and punishment for proposing a heretical theory of the Trinity. In doing so, Abelard used the emergence of power through the confessional subject to discover his own sense of the truth, which had the potential to unbind the *ecriture* of

93 Lacan, 1988, p 299.   94 Southern, 1970, pp 88–90.   95 Ibid.

his subjectivity from the total text.[96] He therefore represented the subjective potential of a unique semblance of truth – his own reality – demonstrating that the subject need not be bound into the spine of some greater story but could instead tear himself from the bind of totality and one absolute meaning. Abelard thus gave meaning to his life by actively negotiating his way within an exchange of words believing that a subject without the capacity to reason is no subject at all, since 'one who does not yet see through reason what he should do has no fault arising from contempt of God'.[97]

When brought before his peers to explain his heresy, Abelard had expected to be able to redeem himself to the guardians of the Word by explaining his thesis logically in his own words. Instead, Abelard was made to burn his work and recite the Creed. Abelard read it 'as best [he] could' but suffered from what he conceived to be disdain and envy of his intellectual findings by his fellow clergy and a denial of his subjective exegesis as a source of truth. Abelard's work is therefore a good example of an individual rebelling against the authority of a Church that demanded his repentance by humbling himself to the point of selflessness by sacrificing his reasonableness to the recitation of divine texts.[98] Abelard demonstrates the dangers – and the possibility of resistance – inherent in a discipline located in someone who is 'truly' individual by rejecting the practice of copying God's *verbum* and the straight-forward reading of God's word from a text. He preferred to interpret, rather than mirror, the Word. Abelard thereby broke from the strict limits placed on reading and proceeded instead 'by locating the authority for making sense no longer in the pages of the past, but in the hands of the reader'.[99] In this regard he placed himself at odds with the general Christian (public) order and its authority.

Abelard empowered himself with meaning – foreshadowing the principle catalytic forces of the Reformation and the struggle between the Roman Catholic Church and the layperson as well as between the authority of the Church and secular rule. These forms of resistance can be traced through to the Reformation of Catholicism, and the struggles by lay people against theological hierarchy, including a monarch who claimed to be divinely

96 Jacques Derrida distinguishes between 'writing' (*ecriture*) and the 'idea of the book'. Derrida discusses the totality of the book as a container for words and meaning. *Ecriture*, on the other hand, is alien to the book in that it does not totalise. The book 'is the encyclopaedic protection of theology . . . against the disruption of writing, against its aphoristic energy, and . . . against difference in general' (Derrida, 1976, pp 18, 30–31).

97 Luscombe, 1971, p 23.

98 Coleman, 1992, pp 135–36.

99 Gellrich, 1985, p 27. Hence, Gratian was to write in his *Decretum* that the heretic displayed intellectual arrogance by preferring their own opinions to those divinely ordained to know and pronounce on such matters of faith (Ullmann, 1967, p 37).

appointed to speak the Word.[100] Indeed, one could read in Abelard's *Historia* the initial traces of democratic society in the sense put forward by Alexis de Tocqueville, who foresaw democracy arising from a social order that could no longer put its faith in the theologico-political authority of the prince.[101] Abelard's body, however, can also be used as an example of how the confessional subject remained under the disciplinary technique of *exomologesis*. By forcing Abelard to read the canon *verbatim* as his own interpretation of the Word was burnt, the Church subjected Abelard to public humiliation by forcing his words and action to accord with the collective memory of the Church. In that regard, Abelard's story is also an illustration of how the Church, and later the sovereign monarch, continued to use practices of *exomologesis* to control individual members of society by means of spectacular forms of public punishment.[102]

The importance of sacraments

The medieval Roman Catholic Church maintained its charge over the souls of Christians as a site of power and knowledge by discounting the tradition of direct absolution from God through contrition and faith (evident in practices of *exomologesis*) in favour of sacerdotal ministration.[103] Initially, the earlier Celtic art of *exagoreusis* prescribed in the penitentials was neither sacramental nor obligatory and it was the penitent and not the adviser who, with amendment and almsgiving, effected the cure.[104] The Church sought to re-evaluate this confessional relationship by regulating the role and authority of the confessor through a renewed interpretation of the gospels of Matthew and John:

> And I will give you the keys of the kingdom of heaven, and whatever you bind on earth will be bound in heaven, and whatever you loose on earth will be loosed in heaven[105]

The early Church had believed these powers to be personal to the respective apostles and it was not expected that the apostles would have any successors. Rather, Christ had spoken of the coming of the end of the world before that

---

100 Grbich argues that the dialogical and structurally conflictual nature of Anglicanism is arguably indistinguishable from jurisprudence, meaning analytical jurisprudence such as that found in the work of H L A Hart. Grbich, 1999, pp 351, 357.

101 Lefort, 1988, p 17.   102 See Foucault, 1979.

103 By 1418, at the Council of Constance, contrition was held not to suffice if a fitting priest could be found. By the Council of Trent, St Victor's definition of contrition became accepted such that a mortal sinner could not be pardoned by a layperson taking auricular confession if a priest was accessible. Lea 1896, Vol. I, p 215.

104 Lea, 1896, p 176.   105 *Matthew* 16:19. See also *Matthew* 18:18, and *John* 20:22–23.

generation had passed away.[106] By claiming to hold the powers of absolution and declaring penance a sacrament, the Roman Catholic Church increased the authority of its clergy to regulate the conduct of their parishioners.[107] The capacity of the Christian priest to forgive sins marked in effect a shift in the capacity of human will to take part in an individual's own salvation in so far as it enabled the self to rationally work to 'improve' itself rather than rely on God's irrational mercy. The shift was one from divine mercy to earthly justice – from faith in God's promise to a calculation of that promise repeated in advance.[108] In effect, the Church had appropriated God's promise and the means to salvation and self-knowledge: *Noverim te, noverim me* (I would know you [God], I would know myself).[109] Christians ceased to be a manifest-ation of sin and became instead brokers of truth – decision makers in the determination of the limits of their own salvation.[110]

The Church officially promulgated these powers of absolution in 1215 in the *Omnis utriusque sexus* decree of the Fourth Lateran Council. Lea has summarised the decree from the Latin as follows:

> All the faithful of both sexes, after they have reached the age of discretion, *must confess all their sins at least once a year, to their own parish priest*, and perform to the best of their ability the penance imposed, *reverently receiving the sacrament of the Eucharist at least of Easter Sunday*, unless by chance he (the priest) should counsel their abstaining from its reception. Otherwise they shall be cut off from the Church during their lifetime and shall be without a Christian burial in death. Whereupon let this salutary statute frequently be made in public in Churches, lest anyone assume by blind ignorance a veil of excuse. However, if anyone with a just cause should wish to confess his sins to another parish priest, let him first seek and obtain permission from his own parish priest, since otherwise that one cannot lose or bind.[111]

The Church, which stood distinct from its members as an overarching cor-poreal body and the proclaimed broker of the truth about salvation, thus

---

106 *Matthew* 24:34; *Mark* 13:30; *Luke* 21:32. See Schaff, 1910, Vol. 5, pp 731–32, 735–37.
107 For a discussion of the ways communities were encouraged to relinquish their traditional forms of worship and systems of kinship, see Kleinschmidt, 2000, pp 36–39.
108 Derrida, 1995, p 41.   109 Augustine, 1990b, Book II, Chapter 1.
110 Southern, 1963, p 113.
111 Emphasis in the original. A later canon ordered all bishops to appoint penitentiaries to their cathedral cities and to all conventional churches. Around 1223, the constitutions of the Bishop of Paris indicate that parish priests were ordered to frequently notify their flocks that all, or at least fathers and mothers of families, should come to confession before Palm Sunday. Lists of all penitents were ordered to be kept and brought to the annual synod. Confession before marriage also became common. Lea, 1896, Vol. I, pp 230–31.

recognised the space of self as a legitimate source of power that could be used to control the conduct of Christians. As such, the Church stood as a beginning for the interdependence of the individual citizen and the secular nation state. The Church took power by situating the interlocution of God's promise within a recognisable obligation owed by the Christian subject to the Church. If the pain of purgatory was not to be greater than necessary, the subject was required to enter into a continuous process of redemption that required an ongoing acceptance of the truth in this world through confession. Thus, according to the *Penitential of Bartholomew Iscanus*, the priest was required to say to the penitent:

> Brother, it is necessary for thee to be punished in this life or in purgatory: but incomparably more severe will be the penalty of purgatory than any in this life. Behold, thy soul is in thy hands. Choose therefore for thyself whether to be sufficiently punished in this life according to canonical or authentic penances or to await purgatory.[112]

This is Christian justice – legitimate power. No longer is one expected to subject oneself to God's mercy and hope for the best. Whether one paid in life or thereafter, one was able to calculate the means by which to redeem God's promise by recognising one's debts and fulfilling them. So it is through Christ's suffering and the skills acquired from confessional practice that each person was afforded the means to conquer sin. The belief that each Christian must 'die and rise with Christ' was underemphasised because their salvation has been made available to them within the temporal world through the confessional.[113] The Christian was not expected to die to this world (in the monastic sense) but instead to erase those elements of the self that did not accord with reason. Humanity was thus able to know itself through itself. Nevertheless, although the good news of salvation was brought closer to humanity, the fact remained that humankind still needed to be saved.

What were once manifestations of sin – the 'complex interaction of body, language, and space' – become the very means to salvation.[114] In as much as the Church was able to control the knowledge of ascertaining God's promise, and by usurping to itself the power of absolution, it possessed a technique of

---

112 McNeil, 1938, p 354.
113 Berman, 1983, p 177. The symbolism of the Eucharistic ceremony again provides an example of this shift in belief. The Mass in earlier times had been a *eucharistia*, a prayer of thanks from the congregation and whose gifts were elevated by the word of the priest to God. During the Carolingian period, particularly as a consequence of the teachings of Isidore of Seville, the Eucharist came to be understood as the *bona gratia*, which God grants the congregation, and which during the height of the Mass descends to them (Jungmann 1959, pp 62–63, 129–30).
114 Spence, 1996, p 4.

disciplinary power with a flexibility and an ability to 'educate consciences' far greater than that based on *exomologesis* and a turning toward or, rather, into the divine and away from the *saeculum* and the jurisdiction of the Church.[115] Importantly, this structure of power operated from the top down but enforced itself at all levels. The self-surveillance and self-discipline necessary for this practice were easily justified and deployed by the promise of the reward of truth and salvation that lay like a 'shimmering mirage' beyond the confessional.[116] These rewards lured the subject toward its object-cause of desire as long as the subject had faith it its own reasoning – a faith based not on God's overwhelming will but on human understanding: *Fides quaerens intellectum* (faith through understanding).

Rectitude, truth and human action were thereby bound together in so far as those who willed what they ought did not sin, since it was only by sinning that they deserted the truth. That, indeed, was the argument of Anselm, Archbishop of Canterbury (1033–1109):

> For if, so long as he wills what he ought, which is why he was given a will, he was in rectitude and in truth, and when he willed what he ought not, he deserted rectitude and truth, such truth can only be understood as rectitude since both truth and rectitude of will were nothing other than to will what he ought.[117]

It was the Church that authorised rectitude and thus controlled individual intentions. Justice became immutable. As Foucault has argued:

> For a long time, the individual was vouched for by the reference of others and the demonstration of his ties to the commonweal (family, allegiance, and protection); then he was authenticated by the discourse of truth concerning himself.[118]

In this way, a confessional discursive space was produced based 'not so much on the permanence and uniqueness of [its] object as on the space in which various objects emerge and are continuously transformed'.[119] In development practice today, this means the construction of discursive bodies around the concepts of the citizen and the nation state in which the peoples of the Third World, and indeed the First World, are given meaning and therefore fulfilment through the construction of ideological paradigms and practices of

---

115 See the exchange between Thomas A Tentler and Willliam J Boyle in relation to the use of *summae* for confessors as an instrument of social control in Tentler, 1974, and Boyle, 1974, pp 103, 137.
116 Foucault, 1998b, p 59.   117 Anselm, 1998a, Chapter 4.
118 Foucault, 1998b, p Vol. I, p 58. Note also Debray, 2004, p181.
119 Foucault, 1989, p 32.

'western' domination as well as professional cartographies of self-awareness that result in an avowed declaration of knowledge.[120] In this way the discursive technique of confession has become 'a condition of possibility for the appropriation of the word of the other, the other as institution, tradition, individual, or even as self'.[121]

Faith through understanding: the texts of Anselm

This section of the chapter takes as its focus the work of Anselm, Archbishop of Canterbury, which is indicative of the move away from the Augustinian reliance on God's inscribing mercy as the guiding force of Christian action toward an incorporation of confessional practice into a 'humane' framework of truth and lawful justice. The first work analysed is Anselm's *Cur Deus Homo*, (Why the God-Man), which reinterprets the Fall of Man from divine will. In this work Anselm attempted to explain 'by necessary reasons' and 'by reason alone' and by '*Christo remoto*' the necessity of the incarnation of Christ without the need for scriptural authority, which had over the centuries 'conspicuously failed to carry conviction'.[122]

In his *Cur Deus Homo* Anselm rejects the long-standing belief that the Fall of Man resulted in a power struggle between God and Satan for the right of lordship over humanity. For approximately the first eleven centuries of Christianity, humanity's fall from God's domination was understood in the same way as a slave who had rejected the authority of the overlord and submitted him/herself to another bond.

This view allowed no role for humanity in its own salvation. It was God and Satan who had the right to fight over the claim to humanity. As the historian R W Southern explains, God became human in order to outwit Satan, who mistook God incarnate (Christ) for his own subject and, thus, illegitimately sacrificed Him. This was taken to be an abuse by Satan of his powers of lordship. As a consequence of this 'illegal' act God was able to save those subjects whom He deemed worthy of salvation.[123] As it is written in the Bible:

> Surely you know that when you surrender yourselves as slaves to someone, you are in fact the slaves of the master you obey – either of sin, which results in death, or of obedience, which results in being put right with God. . . . For though at one time you were slaves to sin, you have obeyed with all your heart the truths found in the teaching you have received. You were set free from sin and became slaves of righteousness. . . . When you are the slaves of sin, you were free from righteousness. . . . But

---

120 See Walker, 1999, p ix.   121 Root, 1997, p 90.
122 Anselm, 1998b, p 260. Southern, 1963, p 91. See also, McIntyre, 1954.
123 Southern, 1954, pp 234–35.

now you have been set free from sin and are slaves of God. Your gain is a life fully dedicated to him, and the result is eternal life.'[124]

For this reason, until the eleventh century, Christ was seen primarily as the conqueror of both death and Satan, enabling the chosen few to return to the kingdom of God.

In Anselm's work Satan was expelled from the equation, and humanity was made the agent of its own redemption through reason. Using feudal imagery, Anselm argued that God created humanity for eternal blessedness, which required perfect and voluntary submission to God. Humanity was alienated from God through its own disobedience. Justice required either that humanity be punished in accordance with its sin, or that humanity provide satisfaction for the dishonouring of God. As for punishment, none would be adequate without frustrating God's purpose again (a second Fall of Man). As for satisfaction, there was nothing humanity could do that would be valuable enough to restore God's honour. Thus, humanity could not make satisfaction. Indeed, only God could. Since only God could, but only humanity was obliged to make satisfaction, Anselm argued it must be made by a 'God-man'. Therefore, Jesus Christ, was born in order to sacrifice himself and so provide satisfaction to God and reconcile humanity to Him. With Christ having sacrificed himself, God then accepted this gift and agreed that recompense would be granted to those who presented themselves to Him as heirs to Christ through baptism. This retelling of Christ's sacrifice as a story of punishment and justice is the same story of justice that would be written by Grotius in the passage cited at the beginning of this chapter.

In line with confessional notions of penance, humanity's salvation was reinterpreted as conditional on the repayment of a rationally determined debt owed to God because of the Fall of Man. Accordingly, it is not the divine power and the ascension into heaven of Christ that enabled the merciful forgiveness of debt, but Christ's descent to earth to repay humanity's debt through suffering and death that redeems. In effect, Christ is the broker of salvation – the ideal confessional subject. Anselm thereby justified the suffering of the Word – of Christ – adding strength to the already common depictions of Christ as a mortal who 'suffered weariness, hunger, thirst, scourging and death on the Cross among thieves'.[125] In addition, it is during

---

124 *Romans* 6:1–22.
125 Anselm, 1998b, Chapter I.3. Accordingly, in the first centuries of Christian practice, the central focus of Christ's crucifixion is his divinity and not his mortality. It is not the sacrifice of his mortal life that is depicted in early medieval art and iconography and worshipped by early Christians, but Christ's superhuman strength and immortality. Christ is portrayed as a king victorious on the cross before his ascension into Heaven. The incarnation of God in Christ on earth and his sacrifice as mortal man, which will represent the means of salvation in later centuries, remains unknown in this period (Kleinschmidt, 2000, p 69).

this period that the Eucharist became not simply a symbol of Christ's mortality but his actual flesh and blood.[126]

The idea that it is sin – that which does not accord with the truth and is wrong – that must be conquered is supported by the change in Christian iconography during this period, from its depictions of Christ reigning from the cross, crowned and wearing the high priestly vestments to Christ shown suffering death for humanity's sins.[127] Christ's mortal life and crucifixion and not his resurrection and divine ascension became the focus of humanity's salvation.[128] Moreover, confession and Christ's mortality were joined as interdependent rituals. In order to partake in Christ's body one was required to purify one's self such that confession was rendered a condition precedent to worthily taking the Eucharist. The Fourth Lateran Council provided the culmination of this belief in its decree of the transubstantiation of the Eucharist, and its declaration that both confession and Communion were obligatory.[129]

As Southern explains, salvation could no longer be limited to a chosen few. Instead, Anselm's argument opened the possibility of salvation to all those who came to God under Christ to redeem their blessedness through submission.[130] In contrast then to the writings of Augustine, Anselm argued that it is divine justice and not humanity's sinfulness that binds humanity to God and divine truth. Justice is thus given meaning by its association with the repayment of debt, not the forgiveness of debt. Here we can see the shift in approach to God's promise away from the recognition of indebtedness to the promise of justice. As a consequence, forgiveness, according to Anselm, must also be understood in terms of justice and not in terms of mercy. For if God were to forgive man's disobedience then He would be making humanity blessed on account of its sin. Anselm concludes that 'Truly such mercy on the

---

126 See Devlin, 1975.   127 Kleinschmidt, 2000, p 75.

128 This was subsequently supported by the Church through the amendment to the Nicene Creed by the proclamation that the Holy Spirit 'proceeds not only from the Father but also from the Son (*filio que*). God the Father, representing the whole of creation, the cosmic order, is incarnate in God the Son, who represents mankind. God, the Holy Spirit, was said not only to have His source in the First Person but also in the Second Person of the Trinity – not only in creation but also in incarnation and redemption. Berman, 1983, p 178.

129 Morris, 1972. The question of the meaning of the Eucharist began to be debated in the 1050s and 1060s, when Lanfranc, then head of the Abbey of Bec in Normandy, and later Archbishop of Canterbury under William the Conqueror, challenged the interpretation offered by the head of a monastic school, Berengar of Tours. Berengar argued against Lanfranc and Pope Gregory VII that the effectiveness of the sacrament, its grace-giving power, did not depend on the transformation of the bread into Christ's body and blood but that its likeness was symbolic. Lanfranc, using the Aristotelian categories of substance and accidents, persuaded the First Lateran Council to denounce Berengar's views and to affirm that the consecrated Eucharist was the miraculously transformed 'true' body of Christ (Berman, 1983, p 173).

130 Anselm, 1998b, Book II, Chapter 19.

part of God would be contrary to himself, it is impossible for his mercy to be of that sort'. This leads Anselm's pupil to say, 'If God follows the method of justice, there is no escape for a miserable wretch; and God's mercy seems to perish'. To this Anselm replies, in language prefiguring discourses of economic restructuring and the refusal to forgive Third World debt today:

> You asked for reason, now accept reason. I do not deny that God is merciful ... But we are speaking of that ultimate mercy by which he makes men blessed after this life. And I think I have sufficiently shown by reasons given above that blessedness ought not be given to anyone unless his sins are wholly remitted, and that this remission ought not be done except by the payment of the debt which is owed because of sin [and] according to the magnitude of the sin'.[131]

Anselm's theory of the incarnation had proved that the rectitude or justice of God required that the price be paid. Mercy was no longer sufficient because it would leave the disturbance of the order of the universe, caused by sin, uncorrected, which in turn would constitute a deficiency in justice and violate the laws of being and becoming. Thus, justice becomes the means by which the redemption of man is attained. It is an economic penal-based justice; a truth that interprets mercy in account-keeping terms. The miserable wretches who do not repent, who do not fall within the justice of men under law, are not subject to God's mercy.

From the eleventh century humanity's progress, its journey toward modernity and the right order of things is limited by – disciplined by – a notion of justice produced within a particular Christian regime of truth or rectitude. This rectitude, the Word of God, is the eternal truth toward which all other truths of will, intellect, fact, word or action are orientated. It is the new Christian code – a rule of law unearthed in the confessional negotiation of the Christian subject. It is a negotiation played out in the apparent rational exchange of human punishment and divine forgiveness, which are brought together into a single economy of justice and rectitude – law and order based on the Reasonable Man.[132] As Anselm argues:

> Observe this also. Everyone knows that the justice of men is under law ... But if sin is neither discharged nor punished, it is subject to no law ... Injustice, therefore, if it is remitted by mercy alone, would be more free than justice, which seems very improper'.[133]

Justice is thus a bounded truth, whereas injustice symbolises the terror of a

131   Ibid, Book 1, Chapter 24.   132   Berman, 1983, p 181.
133   Anselm, 1998b, Book 1, Chapter 12.

promise forsaken. The unjust are outlaws of God's promise, its order and beauty.

The injustice of mercy

Already, in his *On Truth* Anselm argued that something is true 'only by participating in the truth, and therefore the truth of the true is in the true itself'.[134] The preferred means of interpreting the truth, according to Anselm, was by using human reason. Likewise, Anselm's *Cur Deus Homo* was more than an explanation by means *other than faith* of the necessity of Christ's incarnation. This and Anselm's earlier works formed a means of defining the Word in a way that promised salvation to those partaking in the Word – the rule of law – while excluding those who chose not to use their means of 'rational' discrimination in this way. In this sense each Christian remained figurative of the Word in so far as they practiced a discriminating truth of being and, most importantly, of becoming. This was lawfulness: the self-inscribing confessional self. The rationally 'true' subject sought its 'true' signification through confession, a language that was supervised by the supreme truth.

In contrast to Augustine, Anselm believed that it was possible for humanity to discover the truth of living, to know rectitude and the rule of law, *without faith* but with reason, which ultimately seems to amount to the same thing. In both the *Monologion* and the *Proslogion*, Anselm founds his proofs of God in the analogy of human experience and observance. He prefaces his *Monologion* thus:

> For the writing of this meditation they prescribed – in accordance more with their own wishes than with the ease of the task or my own ability – the following format: that nothing at all in the meditation would be argued on Scriptural authority, but that in an unembellished style and by unsophisticated arguments and with uncomplicated disputation rational necessity would tersely prove to be the case, and truth's clarity would openly manifest to be the case, whatever the conclusion resulting from the distinct inquiries would declare.[135]

Human reason is thus accorded the capacity to incorporate humanity into the textual expression of the Word made flesh. Yet, throughout his writings Anselm made clear that the *ultimate* truth was with God, rather than here on earth. Language was supervised by the supreme truth, by making all true signification prior to its signs; it was independent of them, and it could not confer being upon it or withdraw from it.[136] This admission would soon

---

134 Anselm, 1998a, Chapter 2.   135 Anselm, 1986a, p 49.
136 Colish, 1968, p 80.

disappear under the rational sciences and positive laws of the Reasonable Man of modernity only to reappear in the writings of political economists described as the invisible hand of market forces, which are not subject to law but remitted by mercy alone. And as Anselm had used reason to argue, that which is subject to no law but is remitted by mercy alone is freer than justice and seems very improper. This separation of law from mercy in Anselm's work is arguably an act made possible by the space that is opened up within the confessional subject. It constitutes the self through its separation from faith (God) by means of a particular method of speaking the truth. Anselm has become the master creator of God's promise – His Word.

In the same spirit as a penitent distilling the truth about their self from the confession, Anselm distilled the true incarnation of Christ from the Word by defining it in human terms – bringing God down to earth rather than carrying humanity up to heaven. The way to knowledge of God was the *way of incarnation, not revelation*.[137] The Christian subject was no longer the object of divine inscription – a body fading into Word. Instead, Anselm represented a subject who faithfully defined the Word on his own terms.[138] For Anselm, truth was rectitude perceived with reason, and justice was rectitude sought consciously by the will and expressed in right action for the sake of, and by means of, justice itself. The effect was a Christian rule of law, a particular regime of truth that defined the nature and destiny of humanity, its search for salvation and its freedom of thought and action. Human salvation was inevitable if God was to fulfil His original promise to humanity, namely its eternal blessedness. This inevitability was rectitude – God's immutable justice, which became the ultimate authority for the laws of humanity, first in the concepts of divine and natural law but later posited by man as simply rational.

To Anselm it seemed clear that to bring about justice and to do the truth were the same because 'to do the truth is to act well', and to act well is to bring about the Christian rule of law, which is justice.[139] However, in extracting the truth one must also always leave behind an excess of sin, of being otherwise. Indeed, one paid (through penance, suffering, indulgences, martyrdom) to do so. Christian justice was therefore restored in the tragic consequences of truth, a restoration that is discussed in Chapter Three in relation to the European exploration and conquest of the New World.

The subject of exchange

As long as the confessional subject could be contained within a system of totalising truth – in this case of Christian justice – its borders remained solid,

---

137   Berman, 1983, p 175, fn 22.   138   See Colish, 1968, p 59. See also, Evans, 1980.
139   Anselm, 1998a, Chapter 5.

its space sacred and ordered. It is this space of sacred and ordered bondage that secured the subject against the fear of fluidity inherent in the exchange of meaning. But the constitution of the self was never entirely completed. True representation was never returned in exchange for the confession. Thus, the language of confession was released from the limits of Christ's body, but only to break through onto the primordial chaos of language. In this respect confession was a wild force: 'a record of various and changeable occurrences and of irresolute and, when it so befalls, contradictory ideas'.[140]

Hence, during the religious reformation in Europe, the Church lost much of its authority over the confessional subject because it could no longer guarantee the truth about salvation. This, together with the wonders of a newly discovered world, caused great upheaval in the ways that subjectivity was determined and subjectivation took place. On the one hand, there was a trend toward monarchical power as a means to secure the bounds of subjectivity, a trend examined in detail in Chapter Three using the texts of Michel de Montaigne.

This chapter concludes, however, with some thoughts on another remarkable effect of confession, namely the capacity of Christian governance to factor specific obligations and language into a system of exchange. Of particular note is how this capacity marked the beginning of a liquid economy of meaning. The notion that true being had become a matter of negotiation built on containing the threat of betrayal in God's promise provided the ideal conceptual basis for a nascent capitalism that 'degrades men into commodities'.[141] In this process of exchange, there are no political limits to determine the subject, and the individual is absorbed by capital into the machine of production.

This literal realm of exchange was embraced by the merchant classes as the deferred fulfilment inherent in the notion of time as an opportunity for profit. As Pye observes:

> Whether at the level of the discrete subject or at the level of the social field, whether applied literally as final cause or figuratively as global function, the economic metaphor seems to allow for a comprehensive account of the loss of totality. . . .[142]

This is the body of circulation which Karl Marx brought into light as a constantly recurring and totalising cycle into which 'money is a vanishing moment facilitating the exchange of two commodities'.[143] Here the law

---

140   Montaigne, 1958, Book III, Essay 2, pp 610–11.   141   Arendt, 1998, p 162.

142   Pye, 2000, p 19.

143   Spivak, 1988, pp 154, 159. Spivak relies on Karl Marx's *Grundrisse* in making her arguments, particularly 'The Chapter on Money' and 'The Chapter on Capital'. See Marx, 1973.

(justice) links itself to economics. In the same way that the Christian Church had represented itself as having possession of the keys that would unlock the time outside space, the merchants of Christianity began to see their profession as one promising redemption by means of an authoritative knowledge about the accumulation of profit. In this way, humanity could be said to have returned to the will of a Big Other – willing their obedience to an invisible hand. Here the fallen space of humanity is subsumed by time in the continuous exchange of money for time – for money is time. This economic fulfilment was in turn appropriated by the nascent constructions of the nation state and its promise – a merger discussed in later chapters.

As capitalism began to exploit the labour-producing bodies of individuals – the subject of value defined by its capacity to produce more than itself – subjectivity was placed within a produced or disappearing body.[144] That body was not the redeemed body of the merchant. It remained a suffering body awaiting redemption through labour.[145] Here labour is the excess that splits the subject in return for fulfilment through an extraction of surplus value. In this nascent capitalist economy it is thus obedient labour that is given in exchange for subject recognition. A person who cannot be exploited for their pound of flesh is of no worth. The productive value of the subject thus becomes the source of modern capitalism where merchants professed authority and proclaimed the means to salvation. The valueless body was marked with sin, as the capital of merchants began slowly to dispossess the producer from their means of production leaving the working classes as the tragic excess – the 'undifferentiated human labour' that resisted incorporation.

In contrast, the bodies of merchants took on particularly distinguishable identities as they became objects of ingenuity and redemption – self-reliant, independent and competitive – priests of the market. In this respect, the merchant townspeople contrasted themselves to the bodily frailty of the ascetic image.[146] Their spirit was entrepreneurial; their bodies, which had been built in accordance with the appropriation of material prosperity, stood in stark contrast to the depiction of Christ's debt-ridden body. Theirs were bodies redeemed by the spirited labour of others. As Kleinschmidt argues, the 'human body came to be depicted and described as energetic, enduring and as a source of original, not divinely ordained, creative activity'.[147] Merchants earned themselves a body redeemed – a creditable body housing a subjective belief in its own profitability. The penitential manuals were evidence of this

---

144   Spivak, 1988, p 159. The citations from Marx provided by Spivak are her own translations and they are not referenced to the source. See generally, Marx 1973, pp 113–238, 239–50. See Marx, 1930, Vol. 1.

145   See Grbich, 1996a for a discussion of the 'calibration of human exertion according to the needs of financial actors, those imaginary persons and imaginary objects of economic discourse, of the "gold" standard, and of the legal order' (p 139).

146   Kleinschmidt, 2000, p 78.   147   Ibid, p 82.

professional consciousness as well as the recognition of that consciousness by the Church, which sought to regulate the increasingly independent identity of these emerging social groups through the confessional.

Not only did the conceptual space of the human body shift but space itself changed as the monetary economy, constituted around the expansion of urban markets and long distance trade, extended to a measured need for time, particularly with respect to the formation of contractual obligations and money lending. Time became spatial rather than transcendent.

By the thirteenth century, bills of exchange were frequently used, interest became customary, money was used as capital and the merchants were confessing the previously unconfessed sin of wasting time for the purpose of accumulating wealth.[148] Clocks began to appear in urban centres and town governments began to regulate work in terms of time spent. As a consequence, the use of time became a public and externally enforced means of discipline.[149] Meanwhile, scholars revived the Aristotelian concept of time as being linear in nature – the point from which the present and the future had to be derived. The more subjective experiential perceptions of time in rural communities survived in the world outside trade and scholarship.[150] At least within the sovereignty of merchants, time became creditable and available for sale. Time was after all the promise of redemption such that the merchants were not merely appropriating profit but salvation. The mortgaging of time by merchants in their search for profits, which initially had been understood to be in violation of the Christian belief that time belonged to God alone, was suppressed and forgotten. From the perspective of mercantilist experience, time was to be found within space rather than outside it.

This space of creation with its earthly time, like the confessional subject, was no longer understood as a manifestation of sin interrupting divine time. Instead, it was reinterpreted by the clergy, into whose hands the power of absolution had been placed, in a more positive light as a medium of reform and development along which a subject space could be strung. The *saeculum*

---

148   Ibid, 2000, p 25.

149   Kleinschmidt cites the passage of a statute of the Nuremberg Town Hall of 1389: 'The committee of five city councillors shall meet for two hours each before and after lunch time. As soon as all five councillors have assembled, the acting chairman shall turn upside down a sand dial, and all councillors shall sit together for the period of two hours, regardless of whether they have work to do or not' (Kleinschmidt, 2000, p 27).

150   In his *Confessions*, St Augustine wrote of earthly time as an object of inquiry, which humanity could measure at least in small parts. See Augustine, 1955, Book XI. Nonetheless, time generally was experienced subjectively by the medieval European population and its measurement was experienced rather than measured. E.g., the accepted 12 hours of the day and night would be shortened or lengthened depending on the season. As Kleinschmidt reveals from 'the early Middle Ages and up to the thirteenth century, there were few general "objective" standards regarding time and equally few instruments for the precise measurement of time' (Kleinschmidt, 2000, pp 18, 25).

was no longer in decay until the Day of Judgement. Time ceased to represent unfathomable transcendence and became, instead, a process of subjective and objective unfolding. Fulfilment, too, became a process that commenced on earth. Death was no longer a release but a potential shortfall in the promise of a more developed self.

In this sense the Christian world was defined in terms of *becoming*, not *being*, of exchange, not manifest debt, such that its subjects became a function of what time brings.[151] In a manner that precedes the ideas of evolution and historicity of modern western culture, humanity was defined by the sum total of its experience, 'as more than they were when they started'.[152] As a consequence, the penitential practices of western Christianity and the emergence of an entrepreneurial spirit can be said to have swept humanity out of the shadow of sinfulness and into the light of its own development. By the sixteenth century, the Protestant merchant would readily confuse the designs of Providence with their own prosperity and fortune.[153] Capitalism was emerging with its own promise and invisible guiding hand.

Chapter Three explores a rather different shift in Christian conceptions of time and space as a consequence of the period of discovery by the Old World of the New. The discovery of this previously unknown space of creation had marked effects on the philosophies of the Christian world, which had believed itself to be blessed above all others. It is arguable that the discovery marked a radical shift in the conception by the Old World of its own space in relation to time, which adds intensity to the already existing doubts of a region torn apart by conflicts concerning the authority to rule and to interpret the means to human salvation. Moreover, the individual caught within these effects – the subject caught in the time of doubt between its *exomologesis* and its rendering into a 'modern man' of credit was also made to reassess the subjective space of becoming or risk being fragmented into an inexpressible differentiated form.

---

151 Hanning, 1977, p 139.
152 Ibid. In the 12th century there appeared the first European historians who saw history in the West as moving from the past through stages, into a new future. Hugo of St Victor, Otto of Freising, Anselm of Havelberg and Joachim of Floris saw history moving forward in stages, culminating in their own time (Berman, 1983, p 112).
153 See generally, Le Goff, 1980, p 29.

Chapter 3

The age is broken down

The analysis in this chapter puts forward the appreciably post-colonial thesis that the invasion and colonisation of those parts of the world that were discovered by western European powers between the fifteenth and seventeenth centuries gave voice to a renewed embodiment of 'western' subjectivity. The very discovery of the New World was itself a consequence of the 'westernisation' of Christian Europe, since the fall of Constantinople to the Muslim Ottoman Empire in 1453 strengthened the western outlook of Christianity (and literally, its western identity) by closing the trade route from Europe to the east and forcing Christian powers to 'go west'. In doing so, western Europe was made to turn its gaze away from the east and, to paraphrase John Locke, all the world became America.

This chapter explores the impact that the discovery of an unimagined world to the west had on western European identity. In Chapter Two, the disciplinary practices of early Christianity were analysed to demonstrate how conceptions of disciplinary power constituted, marked out, and negotiated the collective Christian body and disciplined the ways in which individual Christians imagined themselves to be. There the forms of subjectivation referred to in Chapter One are described as emerging from practices of repentance based on alternative perceptions of God's promise. The first form of subjectivation was related to the bond of indebtedness between God and His subjects. In that form, the subject wills its own obedience. A second form of subjectivation was where the subject finds within its soul the source of its own will to power and knowledge. There the power of the subject's will was captured by the immutable nature of God's promise, which confined the negotiation of subjectivity to the limits of Christian justice. By claiming to represent the Word and save the soul, Christian governance asserted the means to power and thus secured its authority.

This chapter widens the focus of subjectivation to an examination of territorial bodies (or worlds) and their international (or intersubjective) parts. In pursuing these incorporations of subjectivity, two iterations of a discontinuity in the history of 'the West' that have significance for the emergence of a development discourse in the twentieth century will be investigated. The first involves the emergence of various imperial discourses concerning the discovery of the New World. The second is the religious reformation in Europe and the consequential loss of certainty about the Word and its subject. The Reformation represents a period when the justice of the Roman Catholic Church was returned to the originary violence that had established its authority.[1] As that authority was lost and the Word became subject to new and radical interpretations, Roman Catholic claims to a universal justice and the promise of salvation became more open to interpretation.[2] Textual canons in general lost their cohesion, and yielded their authority to the observations of the named world of astronomers, merchants and anatomists. Hence the discourses forming around the discovery of the New World were tightly intertwined with the discourses of religious reformation and subsequent narratives of Enlightenment. Where there had formerly been 'a place for everything and everything in its right place'[3] now:

> The new Philosophy calls all in doubt
> The element of fire is quite put out;
> The sun is lost, and the earth, and no man's wit
> Can well direct him where to look for it.[4]

Out of this situation, a new symbolic order began to emerge based on faith in universal reason. Human reason thus began its task of binding together a universal family. It is at this juncture that the impossible possibility of universal justice – an international law – emerges. The international law seeks to bind humanity together so that it might be redeemed but does so by representing the necessity for redemption in the separation of the New World from the Old World

During the period of discovery, the quality of previously unknown societies and topographies appealed to and rendered speechless the Christian world.[5] The identity of the New World literally and fundamentally transgressed the borders of Christian identity. Once invaded, however, the New World was colonised like any other Christian subject by subjecting its identity to practices of Christian repentance. The peoples of the New World were brought to justice under an enforced confessional relationship that traded subject recognition in return for the repression of other ways of being and knowing.

In short, the differences discovered in the New World were understood to

1   Derrida, 1992, p 6.
2   In 1517 Martin Luther argued that the basic teachings of the Roman Catholic Church and its practices had no support in the New Testament and must be abandoned. While Protestants maintained that the Bible served as absolute authority, they failed to agree on any one interpretation. Grafton, Shelford and Siraisi, 1992, p 35.
3   Lewis, 1964, p 206.   4   Donne, 1963.   5   Lacan, 1992, p 247.

represent an offence against the justice of the Christian system. Christian justice demanded reparation for the sin of being other than Christian. The very fact of being different was a direct violation of God's Word and a crime against His representative, the imperial sovereign. The point of imperial violence was to respond to this perceived transgression by spectacularly reconstituting the universal authority of the Christian religion and its respective sovereign representatives.[6] The violence of imperial invasion was not merely an act of conquering, nor did it merely attempt to make equal what was new.[7] The violence of imperialism brought 'into play, at its extreme point, the dissymmetry between the subject who had dared violate the law and the all-powerful sovereign who displayed his strength. . . . the punishment [was] carried out in such a way as to give spectacle not of measure, but of imbalance and excess; in this liturgy of punishment, there [had to be] an emphatic affirmation of power and of its intrinsic superiority'.[8] The New World was thus forced to repent publicly.

The period of discovery was a time when the tortured, colonised bodies of the New World were inscribed as subjects by a violent imperialism that produced the truth of their transgression.[9] The only way in which this 'truth' could exert all its power was for the colonised world to repent and bind itself to the obligations of an imperial promise. As Foucault would write in relation to the accused of medieval law, 'the criminal who confessed came to play the role of living truth'.[10] The New World was made to perform the truth about itself as a transgressive subject by sacrificing bodies to marks of race, primitivism and heresy in the same way that early Christians performed their status as a penitent.

The marks of primitivism and savagery were further developed by Enlightenment narratives about the New World such that the Old World was able to imagine itself into a time that is both within and outside the bounds of Christian justice. From the moment of the discovery of the New World, the Christian religion enabled the Old World to take up Christ's promise anew, in order to represent itself in an historic dimension as the broker of the New World's salvation.

Since the Incarnation, the Christian Church had been fulfilling its side of humanity's covenant with God by performing its missionary duty of redemption. By violently marking out the transgressive condition of the New World, the Old World embarked on the further mission of saving the New World from its space of unredeemed sinfulness. This mission would have two superior proselytisers: those claiming political authority and espousing universal justice, and those practising mercantilism and espousing material profit. Both proselytisers authorised and used the increasingly superior

6 Foucault, 1979, p 48.   7 Augustine 1966, Book I, Chapter 12.21.
8 Foucault, 1979, pp 48–49.   9 Ibid, p 35.   10 Ibid, p 38.

authority of territorial or monarchical sovereignty and its links to the body politic and territorial space.

By marking out the New World in this way, by refusing to enter into mutual negotiations of recognition, the Old World created an object of desire more real than God. The western subject began its journey of self-realisation by moving away from God to seek the answer in the reply of the New World Other. In a sense, the New World represented the very object of desire. For what can be more desirable than the intrigue of a place that exists beyond signification? A world not yet confessed.

Like God, the New World held promise. This promise attracted the monarchs of western Europe and their merchant explorers to journey into the New World in search of new territories, human subjects, gold and spices. The promise drove the understanding of exchange as being based not only on the expectation of material reimbursement and the opportunity for profit but also on the promise of subjective determination. It is a promise best symbolised in the numerous searches for the lost city of Eldorado; a search begun by the Spanish but soon taken up by all seafaring nations of Europe.[11] It is arguably at this juncture that the will of the sovereign monarch and the merchants' entrepreneurial spirit merged in a joint venture that promised redemption by means of an authoritative knowledge about the accumulation of profit and the colonisation of (real) property.

At home in imperial Europe, the Roman Catholic Church lost the power to interpret the Word, and individual subjects began to confess their allegiance to the jurisdiction of sovereign monarchs in order to obtain recognition as a 'true subject'. The promise made by the sovereign monarch, and backed by the entrepreneurial spirit, secured for the Old World its continued faith in its own identity. Western subjects were bound to this promise out of fear that their very subjectivity would otherwise disappear into the increasingly liquid economy of meaning and transformation of the early modern period. The work of scholars such as Jean Bodin, Hugo Grotius and Michel de Montaigne are used here to explore the instability of power and identity in western Europe during the period of religious reformation and the Enlightenment. The further 'nationalisation' of subjectivity will be taken up in Chapter Four, which discusses in greater detail the transformation of Christian disciplinary practices into bio-political techniques used by the state to regulate the conduct of individuals in accordance with the conception and desires of nation.

11 The legend of Eldorado became a popular object of literature and speculation as well as ground for numerous exploratory excursions by European mercantilists during the later half of the 16th century. Perhaps the most well known of the many European missions established to find Eldorado is that of Sir Walter Raleigh, who undertook two explorations on the commission of English monarchs. His first expedition sailed in 1595 and is the subject of Raleigh's travel text, *The Discovery of the Large, Rich, and Beautiful Empire of Guyana* (1596). The second set sail in 1616.

This chapter begins by setting the scene of discovery through the texts of Christopher Columbus. The aim is to give the reader a sense of the wonder brought about by the discovery of the Americas. At stake was not transformation, but the reformation, the recasting or refounding of western justice. By reading the texts of Columbus, the reader is asked to consider what happens when the confessional subject encounters a world that refuses to take part in the significance of a Christian truth. If, as Lacan points out, the subject must arouse in the other a desire to know, in order that a path to truth be found by way of another who seems to represent it, did Columbus suffer the betrayal of God's promise, as well as 'all those aspects of the world – friend, family, country, cause – that the self is made up of'?[12] At the moment of discovery, Columbus sailed into a time 'before the law' where he 'cannot manage to see or above all to touch, to catch up to the law'.[13] Columbus arrives at the aporia of the unfathomable singularity of another promise of justice. In that moment he is made speechless but is soon forced to make his decision, to take responsibility for the discovery of the Other.

> This anxiety-ridden moment of suspense – which is also the interval of spacing in which transformations, indeed, juridico-political revolutions take place – cannot be motivated, cannot find its movement and its impulse (an impulse which cannot itself be suspended) except in the demand for an increase in or supplement to justice.[14]

In this instance, the determination of Christian justice heeds that call.

Speak of the devil: the consequences of naming

On 3 August 1492, Christopher Columbus sailed for the Indies and discovered, instead, the Caribbean islands. In describing his explorations, he became lost for words, beginning with comparison: 'the weather is like April in Andalusia';[15] 'the sea was as smooth as the river at Seville'.[16]

However, soon he found that no comparisons could be made:

> During that time I walked among the trees, which were the loveliest I had yet seen. They were green as those of Andalusia in the month of May. But all these trees are as different from ours as day from night and so are the fruit and plants and stones, and everything else. It is true that some trees were of species that can be found in Castile, yet there was a great

---

12 Cohen, 1969, p 29.   13 Derrida, 1992, p 993.   14 Ibid, pp 21–22.
15 Cohen, 1969 pp 37, 42.   16 Ibid, p 43.

difference; but there are many other varieties which no one could say are like those of Castile, or could compare with them.[17]

Columbus's astonishment, his inability to articulate, grows stronger in his writings the further he travels:

> It grieves me extremely that I cannot identify [the birds and trees], for I am quite certain that they are all valuable and I am bringing some samples of them and of the plants also.[18]

The inability of Columbus to speak of the New World literally pains him. His inability to speak of what he observes forms a non-negotiable presence that cannot be denied nor confirmed. The experience is painful for its very 'unshareability' – 'through its very resistance to language'.[19] Columbus indeed feared that he would not be believed: 'Your Highness must believe me that these islands are the most fertile, and temperate and flat and good in the whole world.'[20] The further he travelled, it would seem, the more he became removed from the symbolic jurisdiction of his sovereign monarchs and their rule of law. More painful still, perhaps, was that his inability to describe what he saw was also an inability to assess its (redeeming) value:

> Everything on all these coasts is so green and lovely that I do not know where to go first, and my eyes never weary of looking on this fine vegetation, which is so different from that of our own lands. I think that many trees and plants grow there which will be highly valued in Spain for dyes and medicinal spices. But I am sorry to say that I do not recognise them.[21]

In short, Columbus, Admiral of the Roman Catholic monarchy of Ferdinand and Isabella, was unable to confess the truth of his discoveries to them:

> Very often I would say to my crew that however hard I tried to give your Highnesses a complete account of these lands my tongue could not convey the whole truth about them nor my hand write it down. I was so astonished at the sight of so much beauty that I can find no words to describe it.[22]

---

17 Ibid, pp 64–66. Or, 'The fish here are surprisingly unlike ours. There are some the shape of dories and of the finest colours in the world, blue, yellow, red and every other hue and others variously flecked. The colours are so marvellous that everybody wondered and took pleasure in the sight' (Cohen, 1969, p 65).

18 Ibid, p 70.   19 Scarry, 1985, p 4.   20 Cohen, 1969, p 67.   21 Ibid, p 69.

22 Ibid, pp 77, 83–84.

Columbus had lost the normative link between fact and value. The promise that drove Columbus to speak had fallen into crisis. Without language, the traffic of value and truth was subject only to silence. Contrary to what Columbus believed, his masters were nothing. Certainly, in the realm of this New World, there was no possession because there was as yet no language to describe it. Columbus was driven by the force of Christian promise to reproduce himself, to prove himself – to exclaim after waking from the Cartesian nightmare: 'I think therefore I am'. This drive came from the violence of origin – from the pain of unshareability that 'does not simply resist language but actively destroys it, bringing about an immediate reversion to a state anterior to language, to the sounds and cries a human being makes before language is learned'.[23]

In discovering the beautiful wonders that could not be put into words, that defied confession, the Roman Catholic Columbus experienced a torture of his knowledge and representation. His possession of the New World could not be translated or – in economic terms – exchanged with the world from whence he had come. In Roman Catholic terms, Columbus was unable to confess and was thus left deprived of redemption and, so, salvation. The language of the Old World had been cast into doubt in its relation to a new world. Columbus had sailed to the boundaries of his jurisdictional limit. Yet, ironically, Columbus had faced the likes of God. The Old World in discovering the New World had passed beyond the signifier and apprehended the momentary presence of an unmediated subject – the vanishing of the subject together with the end of speech. For Columbus it was a terrifying and faithful experience – one that is immediately repressed by an aggressive repossession of an unredeemed world. How was Columbus to speak of the Other? How would he be able to confess what he desired? The unknowable became the unnamed. Columbus called the New World back into the Old World by naming the New World and his pain was assuaged as it was transformed into outrage, indignation and outright denial. This renaming sought the redemption of sin from the imperfect fragmentation of the whole.

The violence of naming

Columbus's confession made valuable what could not be named, 'guaranteeing that the continuous deferrals of language are not babble but meaning'.[24] By refusing to confess his belief in any other order than his own, Columbus sought to maintain not only the coherency of the Word, but also its superiority.[25] As a consequence, the contemptuous confidence with which Columbus

23 Scarry, 1985, p 4.   24 Foster, 1987, p 11.
25 As Cheyfitz observes, this practice of naming has other effects. E.g. the term 'cannibal', which first appeared in Columbus's logbook to describe a particular group of people, it

reacted to the threat of his inability to know and represent the New World was meted out by physical violence, but also evidenced discursively in his immediate assimilation of the New World into the Old World by the violent and professedly Christian practice of naming – of symbolically encompassing the New World into the body of Christian territory:

> And as from this island I saw another larger one to the west, I hoisted sail to run all that day till light, since I should otherwise not have been able to reach its western point. I named this island Santa Maria de la Concepcion. . . . Generally it was my wish to pass no island without taking possession of it.[26]

'Mastery begins', as Derrida reminds us, 'through the power of naming, of imposing and legitimating appellations':

> This sovereign establishment [*mise en demeure souveraine*] may be open, legal, armed, or cunning, disguised under alibis of 'universal' humanism, and sometimes of the most generous hospitality. It always precedes culture like its shadow. . . . And all culture, we are also reminded, is colonial.[27]

Like Jesus Christ's apostle, Peter, Columbus calls the New World to be baptised in the name of Jesus Christ: 'For the promise is for you and your children, and for all who are far off as many as the Lord our God shall call to Himself'.[28] Baptism in the name of Jesus Christ or 'christening' involved one's rebirth into the body of God, which gave Christians the opportunity to reconcile themselves to the promised 'fullness of Him who fills all in all'.[29] The effect of naming was a means by which the Church secured a collective identity by marking out and identifying its members. In doing so, the Church restructured traditional bonds of family and kinship, and began its mission of converting difference into otherness.

Christening or name-giving cannot be mistaken here with gift-giving. Naming here is an act of confession – of splitting the subject into a particular form. As Laclau suggests, if the unity of the signifier is the retroactive effect of naming itself, then naming is not just the pure nominalistic game of attributing an empty name to a preconstituted subject. It is the discursive construction of the object itself.[30] As Derrida has written:

came to mean one thing in western languages: 'For Europeans this term will be part of a diverse arsenal of rhetorical weapons used to distinguish what they conceive of as their "civilised" selves from certain "savage" others, principally Native Americans and Africans' (Cheyfitz, 1997, p 42).

26 Cohen, 1969, p 60.   27 Derrida, 1998, p 39.   28 *Acts* 2:38, 39.
29 *Ephesians* 1:23.   30 Laclau, 1989, pp ix, xiv.

One can have doubts about it from the moment when the name not only is nothing, in any case not the 'thing' that it names, not the 'nameable' or the renowned, but also risks to bind, to enslave or to engage the other, to link the called, to him/her to respond even before any decision or any deliberation, even before any freedom. An assigned passion, a prescribed alliance as much as a promise'[31]

Columbus sought to demystify the New World by inscribing it with words in order to make it represent itself as a Christian subject.[32] In this way Columbus discharged the divine right of his monarchs to inscribe the Word onto the New World in order to re-establish the economy of Christian justice through redemption.

The discourse of the New and the Old Worlds, of colony and empire, of developing and developed had begun. The repression by the Old World of its relationship to the New World is never enough to hold back the sense of doubt (of itself, of the Other) and so the Old World continues to secure its identity, and the identity of the Other, by discursive acts driven by the desire to name and to represent what it has not signified – to bring the New World into the fantastic frame that stimulates desire, exactly because it promises to cover over the lack of totality.

When all's said and done, the christening of each island by Columbus was not just a symbolic act of possession, whereby each island was incorporated into the body (and normative/symbolic order) of the Church. It was also a suppression of the pain of the non-negotiable presence by the consciousness of language. Columbus refused, indeed was unable to, absolve himself of his own knowledge and beliefs, nor his underlying Christian faith, which verified them. His return to God was short, but by speaking he was returned to earth to re-master history.

Columbus was not alone in this practice. His contemporary, Amerigo Vespucci, also felt obliged to christen the New World; indeed, America becomes his namesake. Vespucci emphasised in his travel writings that the peoples he encountered were 'so barbarous', 'their customs so varied and diverse and different from our affairs and methods' that familiar terms could not apply.[33] He began his account of the 1497 voyage by stating that:

> This voyage lasted eighteen months, during which I discovered many lands and almost countless islands (uninhabited as a general rule), of which our forefathers make absolutely no mention. I conclude from this that the ancients had no knowledge of their existence.[34]

31 Derrida, 1995, p 84.   32 See Derrida, 1989, p 3.
33 Grafton, Shelford and Siraisi, 1992, p 84.   34 Ibid.

The New World was conceived by Vespucci as unknown – brought into existence by his discovery: 'I may be mistaken; but I remember reading somewhere that the [ancients] believed the sea to be free and uninhabited. Our poet Dante himself was of this opinion'.[35] The coherent organising systems of the ancient scholars had made no room for new discoveries. In the same period Ptolemy's *Geography*, the basic canon of medieval geography, was declared to be out of date, becoming instead an historical rather than a scientific text. In his *Mundus Novus*, Vespucci cites the many trees of the New World as proof that 'Ptolemy did not touch upon a thousandth part of the species of parrots and other birds and the animals too, which exist in those same regions'. In addition, the new stars of the Southern Cross inspired Vespucci to think that he himself should produce 'a book of geography or cosmography, that [his] memory may live with prosperity' and thus start a new canon based on contemporary observations.[36] Similarly, Michel de Montaigne writes:

> Ptolmey, who was a great man, had established the limits of our world; all the ancient philosophers they had its measure, except for a few remote islands that might escape their knowledge. . . . it was heresy to admit the existence of the Antipodes. Behold in our century an infinite extent of terra firma, not an island or one particular country, but a portion nearly equal in size to the one we know, which has just been discovered. The geographers of the present time do not fail to assure us that now all is discovered and all is seen.[37]

The recognition of the New World also created, however, a sense of redundancy whereby the Old World was seen doubled in the other. It was no more the unique creation of divinity but possibly a world that was replaceable, secondary, moving from 'having an assurance of immortality . . . [it] becomes the ghastly harbinger of death'.[38] In his treatise on the origins of the indigenous American peoples, the jurist Hugo Grotius wrote:

> [If it is agreed that] these peoples are not Germans on the grounds that many of their words reveal them not to be so, then they will not be descended from any people because their words are not like those of any other people; then we must believe, with Aristotle, that they have been present throughout all eternity, or that they sprung from the Earth, as the legend has it about Sparta, or from the ocean, as Homer would have it, or before Adam there were other unknown men, as has

35 Ibid.   36 Ibid, p 85.   37 Montaigne, 1958, pp 318, 430.
38 Freud, 1958, p 141.

recently been imagined by some in France. If these things are believed, I see a great danger to piety; if my theses are believed I see no danger at all.[39]

Grotius's attempt to avert the danger of diverse languages to universal Christian piety relied on a universalising incorporation of humanity. If God's promise was to assume responsibility for His confessed body of subjects, then it had to be iterable in each re-contextualisation without losing the meaning of God's original promise.[40] Grotius manages to contain the meaning of diverse languages by interpreting their diversity as a natural outcome of humanity's creation. According to Grotius, sin had caused the Word to enter into diverse contexts where God's promise had been forsaken by the misinterpretation of His Word. Grotius maintained that 'from the start . . . all of humanity was diffused into all parts of the world either from the time of Noah or from the time of the erection of the Tower of Babel'.[41] As such, all peoples were bound by the same promise of universal language under the laws of Christianity. Underneath this trope of universal Christianity, of course, Grotius was constructing the legitimate claims of the Swedish monarchy to New World territory on the basis of ancestral links between the Lapps and 'these people'. Church and secular interests remained intertwined in their search for the promised land. As Crystal Bartolovich notes, 'the limits to the potential commodities and colonies had not yet been reached, encouraging an orientation toward limitless accumulation rather than zero-sum rivalry'.[42] The idea that humanity did not share a common history was impossible to grasp. Likewise today, all of humanity is grouped into a single trajectory of development based on 'universal' rights to democracy, material wealth and freedom. None of these concepts, however, have common meanings. As Martti Koskenniemi has written, to speak of democracy as a 'universal value' is to 'obscure the terms of particular struggles'.[43]

Despite the real differences in language, and the fear produced by words 'not like those of any other people', one was expected to have faith in the universal claims of Christianity or to face the danger of irreligiosity and redundancy. Without this faith, the confessional subjects of Christianity were brought to the same unnegotiable realm of unshareability that Columbus had

---

39 Grotius, *De Origine Gentium Americanarum* (On the Origin of the Native Races of America), in which he argued that the indigenous peoples of North America came from Scandinavia, those of Central America from Ethiopia, and those in South America from China (1884).

40 For a discussion of iterability, see Derrida 1988, p 20.

41 Grotius, 1884.

42 Bartolovich, 1998, pp 204, 228.   43 Koskenniemi, 2000, p 437.

experienced in the New World. Hence, the Jesuit Joseph Lafitau, who spent five years in a Canadian mission, was concerned that:

> this argument [of the universality of Christian belief based on consent] falls, if it is true that there is a multitude of diverse nations brutish to such an extent that they have no idea of a god, nor any established customs to render the cult that is due him; for on that basis the atheist seems to be correct in concluding that if there is nearly a whole world of nations who have no religion, the religion found among others is a world of human prudence and an artifice of rulers who invented it to lead peoples by the fear born of superstition.[44]

Etymological explanations of a universal Christianity therefore began to merge slowly with historical fact and were adopted by the enlightened natural and social sciences. Jean Bodin's belief that the Scriptures of Moses were the key to all true history is illustrative. Bodin traced all peoples back to the three sons of Noah, claiming that etymology could prove this surmise by identifying the similarities of diverse languages.[45] Bodin sought to explain differences between peoples according to geography, while maintaining that their common humanity and universal heritage could be drawn from his etymologies. The former was in turn drawn from the traditional taxonomy of stereotypes elaborated by the Hippocratic doctors and astrologers of the Ancient and Middle Ages.[46] As Nebrija observed to Queen Isabella of Spain, 'language has always been the companion of empire'.[47] In this 'tragic economy', the peoples of the New World had to 'learn the language of their masters, of capital and machines; . . . lose their idiom in order to survive or live better.[48]

Anticipating imperial narratives of nineteenth-century orientalism, Bodin's work studied, saw, and observed objectified peoples, facilitating as he did so, the colonising mission. Bodin was able to confirm, with the apparent authority of a new psycho-geographical science, the traditional accounts that those in the south of Europe were contemplative and religious and those in the north were active and strong, while the people of the middle regions were prudent and thus adept at government.[49] The peoples of Europe were all,

44 Lafitau, 1734.
45 Bodin also refuted the medieval and ancient claims that people were descendant from gods and the 'pretensions to divinity on the part of some men who thought they would be gods when they had ceased to be human' (1966, p 334).
46 Grafton, Shelford and Siraisi, 1992, pp 121–22.
47 In 1492, Antonio de Nebrija published the first grammar of a modern European language, *Gramatica de la lengua castellana* (1980, p 97).
48 Derrida, 1998, p 30.
49 The Southern Hemisphere, while mentioned, was not discussed by Bodin. Other characteristics he based on the movement of particular planets, and on the functions of the brain, the

nonetheless, descendants of an original Christian, Noah. All of humanity, therefore, ought to acknowledge their commensurability, the iterability of God's promise, in order to promote peace and amity.

> Nowadays, . . . we have seen it come about that no region is so fecund that it does not urgently need the resources of others. . . . [N]ature constantly imposed these laws [of exchange] and lasting allegiances on certain regions. For what purpose, finally, if not that the peoples should unite their possessions and ideas in mutual commerce and thus strengthen peace and friendship?[50]

Diversity was thus rendered into order by natural economic laws, the rules of etymology, and the natural laws existing between peoples in pursuit of peace, amity and friendship. Doubt raised by the differences within and among peoples was explicable and certainty arose from what seemed to be a chaos of representation and form. The globalisation of the world was as clear as the performance of God's promise to redeem His people. Like the Europeans who would follow him, Columbus was fitted with more than gunpowder, superior weaponry, armour and navigational instruments. His was a religious culture that assumed its own universality – a culture with developed hierarchies of obedience and a religious ideology grounded in martyrdom and a tortured God-man.[51] As Greenblatt observes:

> Such was the confidence of this culture that it expected perfect strangers – the Arawaks of the Caribbean, for example – to abandon their own beliefs, preferably immediately, and embrace those of Europe as luminously and self-evidently true. A failure to do so provoked impatience, contempt and even murderous rage.[52]

Once united in mutual commerce humanity would be assured of peace. The laws imposed by nature represent here the Word of God transposed into the modern discourses of universalism. The universalising force of law was bound by the Providence of God; guided by the entrepreneurial spirit. God's providence was understood by the imperial monarchs as no less than an opportunity for profit. By determining God's promise in this way, by making it (re)presentable as Providence, 'there is no longer promise, there is only calculation . . . all will already have happened – all is beforehand, repeated in advance'.[53] In this moment, it is possible to perceive a global market

heart and the liver, which were attributed to the southern, temperate and northern regions. See Chapter V of Bodin, 1966, p 85.

50 Bodin, 1966, p 336.   51 See the discussion of martyrdom in Chapter Two, above.
52 Greenblatt, 1991, p 9.   53 Derrida, 1995, p 41.

beginning to make its own promises to monarchs and merchants alike.[54] In this sense, by grounding law in the origins of a universal humanity, Christian justice continued to lay to rest the crisis of identity wrought on western Europe by the reformation of its religious authorities and the discovery of a New World. Difference was neither recognisable nor recognised. The good news was that all of humanity had links to Christianity and were subjects to the Word and its salvation. This counted as good news however, only if, as Linda Woodhead notes in her very short introduction to Christianity, 'you also believe in some very bad news: that human beings need to be saved from something and are incapable of saving themselves'.[55]

By investing the New World into its economy of desire, the Old World was able to preserve its sense of identity within its own unique Christian discourse of salvation and its correlated account of its loss of totality. This economy was, to borrow from Marx, 'a very Eden of the innate rights of man'.[56] Like the early Christian Church, the Old World continued the Christian mission of marking, with language and violence, the peoples of the New World, who had remained until then seemingly unmarked, and unredeemed 'beyond the limits allowed'.[57]

The violence of imperialism

The Old World colonisers carried with them all of the disciplinary techniques of the confessors. In the first 50 years after the Spanish invasion of the Inca and Aztec peoples, the Spanish overthrew temples and prohibited the practice of indigenous religions. Missionaries were trained to do more than denounce and convert. Their medieval discipline of hearing confession endowed them with skills in observation and investigation. The tools of the Inquisition, with which the Church had sought out women accused of witchcraft and Jewish recidivists in Europe, provided them with a set of questions to ask about beliefs and rituals in the Americas. Churches and religious communities were built in the New World in much the same way that these institutions had been spread across Europe.

The missionaries learnt the indigenous languages and translated into them both the basic documents of the Roman Catholic faith and the manuals for hearing confession.[58] As a consequence, the missionaries and those trained in the religious schools of Europe were able to collect intimate knowledge of indigenous religions in order to eliminate surviving traditions and negotiate their way into the souls of men.[59] They used systematic questionnaires, repeated interviews and other practices proleptically reminiscent of modern

---

54 See generally, Le Goff, 1980, p 29.   55 Woodhead, 2004, p 25.
56 Marx, 1976–81, p 152.   57 Deleuze and Guattari, 1983.
58 Cohen, 1998, p 1. See also, Abbott 1996.   59 Grafton, Shelford and Siraisi, 1992, p 132.

fieldwork. Their systematic studies, clarified by glosses and illustrations, explained the calendars, the divinatory rituals, the gods, the customs, the rhetoric and the morality of this strange New World, thereby eliminating doubt and producing a 'shareability' of representation of the New for the Old. In doing so, they tortured the voice of the New World into a state anterior to language, to the frozen sounds and cries of multiple, mutable cultural traditions, 'producing a solid and immobile text and commentary, unchanging if readily accessible in form, and as divergent in character from its oral sources as its illustrations'.[60] This tortured voice confessed its savagery in order to arrive at truth.

In 1550 the Basel professor Sebastian Munster published his *Cosmographia* containing more than 1,000 pages comprising an encyclopaedic survey of the world's lands and peoples. Maps of the world were given borders and definition and showed the independent existence of the Americas to the west, although in the text Munster denied their existence.[61] The scientific gaze thus begins its observation of the world in spite of, and in opposition to, the Word and its diminishing authority. The world that had previously defied words began slowly to slip under the signifying text of the scientific canon. The information was not collated in order to produce a pluralism shared, but rather classified to produce a single, universal understanding. Observed facts were thus classified in the classical manner into the traditional canon of the scholastics of the Old World. For, as Homi Bhabha notes in a slightly different context:

> [t]here is in such readings a will to power and knowledge that, in failing to specify the limits of their own field of enunciation and effectivity, proceed to individualise otherness as the discovery of their own assumptions.[62]

These ethnographic, geographic and historical narratives employed 'a system of representation, a regime of truth . . . structurally similar to realism', which produced the New World as a fixed reality 'Other' than the Old and yet still completely knowable and visible.[63] The 'shareability' and certainty that the discourses about the New World sought to produce were meant only to assuage the pain of doubt – of lack – felt by the Old World by converting the New World. A new 'reality' was thereby created like the reality later to be produced by orientalists. As Said has noted:

> the tense they employ is the timeless eternal; they convey an impression of repetition and strength . . . . For all these functions it is frequently enough to use the simple copula is.[64]

60 Ibid.   61 Ibid, p 101.   62 Bhabha, 1986, pp 148, 154.   63 Ibid, p 156.
64 Said, 1978, p 72.

The New World was thus confessed – inscribed with the same cruel and arbitrary marks of rationalisation to render it capable of exchange within the debtor–creditor relation that had been used to breed the Christian body.[65] The guilty subject was made herald of its own condemnation; its punishment the revelation of truth.[66]

Portending of the International Monetary Fund (IMF) and World Bank data collection, and in the traditional model of a penitential manual, Munster sent surveys to European scholars to enrich his systematic classification of peoples and their genealogies, customs and resources.[67] A survey, which was sent to a Swedish scholar, asks for a list of rulers and boundaries, an assessment of royal revenues, and a description of any monsters.[68] It is, 'on the one hand, a topic of learning, discovery, practice; on the other it was the site of dreams, images, fantasies, myths, obsessions and requirements'.[69] Munster's *Cosmographia* was not a history of the world but an order in which peoples stood in a timeless space – a 'static system of "synchronic essentialism", a knowledge of "signifiers of stability" such as the lexicographic and the encyclopaedic'.[70] It formed the model apparatus for an emerging colonial discourse 'that turns not only on the recognition and disavowal of racial/ cultural/historical differences' as Bhabha has argued, but also on the perceived differences in destiny. It should not be forgotten just how important the Old World saw its own predestination – how much its present was informed and signified by its Fall from Grace and its eventual salvation. Its very identity hinged on this discourse of salvation.

Here we see the Christian rule of law at work. This is Anselm's rectitude; it is a justice that demands confession and repayment before forgiveness. All that was new and different was to be incorporated into the 'old' and this totality of objects was then to become subject to a new method of speaking the truth that would succeed where the ancient authorities had failed. The violence of imperialism possessed its own liturgy of punishment that marked the colonised world, either by the scars it left on the bodies of colonised peoples and their territories, or by the spectacle inscribed onto the collective memory of all people involved. Even as it purged the colonised world of its transgression, imperialism did not reconcile; 'it trace[d] around or, rather, on the very body of the condemned [world] signs that must not be effaced'.[71] Today, the world still remembers imperialism's exhibition, 'the pillory, torture and pain duly observed'.[72]

By positing imperialism within a redemptive frame, the colonised peoples

---

65 See above, Chapter Two; and Deleuze and Guattari, 1983, p 190.
66 Foucault, 1979, p 43.   67 Grafton, Shelford and Siraisi, 1992, p 100.
68 Ibid, p 106.
69 Bhabha, 1986, pp 157–58. Bhabha is here discussing Said's analysis of orientalism.
70 Ibid, p 157.   71 Foucault, 1979, p 34.   72 Ibid.

were denied the discourse of martyrdom as a narrative of resistance to European conquest and its 'normative world-building' that constitutes 'law' by placing 'bodies on the line'.[73] Instead, the New World was forced to represent humanity's sinfulness, subject to the austerity measures of Christian justice. As Grbich has observed, colonised peoples, the New Hollander, or native, 'marked the boundary of a way of thinking, a culture, where Reason would provide sufficient grounds for how the citizen could satisfy himself of a moral system and a moral judgment'.[74] As Lacan points out in an analysis of the universal laws of Creon in Sophocles' play, *Antigone*:

> before the ethical progression that from Aristotle to Kant leads us to make clear the identity of law and reason, doesn't the spectacle of tragedy reveal to us in anticipation the first objection? The good cannot reign over all without an excess emerging whose fatal consequences are revealed to us in tragedy.[75]

The New World, which is marked out as sin – the manifestation of debt within a Christian economy of desire – became the excess of Old World rectitude and truth. 'In the "excesses" of torture, a whole economy of power is invested'.[76] Indeed, the tragic excess of the reign of the Spanish was not lost on European scholars. Michel de Montaigne had this to say of the conquest of the Mexican king by the Spanish:

> After this victory, his enemies, not finding all the gold they had promised themselves, first ransacked and searched everything, and then set about seeking information by inflicting the cruellest tortures they could think up on the prisoners they held.[77]

A 'just war' so far, it would seem:

> But having gained nothing by this, and finding their prisoners' courage stronger than their torments, they finally flew into such a rage that, against their word and against all law of nations, they condemned the king himself and one of the principal lords of his court to the torture in each other's presence. . . . They hanged him later for having courageously attempted to deliver himself by arms from such a long captivity and subjection, and he made an end worthy of a great-souled prince.[78]

---

73 Robert Cover describes martyrdom as the refusal to allow a particular reality or world view to be destroyed. Cover argues that the 'triumph [of martyrs] – which may well be partly imaginary – is the imagined triumph of the normative universe – of Torah, Nomos – over the material world of death and pain.' See Robert Cover, 1986, pp 1604–05.

74 Grbich, 2005.   75 Lacan, 1992, p 259.   76 Foucault, 1979, pp 34–35.

77 Montaigne, 1958, p 696.   78 Ibid, pp 696–97.

The line between 'lawfully' colonising the territories of the Mexican people and unlawfully condemning, torturing and murdering their king is less than arbitrary. Like Antigone, the Mexican king's defiance of the law of nations – his martyrdom at the hands of imperialism – emerged as tragic excess in the Christian search for Eldorado. His debt could never be paid.

Montaigne brought to light this excess in order to shift the gaze away from the New World onto the Spanish invaders, thus problematising the readers' ability to identify who in fact is really suffering from a pain resistant to language, from wonder and astonishment:

> For as regards the men who subjugated them, take away the ruses and tricks that they used to deceive them, and the people's natural asto-nishment at seeing the unexpected arrival of bearded men, different in language, religion, shape and countenance, from a part of the world so remote, where they had never imagined there was any sort of human habitation, mounted on great unknown monsters, opposed to men who had never seen not only a horse, but any sort of animal trained to carry and endure a man or any other burden; men equipped with a hard and shiny skin and a sharp and glittering weapon . . . add to this the lighten-ing and thunder of our cannon and harquebuses – capable of disturbing Caesar himself . . . eliminate this disparity, I say, and you take from the conquerors the whole basis of so many victories.[79]

In his description of the conquest of the peoples of Mexico, Montaigne highlighted the hypocrisy inherent in the emerging law of nations as the arbiter of a determined Christian justice and universal reason, together with nature's providential imposition of economic globalisation.[80] The Old World indulged the New World only in exchange for life and profit. This was reasonable because it was just. It was just because:

> blessedness ought not be given to anyone unless his sins are wholly remit-ted, and that this remission ought not be done except by the payment of the debt which is owed because of sin [and] according to the magnitude of the sin.[81]

Universal laws in the political and economic domains regulated the exchange of life with other forms: of gold, souls and territory. The cries of the great-souled princes were silenced under the force of an emerging law of nations. The speech of the New World subject was made subordinate to the ruses and tricks of a greater significance.

---

79 Ibid, p 694.   80 See Chapter V of Jean Bodin, 1966, p 85.
81 Anselm (1998b), Book 1, Chapter 24.

The New World was thus drawn into the confessional narrative of the Old World – an exchange in which the Old World was still attempting to maintain its fantasy of chosenness by proclaiming itself the confessor of humanity, the redeemer of salvation. Out of this recognition emerged a desire by the Old World to constitute itself as autonomous, independent of the inscribing forces of a transcendent debtor. Its originary myth was set to be retold.

While humanity's Fall from God continued to explain retrospectively humankind's incomplete fulfilment, a new means to salvation began to present itself. Imagine the New World as the original place from whence the Old World had come. This New World is at the beginning of creation, far from God's forgiveness but the Old World is closer to redemption – it is, let us say, the First World. Could not the Old World take the place of the Word, of Christ the Broker, outright? The possibility of atonement already recognised as one attainable through a confessed negotiation was transposed by the Old World onto an economy of discursive exchanges acted out through practices of imperialism, brute conflict and, in modern times, development. The effect of this new economy was a series of discourses or power-relations that aimed to shape the desire for the Other into atonement for the sense of loss in western culture.

Humanity was to be measured by the distance it had travelled from the separation of nature/creation/sin into the unity of rationality/transcendence/law. The peoples of the New World were manifestly considered part of nature and thus located in close proximity to the time of original sin:

> These nations [of the New World], then, seem to me barbarous in this sense, that they have been fashioned very little by the human mind, and are still very close to their original naturalness. The laws of nature still rule them, very little corrupted by ours . . . for it seems to me that what we actually see in these nations surpasses not only all the pictures in which poets have idealized the golden age and all their inventions in imagining a happy state of man, but also the conceptions and the very desire of philosophy.[82]

In his own writings, Montaigne sought to challenge these claims of superiority of the Old over the New, but he nonetheless assumed this ability 'to know', placing both worlds into a universal history in which the 'elders' have done nothing to raise 'their infants' correctly:

> If we are right to infer the end of our world, and that poet is right about the youth of his own age, this other world will only be coming into the light when ours is leaving it. The universe will fall into paralysis; one

82 Montaigne, 1958, pp 150–52.

member will be crippled, the other in full vigor. I am much afraid that we shall have very greatly hastened the decline and ruin of this new world by our contagion, and that we will have sold it our opinions and our arts very dear. It was an infant world; yet we have not whipped it and subjected it to our discipline by the advantage of our natural valor and strength, nor won it over by our justice and goodness, nor subjugated it by our magnanimity. Most of the responses of these people and most of our dealings with them show that they were not at all behind us in natural brightness of mind and pertinence.[83]

He concludes with the paradox that this 'young world is very old, living at the end of history'. Indeed, the golden age was coming to an end in order that the search for Eldorado could begin. One could also conclude that the promise of God had allowed this historicised account to be told.

The making of gold[84]

At the end of the fifteenth century, time in western Europe was still knowable. Christians still believed that time would eventually stretch space back into itself as the world was brought to an end and humanity to judgement. The unification of the world by travel seemed to herald the approach of the end of history itself. This conviction continues into the present, evident in claims of an end to history such as Fukuyama's *End of History and the Last Man*.[85] In his later writings Columbus would conclude that the unification of humanity, following the conversion of the Chinese and a crusade against the Muslims, would precipitate the Last Judgement and perhaps a return to the Real, to that place of 'everlasting continuance' in which the self 'needeth no good' and is forever at rest.[86] Yet, the 'primitive' nature of the peoples newly discovered seemed to indicate otherwise. The emergence of ethnographic comparisons made possible a humanity that, rather than inevitably deteriorating over time, progressed through increasingly sophisticated stages of civilisation. Indeed, such superiority was essential if the violent appropriation of the New World by the Old World was to be justified. This, in turn, had a similar effect on the interpretation of space and time, as did the changed bodies of the emerging merchant and knightly professions.

Montaigne found these consequences in more ancient texts concerning the proper interpretation of human history. In his essay *Of Coaches*, Montaigne compared two conflicting observations of Lucretius in the *De Rerum Natura*.

---

83 Ibid, p 693.
84 A chapter on the 'The Making of Gold' is included in Francis Bacon's *Sylva Sylvarum, or a Naturall Historie in Ten Centuries* (London, 1627), which was part of Bacon's unfinished *Instauratio Magna*.
85 Fukuyama, 1992.   86 Augustine, 1955, Book 13 Chapter 38.53.

Lucretius began with an observation of nature, stating that the 'age is broken down, and broken down is the earth' but in Book Five he stated:

> The universe, I think, is very new,
> The world is young, its birth not far behind;
> Hence certain arts grow more and more refined
> Even today; the naval art is one.[87]

Montaigne then discussed the discovery of another 'young' world in his own times:

> Our world has just discovered another world (And who will guarantee us that it is the last of its brothers, since daemons, the Sibyls, and we ourselves have up to now been ignorant of this one?) no less great, full, and well-limbed than itself, yet so new and so infantile that it is still being taught it's A B C; not fifty years ago it knew neither letters, nor weights and measures, nor clothes, nor wheat, nor vines. It was still quite naked at the breast, and lived only on what its nursing mother provided.[88]

This passage illustrates Montaigne's clear perception of a world that still existed in a pre-linguistic realm, which is associated here with the bond between mother and child. This is not because the New World in fact had no language of its own, but because it was not recognised by the symbolic order of the Old World.

Such representations of the 'New World peoples' as 'primitive' in time, relative to the 'civilised' peoples of Europe also enabled new meanings to be

---

87 Montaigne, 1958, p 693.
88 Ibid, This perception of superiority fell easily into place with existing Christian belief in the superiority of humanity over all creatures and what Samual Purchas, writing in the early 17th century, was to call the European's 'literall advantage':

> God hath added herein a further grace, that as Men by the former exceed Beasts, so hereby one man may exceed another; and amongst Men, some are accounted civill, and more both Sociable and Religious, by the Use of letters and Writing, which others wanting are esteemed Brutish, Savage and Barbarous.

He adds:

> By speech we utter our minds once, at the present, to the present, as present occasions move (and perhaps unadvisedly transport) us: but by writing Man seemes immortall, conferreth and consulteth with the Patriarks, Prophets, Apostles, Fathers, Philosophers, Historians, and learnes the wisdome of the Sages which have been in all times before him; yea by the translations of learning the Languages, in all places and Regions of the World: and lastly, by his owne writings surviveth himself, remaines (Litera scripta manet) thorow all ages a Teacher and Counsellor to the last of men: yea hereby God holds conference with men, and in his sacred Scriptures, as at first in the Tables of Stone, speakes to all. (Cited in Greenblatt, 1991, p 10.)

given to perceptions of the ancestors of contemporary Europe. Thus, Lafitau concluded in his argument on the universality of Christianity:

> I compared these customs, and I admit that, if the ancient authorities gave me insights to support some successful conjectures with respect to savages, the customs of savages gave me insights to understand more easily and to explain many things found in the ancient authors.[89]

In this way the history of peoples was transformed into the history of humanity, which stretched chronologically from a primitive origin to a civilised presence. Already, Bodin had observed in his *Method for the Easy Comprehension of History*:

> Although nothing is more remarkable in the whole nature of things than the magnet, yet the ancients were not aware of its use, clearly divine, and whereas they lived entirely within the Mediterranean basin, our men, on the other hand, traverse the whole earth every year in frequent voyages and lead colonies into another world, . . . in order to open up the farthest recesses of India.[90]

Bodin rejected the claim that the ancients 'were the inventors of the arts and to them the glory ought to go'. He concluded that no one 'can doubt that the discoveries of our men ought to be compared to the discoveries of our elders; many ought to be placed first'.[91] Hence, he argued that neither age was superior but that knowledge was accumulative in so far as modern peoples had improved upon the ancient knowledge of astrology, discovered the use of the compass (the magnet) and built 'engines of war' and the printing press. Instead of deteriorating from a golden age to one of silver then to bronze, iron and finally to clay, Bodin argued that each age progressed in relation to the former. Those who bemoaned the loss of the golden age did no more than bemoan their youth.[92] In this way any argument that the peoples of the New World were somehow 'closer' to God because of their 'primitive' nature, which could be likened to the state of Eden, could be rejected. Instead, closeness to God, and ultimate salvation, was argued to lie in the future-perfect present.

> So they who say that all things were understood by the ancients err not less than do those who deny them the early conquest of many arts.

---

89 Lafitau, 1734. In a similar vein, the discovery of the non-European world and the discovery that the ancients were not wiser than the moderns subsequently found depiction in the art of John White, who used the discovery of peoples in Virginia as the models for his depiction of the ancient Picts and Britons (Grafton, Shelford and Siraisi, 1992, p 126).
90 Bodin, 1966, p 301.   91 Ibid, p 301.   92 Ibid, pp 296–99.

Nature has countless treasures of knowledge which cannot be exhausted in any age.[93]

Bodin's historical analyses would not have been possible were it not for the reinterpretation of time by the clergy as a medium of reform and development – as an opportunity for profit within space rather than outside it. These conclusions, combined with the discovery of the New World, enabled Bodin to argue that humanity was part of a single universal history, which had 'a beginning and an end':[94]

Those who think that they can understand history without chronology are as much in error as those who wish to escape the windings of a labyrinth without a guide.[95]

As Bodin observed, '[a]bout this knowledge the ancients could write nothing, since they were ignorant of regions and places which not so long ago were opened up'.[96] Time had become linked to the chain of desire along which western culture could continuously constitute itself. The end was no longer in focus. When 'its fall will take place, not even angels know – certainly no one of the mortals'.[97] The end of experiential time places human history on a path that connects space to time (and progress). Montaigne's paradox of a young world at the end of a history not its choosing was no paradox – rather the New World was merely seen to be moving forward in time toward a common point of historical completion. 'European' history stood at the crossroads of two fantasies. The one of decline in which fulfilment was to be found in the time of God and the second one of progress where the mystery of wholeness would be revealed on earth. The end of the New World, then, in Montaigne's work, signified only the beginning of a more universal history; one which the Mexicans understood 'as we do':

The people of the kingdom of Mexico were somewhat more civilised and skilled in the arts than the others. Thus they judged, as we do, that the universe was near its end, and they took as a sign of this the desolation that we brought upon them.[98]

Montaigne illustrates the ultimatum of his times. If the Old World of Christian Europe was to justify its conquest and destruction of the New World then it had to believe that it held the promise of salvation – that the conquest of the New by the Old signified the Fall of one world into the promise of another. The colonisation of the New World was justified

---

93 Ibid, p 302.   94 Ibid, p 319.   95 Ibid, p 303.   96 Ibid, p 85.
97 Ibid, p 333.   98 Montaigne, 1958, pp 697–98.

figuratively by the Old World by its promise that the two worlds belonged to a single history. Moreover, by binding all of humanity to the same promise, which was subject to a particular Christian system of justice, the New World was also obliged to recognise its debts to that justice. By mapping western European providence onto the New World, the Old World located itself figuratively in that previously unredeemed time possessed by God alone. The emergence of the western world was thus located in the Fall of the New World into the space of pre-modern time; the origin becomes a place where the Old World already was but also what it had cast out; it was that part of itself, which was denied. Europeans, with their allegiance to themselves as the chosen ones, were able to assert themselves as complete while casting New World peoples as barbaric and incomplete. Despite having narrated itself into a time outside of space, the Old World existed nonetheless within this world. Both worlds – Old and New – began at the same moment. By positing the New World in a space that is chronologically prior to that of the Old World, the Old World marked out the New World as an immanent space, which enabled the First World to speak from a transcendent time of promise – to produce a sense of completion and authoritative determination. The New World was, however, left to embody the incarnation of time in space and all that this space represented in terms of irrationality, femininity, primitivism and physicality.[99] The New World was deemed to be both the cause and effect of its own place in history and development. The New World was not, however, in another world but of the same world at the same time but not necessarily of the same history.[100] The result was the fetishisation of a transcendent presence in which the Old World came to idolise itself. The Old World was no God and it had no place in time outside of space. Thus, the Old World merely reduced transcendence into the immanence of itself.

The New World was in turn fetishised and fixated upon as an object, while its colonisation by the Old World continued to bind it to a universal destiny – an either/or between death and life. In the process of this universalisation of western Christian justice, the once 'foreign and distant' New World acquired a status 'more rather than less familiar'. The Old World therefore vacillated between its 'contempt for what was familiar and its shivers of delight in – or fear of – novelty'.[101]

Indeed, development theory today can be characterised not by an incapacity to accept Third World lack, but rather by its incapacity not to view Third World peoples as lacking. Development discourse transposes the 'seeable'

---

99 Hence, the alterity presented by the New World is not the only source of interrogation, torture and murder upon medieval western knowledge. The apostate doubt perceived to rest in the irrationality of nature and women is also to be cordoned off in the separation of the mind from the body, i.e. the systemic 'witch-hunts' that took place during this period.

100 See Beard and Pahuja, 2003.   101 Said, 1978, pp 58–59.

differences into a theoretical framework that defines the seeable – be it racial, cultural, social, economic or political.[102]

Guaranteeing the convertibility of form

As the New World was being discovered by European explorers, the age of reason was dawning. Its aim would be to substitute humanity's belief in divine intervention for empirical observations and causal reasoning. Imperial Europe had ceased to repent and had turned its mind to the reason of man so that humanity might know its purposes and desires. Humankind now sought to bind itself to reason. The desire to seek faith through understanding had transformed the split between God and humanity into one between nature and rationality, mercy or justice. This western will to power would come to be described by Francis Bacon as a 'masculine birth of time' – one in which 'man' is distinguished through detachment, rationality and transcendence of the body from the 'alien world'.[103] The Christian Empire rising from the west of Europe would now lay down the Word – the law. Reason was to be used not to prove the existence of God but to prove the existence of humankind. The 'blind determinism of Providence' was left to govern 'the mechanistic-material realm of physical nature' and the yet unobserved and unnamed spaces of the New World.[104] The doubt of the age inspired a corresponding impulse 'to sharpen boundaries, to render meanings more precisely', or in other words, to define the terms of humanity's promise.[105] Diversity, at least in so far as it presented itself in peoples, was prevented from undermining the word of reason. Humanity was to be divided into the rational and the irrational. The confessional self continued its task of asserting and marking difference to redeem itself and arrive at salvation. As Lamore comments in relation to the constitution of the subject in the early modern period, '[m]an appeared to become fully man only when he settled in advance upon the forms through which he would encounter the things in the world'.[106] The challenge was to discover ways of making sense of the new in the resolve to order the conditions for experience rather than allow experience to dictate the order of humankind.

Reason did not install itself easily. In that long sixteenth century, the doubt over knowledge and truth was only as certain as humanity – a humanity which accorded to 'piety only the services that flatter our passions'.[107] This

---

102   See Beard and Pahuja, 2003, p 82.   103   Merchant, 1980, p 169.
104   William Pietz, 1993, pp 119, 138. Peter van der Veer writes that:

> In fact, what we have to realise is that the very distinction between religious and secular is a product of the Enlightenment that was used in orientalism to draw a sharp opposition between irrational, religious behaviour of the Oriental and rational secularism, which enabled the westerner to rule the Oriental (van der Veer 1993, p 39).

105   Agnew, 1986, p 10.   106   Larmore, 1981, pp 108–09.
107   Montaigne, 1958, p 323–24.

condition of doubt was no more evident than in the work of Montaigne. His texts have thus far been relied upon to demonstrate the hypocritical underpinnings of the relationship forged by the Christian world with the world it had newly discovered. The texts will be relied upon in the remainder of this chapter to examine the uncertainty of Montaigne's times, and the more personal crises of representation that were produced as individual social and communal identities were being brought into question by the discovery of the New World, the religious wars in Europe and a nascent liquid market.

Referring to the New World, Montaigne writes:

> I once saw among us some men brought by sea from a far country. Because we did not understand their language at all, and because their ways, moreover, and their bearing and their clothes were totally remote from ours, which of us did not consider them savages and brutes? Who did not attribute it to stupidity and brutishness to see them mute, ignorant of the French language, ignorant of our hand kissings and our serpentine bows, our deportment and our bearing, which human nature must take as its pattern without fail? Everything that seems strange to us, we condemn, and everything that we do not understand . . .[108]

The signs of strangeness spoken of here by Montaigne are those very signs of wonder felt by Columbus, representative of that gap in his knowledge which was without a familiar name or attributable words; that which was monstrous and disordered:

> How many things we call miraculous and contrary to nature! This is done by each man and each nation according to the measure of his ignorance. . . . For to us, to go according to nature is only to go according to our intelligence, as far as it can follow and as far as we can see; what is beyond is monstrous and disordered.[109]

Montaigne observed that 'knowledge is a great and useful quality' but that it is by no means 'in its power to make us wise and content' nor is it 'the mother of all virtue'.[110]

> Besides this infinite diversity and division, it is easy to see by the confusion that our judgement gives to our own selves, and the uncertainty that each man feels within himself, that [knowledge] has a very insecure seat. How diversely we judge things! How many times we change our notions! What I hold today and believe it with all my belief; all my tools and all my springs of action grip this opinion and sponsor it for me in every way

108 Ibid, p 345.   109 Ibid, p 391.   110 Ibid, p 319.

they can. I could not embrace or preserve any truth with more strength than this one. I belong to it entirely, I belong to it truly. But has it not happened to me, not once, but a hundred times, a thousand times, and every day, to have embraced with these same instruments, in this same condition, something else that I have since judged false.[111]

What, in fact, Montaigne was missing was the signifier of faith: the early Christian's 'ultimate subordination' to the Word of divine inscription;[112] a symbolic order to exclude or repress the fear of the unfathomable promise. Without it, human understanding becomes a bestiary of images, monsters and superstition. Montaigne understands this ambiguous state as one resulting from the inability to know God – the inability of humankind to locate the desire of the Other. The Christian soul could no longer recognise itself, nor indeed authorise itself, within traditional confessional narratives of religion, family and estate.

The authority of the canon had fallen, boundaries between Worlds were distorted; the peril of borderless relativity threatened to engulf the Old World as it was reduced to becoming the passive object of the *jouissance* of the Other.[113] Where does knowledge end and the monstrous and disordered begin?

Determining the promise guaranteed the Old World's existence 'sustaining the fantasy of an *adaequatio* between language and the world'.[114] As Montaigne observed, being is a mere interpretation – the staggering passing of subjectivity from day to day, minute to minute. One could not represent more than this; to do so would be to enter into the unredeemed wild of the New World. 'I cannot keep my subject still', writes Montaigne:

> It goes along and staggering, with a natural drunkenness. I take it in this condition, just as it is at the moment I give my attention to it. I do not portray being: I portray passing. Not the passing from one age to another ... but from day to day, from minute to minute. My history needs to be adapted to the moment. I may presently change, not only by chance, but also by intention. This is a record of various and changeable occurrences, and of irresolute and, when it so befalls, contradictory ideas: whether I am different myself, or whether I take hold of my subjects in different circumstances and aspects.[115]

Security against this roving subject could be found only within language in a chain of signification, although that knowledge of one's self was merely an

111 Ibid, p 423.   112 See Chapter Two, above.
113 See Verhaeghe, 2000, p 92.   114 Stavrakakis, 1999, p 25.
115 Montaigne, 1958, pp 610–11.

observation. The subject alternately appeared and disappeared in the continuous movement from signifier to signifier.[116] 'Painting myself for others', wrote Montaigne,

> I have painted my inward self with colours clearer than my original ones. I have no more made my book than my book has made me – a book consubstantial with its author. . . .[117]

In his essay most devoted to the question of doubt, famously summed up in his question, 'What do I know?' (*Que sçais-je?*), Montaigne argued that 'it is like that if the soul knew anything, it would first of all know itself; and if it knew anything outside of itself, that would be its body and shell before anything else'.[118] He adds:

> We are nearer to ourselves than the whiteness of snow or the weight of stones are to us. If man does not know himself, how does he know his functions and powers? Not that it is impossible that some true knowledge may dwell in us; but if it does, it does so by accident.[119]

Is snow white? Is it certain 'whether there is anything or whether there is nothing' or 'whether there is knowledge or ignorance' or 'whether we live'?[120]

> Our disputes are purely verbal. I ask what is 'nature', 'Pleasure', 'circle', 'Substitution'. The question is one of words, and is answered in the same way. . . . You would finally drive the respondent to the end of his lexicon. We exchange one word for another, often more unknown. . . . It is the Hydra's head.[121]

In the work of Montaigne we can perceive the link between the loss of words caused by the discovery of the unnamed New World, the loss of the Word in the religious wars of the Reformation, and the impossibility of naming his own subjectivity. His work exemplifies the struggle of each subject to know itself, construct its ego and to recognise itself in the gaze of the other. 'Others do not see you, they guess at you by uncertain conjectures; they do not see so much your nature as your art'.[122] The subject's 'ruling pattern' remains

---

116 See Lacan, 1978, p 205.   117 Montaigne, 1958, pp 503–04.
118 Raymond Sebond, whose 'Natural Theology' had been translated by Montaigne, had argued that humankind could learn all about God and religion by reading in the book of God's creation, the world. Montaigne refutes this and in his apology to Sebond he writes a sustained argument on the impotence of unaided human reason. In doing so, he argues the impossibility of the injunction to 'know thyself' (Montaigne, 1958, p 393).
119 Montaigne, 1958, p 421.   120 Ibid, p 391.   121 Ibid, pp 815, 818–19.
122 Ibid, p 613.

hidden[123] while disease, guilt, sin, vice, ugliness, 'corruption and filth' – the constant companions of humankind – distinguish the 'still, quiet centre of being'. This abstraction from being is the confessional subject emerging from a still and quiet centre into the cacophony of custom and the signifying power of the Word.

Thomas Hobbes would soon write that:

> A person is he whose words or actions are considered, either as his own, or as representing the world or actions of an other man, or of any other thing to whom they are attributed, whether Truly or by Fiction. When they are considered as his owne, then is he called a Naturall Person: And when they are considered as representing the words and actions of another, then is he a Feigned or Artificiall person. The word Person is latine . . . as *Persona* in latine signifies the *disguise*, or *outward appearance* or a man, counterfeited on the Stage; and sometimes more particularly that part of it, which disguiseth the face, as a Mask or Visard: And from the Stage, hath been translated to any Representer of speech and action, as well in Tribunalls, as Theaters. So that a *Person* is the same that an *Actor* is, both on the Stage and in common Conversation.[124]

Hobbes viewed the natural person as an actor – like Montaigne he recognised no centre of being – there was no subject underneath the mask. Instead, there existed a space for self-representation. To know thyself, like any acquisition of knowledge, emerged from translation and interpretation.[125] In speaking of interpretation and commentary, Montaigne argued that by 'diluting the substance we allow it to escape and spill it all over the place'.[126] He likened the search for truth to Aesop's dogs who, discovering something like a dead body floating in the sea and being unable to approach it, attempted to drink up the water and dry up the passage, choking in the attempt.[127] 'There is no end to our researches; our end is in another world'.[128] God's promise was no longer considered powerful enough to bind humanity to the Word.

Language – the Word – according to Montaigne had lost its original grounding power and it, too, took part in this constant movement. Its rule of law seemed unable to guarantee the stability of language on which the medieval order depended.

> The worst thing I find in our state is instability, and the fact that our laws cannot, any more than our clothes, take any settled form. It is very easy to accuse the government of imperfection, for all mortal things are full of it. It is very easy to engender in a people contempt for their ancient

123 Ibid, p 616.   124 Hobbes, 1991, p 112.   125 Judovitz, 1988, p 19.
126 Montaigne, 1958, pp 815–17.   127 Ibid.   128 Ibid.

observances; never did a man undertake that without succeeding. But as for establishing a better state in place of the one they have ruined, many of those who have attempted it have achieved nothing for their pains.[129]

Montaigne feared that an autonomous confessional subject was not constant enough to become the new symbolic lawmaker of humanity in a period when people were moving away from 'ritual, kin and proscriptive bonds' and toward 'contractual, commutable and convertible' forms of exchange.[130] The self was as empty as the fetishes of capital. Montaigne argued, 'We have no communication with being'.[131]

At the heart of this crisis of representation was the emerging liquid market in Europe and its apparent 'capacity to commute specific obligations, utilities, and meanings into general, fungible equivalents'.[132] As Pye argues, 'It is the constitutive force of economy – the prospect that one might be reduced to a commodity or mere factor in a system of exchange – that prompts fear and shame'.[133]

The greatest doubt arose from taking what was said for granted, so that:

> men no longer consider what the coins weigh and are worth, but each one in turn accepts them according to the value that common approbation and their currency give them. Men do not argue about the alloy, but about the rate of exchange: thus all things are accepted equally.[134]

Culture and society thus became negotiable against the 'immense collection of commodities' subject to an exchange in which 'the individual commodity appears as its elementary form'.[135] As Ebert has argued, materialism as a praxis of labour through which 'humans act upon external nature and change it, and in this way simultaneously change themselves' is what makes the discursive possible, 'it explains the discursive'.[136]

Political material

In order to secure self-identity, the modern subject entered into two kinds of negotiation: discursive and material. The first arose out of the relationship between the subject and the monarch; the second from the extraction of value from a person's labour. The first would, to a certain extent, regulate the terms

---

129   Ibid, p 498.   130   Agnew, 1986, p 8.   131   Montaigne, 1958, p 455.
132   Money begins 'to talk'; the written word is again embellished with value and meaning. Already, the scholastic writer John of Salisbury had claimed that a written conveyance could represent the terms rather than the mere existence of an agreement. Written words, he argued, 'speak voicelessly the utterances of the absent'. Cited in Agnew, 1986, pp 29–30, 42.
133   Pye, 2000, p 18.   134   Montaigne, 1958, p 420.   135   Marx, 1976–81, p 125.
136   Ebert, 1996, pp 34–35.

of the latter but also masked the latter in so far as it reduced the exploitation of peoples' lives and labour into a negotiation of linguistic differences.[137] In both forms of negotiation, the confessional subject was exchanged freely not as an object as such but as a value within 'a system that traffics only in abstractions, idealisations, prejudices, and their ciphers and markers'.[138]

The first form of negotiation – between the sovereign monarch and the subject – is that which Montaigne identifies as the best means of stabilising the value of humankind. To obstruct the insidious developments of his times, society was to secure the power of one man because, 'it is easier to safeguard him by good education and advice, from the effects of that poison'. Montaigne was an ideologue of the 'cult of the government's will'.[139] He stated that one of the principal merits of the Christian religion was its 'precise recommendation of obedience to the magistrate and maintenance of the government'.[140] Thus, in a period when Christians also went by the same title as Perigordians or Germans, it was those latter titles that were the more secure.[141] Montaigne observed:

> Society in general can do without our thoughts; but the rest – our actions, our work, our fortunes, our life – we must lend and abandon to its service and to the common opinion. . . . For it is the rule of rules, and the universal of laws, that each man obeys those of the place he is in.[142]

Bodies, labour, commodities were to be abandoned to the force of the juridical sovereign. This power 'of a monarch' would in turn guarantee the 'good government' of the state and the stability of a regulated exchange rate. Unlike the unfathomable, unspeakable subjection to a divine being, the sovereign monarch's *raison d'être* was rationalised to become the very model of faith through understanding. Statecraft was becoming the art of knowing the promise.

Montaigne declared that, 'it takes a lot of self-love and presumption to have such esteem for one's own opinions that to establish them one must overthrow the public peace and introduce so many inevitable evils'.[143] Anyone who chose to place the private realm first, 'meddles with choosing and changing, usurps the authority to judge'.[144] It was the unreasonable abuse of internal liberty 'to make it serve our frivolous and private fancies' that had to be controlled. One had to follow 'the common and legitimate arrangement' or be inscribed as psychotic – an ungovernable savage.[145] The anarchic speech of the psychotic ignored the rule of law and served instead to 'manipulate and agitate a crowd and a disorderly populace'; it served to persuade 'the herd' and 'the ignorant' in a state where 'things were in perpetual turmoil'.

137 Ibid, p 40.   138 Keenan, 1993, pp 152, 175.   139 Pietz, 1993, p 141.
140 Montaigne, 1958, pp 87–88.   141 Ibid, p 325.   142 Ibid, p 86.
143 Ibid, p 87.   144 Ibid, p 88.   145 Ibid, pp 278, 289.

> The ordinary discipline of a state that is in a healthy condition does not provide for these extraordinary accidents; it presupposes a body that holds together in its principal parts and function and a common consent to its observance and obedience.[146]

In such a case, speech could offer itself as 'a medicine' though a very dangerous one, for it appealed precisely to the constant oscillation of the private being and not to the loyalty of the public one. 'The commonwealths that kept themselves regulated, like the Cretan and the Lacedaemonian', wrote Montaigne, 'made little account of orators'.[147] Free speech either set off anarchy or it was of use only where anarchy already reigned – a lesson already taught to Abelard by the Roman Catholic Church.[148]

Divine laws, social laws, and sovereignty of the magistrate, these all formed a coherent body that dissolved under any usurpation of mastery.[149] Montaigne's reverence for, and fear of, speech was the same as that which prompted the disciplinary practices of the medieval Church. Given the power of language held by each individual, Montaigne considered the intervention of the private into the public realm was a potential usurpation of sovereignty and appreciated the existence of law's judge as 'guarantee both of law's material presence and the possibility of justice'.[150]

State sovereignty was the only practical means to secure order, according to Montaigne, because its promise of justice was secure – already determined. He wrote of the many people who had been punished for a crime of which they were innocent and concluded that the decisions of the judges must be final. The innocent, even when later proven to be so, are sacrificed to the 'forms of justice'[151] and their claim to 'universal validity'.[152] This seems to be the same form of justice described by Grotius and referred to in Chapter Two. Here justice is the promise that cannot be betrayed.

The juridical rule of law thus becomes immutable – the ultimate limit beyond which the subject ceases to be fully human. The sovereign ruler is a Leviathan who can enable the functioning and ongoing construction of the Old World – a new God-man sitting at the head of the old monotheistic patriarchal system. He will live like the God-man, not a real man but an ideal man, who 'by his particular position of outside, functions as a kind of guarantee' of justice, its rule of law and the human rights and freedoms that are fundamental to it.[153] Hence, Montaigne wrote:

> Law is thus constituted by the ordered subject as it also constitutes that

---

146 Ibid, p 98.   147 Ibid, pp 221–22.   148 Reiss, 1986, pp 115, 131.
149 Montaigne, 1958, p 51.   150 McVeigh, Rush and Young, 2002.
151 Montaigne, 1958, p 820.   152 Lacan, 1992, p 259.
153 See Verhaeghe, 2000, p 91.

subject. Without the law the subject has no means to direct and to rationalise the otherwise borderless reason within.[154]

The justice meted out by the head of state is the only means to guarantee stability and unity. The laws take their authority from possession and usage; it is dangerous to trace them back to their birth.[155] Just as in Anselm's picture of rectitude, law, order, justice and humankind were bound together into a divine truth and single way of being and becoming. Monarchy and profit became two sides of the same coin circulating in a realm of bodies, labour and subjectivity.

The limits of the rule of law would be set through a variety of technologies: sexual repression, physical discipline, judicial torture and interrogation to predicate a modern confessional subject. From the sixteenth to the eighteenth centuries, national sovereignty would be increasingly imposed by the rule of law onto the whole of society through the bruised and tortured bodies of outlaws – a reminder that bodies and their inherent value belonged to the monarch and to God.[156] This inscription of national sovereignty by the imperial violence of colonisation was the same pain imposed by the early Christian Church on penitents in their performance of *exomologesis*, and it is the same violent inscription of identification employed by many international development agencies on the peoples of the Third World today.

A belief in the Leviathan as universal arbiter of subjectivity allowed Hobbes, in his *Philosophical Rudiments Concerning Government and Society*, 'not to point which are the laws of any country, but to declare what the laws of all countries are'.[157] Universal justice secured control over the errant confessional subject of a pre-modern, pre-rational unredeemed age. While the private natural person could be recognised by their ownership of their words and actions, it was sovereign authority that granted this ownership; a sovereign authority that was vested in an artificial person who represented the words and actions of the entire nation.[158]

But how could such a figure be more than it was? Through faith in an incarnational account of the monarch's authority, which recalls the same belief in the promise offered by the Old World in its relation to the New World. The medieval philosophers had spent centuries perfecting the practice known as '*Credo quia absurdum*' (I believe because it is absurd).[159] As Slavoj Zizek argues, the transubstantiated body of the sovereign 'is an effect of the performative mechanism . . . we, the subjects, think that we treat the kings as

154 Montaigne, 1958, p 272.   155 Ibid, p 440.
156 See Muchembled, 1985, pp 202–08.   157 Hobbes, 1983, p 37.
158 Hobbes, 1991, pp 112–15. See also, Greenblatt 1986, pp 210, 222.
159 Verhaeghe, 2000, p 96. See Freud, 1953, p 74.

a king because he is in himself a king, but in reality a king is a king because we treat him like one'.[160]

Hence, the fantasy of sovereignty acquired its signification, and thus its power from the faith the body politic had in it. Religion, ethnicity and emerging forms of nationalism are used as sovereign marks to interpellate juridical subjects. These subjects will themselves into the monarch's body, and in so doing they negotiate the nature of the monarch's rule. Beyond this shared faith in the sovereign exist savages and outlaws. By cleaving the king in two, the mystical and immortal body guarantees the stability and permanence of the state – the rational conscience – as against the present, particular and mortal body subject to the laws of any given society. The sovereign monarch, then, is someone possessed, inhabited by another body – the body politic – most truly present in their demise. The monarch is 'that magical surplus, the true and invisible mark of sovereignty', 'the hypostatized embodiment of the symbolic as such'.[161]

Emerging from the Middle Ages into the birth of masculine time and affirming itself in theories of divine right toward the end of the sixteenth century, the theory of the double body guarantees the stability of the Word (and the subject). The Leviathan stands in the position of authority binding the subject as one 'as if from wax' out of 'so many contrasting figures'.[162] For, as Montaigne argued, humanity could not stay in form if left scattered amongst its individual fragments, which are 'weak in every direction'.

So it was that in 1578 Aegremont Ratcliffe could refer to the 'Politique bodie' as 'societie . . . in general':[163]

> For as there is a divine coherence between members of the bodie, though they haue all a distinct and perculier office, yet they all minister to the common societie: so in like manner we being members of that bodie, whereof Christ is the head, ought to bend our actiuitie for the health & welfare of the same.[164]

Both the monarchy and the confessional self could thus be remedied through confessional narratives applicable to the body politic. The body politic itself became an object of salvation in early modern discourse because it was bound to the same promise of justice and Christian rule of law. Social,

---

160   Zizek, 1989, p 146.   161   Pye, 2000, pp 45–46.   162   Montaigne, 1958, p 323.
163   Sherman, 1997, p 107.
164   In a study of his work on the Elizabethan commonwealth, Sherman cites many examples of how the term 'commonwealth' became synonymous with the 'body politic' and he suggests this was often done using medical analogies of diagnosis and prescription. In effect, the employment of this imagery served to naturalise the body politic lending it not only an 'aura of immutability', as Sherman argues, but also objectifying it for (political) scientific observation (Sherman, 1997, pp 107–08).

economic and religious reform became the objectives of a 'godly' and 'perfect Commonwealth'.[165] Economic growth was not yet the express objective of the state but, like any Christian body, redemption from the Fall was.

The new sovereign body politic thus became the signifier of fulfilment. With this body it would be possible to discover the promised land – to reach salvation. This real presence of the power of the state was no more evident than in its guarantee of the great signifier of value – money, which in turn defined the value of each subject. In the same way that 'the sacramental host also is, at the moment of consecration, a "narrative" reiteration of the historical sacrifice of Jesus Christ', the coin (backed most often by gold) represented the redemptive power of the absolute monarch.[166]

Paradoxically, it is the coin – the root of all evil – that immediately robs the sovereign of its name. Thus the Emperor in Wilhelm Goethe's *Faust* bemoans his lack of control over the paper money he has authorised with his name, which was now being copied by 'conjurers'.[167] As Jochen Hörisch comments, '[n]ow everyone may find salvation in this sign that is not exactly exclusive'.[168] The sign of the cross had run out of credit and, similarly, the sovereign's signature, 'the decisive power of the king's word is replaced by the silent power of money as the social and national agency of governance', which because it is ratified by the Emperor, must be made to count.[169]

> He who is used to justifying his legitimacy through transcendence, and relying on this godly guarantee of, or cover for, his earthly authority, is forced to let the legality of the money count.[170]

It is arguably here in this slippage of sovereignty that cycles of labour valorisation, monetary realisation, and capital accumulation emerge from the sovereign realm of economic exchange to stabilise the subject by its labour through the force of the sovereign's law. The formless subject described in Montainge's texts is to be redeemed through the security of its 'value' and re-formed in a signifying chain of subject, commodity, capital and back again to the subject form.[171] As Grbich writes:

---

165 John Booty, 'Communion and Commonweal: The Book of Common Prayer' cited in Sherman, 1997, p 111.
166 Marin, 1988, p 128.   167 Hörisch, 2000, p 12.   168 Ibid, p 11.
169 Ibid, p 12.
170 Ibid. At first it was the church and the market cross that provided a visible form of security allowing honourable pledges and oaths to be performed in the presence of sacredness; and although juridical sovereignty wrested power from the Church from the 10th to the 17th centuries, the practice of 'Sunday' marketing continued for a much longer period. By the 17th century the 'fully autonomous and creditable commercial instruments' were all that was left of the ceremonial and personal rite from which they had originated. Cited in Agnew, 1986, pp 29–30, 42.
171 Pietz, 1993, p 149 citing Marx, 1971, pp 494, 498.

The axiomatics of imperialism included learning to analogise the miracles of western money to the narratives of Christian eschatology – the doctrines of death, judgment, heaven and hell, mediated by the tropes of Christ's redemption and resurrection. Just as the name of God was being foreclosed in the practices of a secular Enlightenment, biblical stories of suffering and abjection needed new characters to form the ground of new actions.[172]

In the modern age, it will be the extraction of labour, rather than the confession of sin, that will mark out the true subject from the faithless outlaw. Humanity becomes indistinguishable from the commodity. It is the 'ghostly residue that names the pragmatic necessity of likeness in exchange. To be alike is to be abstract, which is to say, to be a ghost – to be human or a commodity'.[173] Money thus acts as the totaliser of a society of individual fragments in a temporal sense in the same way that the sovereign monarch incorporates the body politic in a spatial sense. In these ways, God is erased as space is subsumed by time. Voltaire (1694–1778) wrote:

Go to the Exchange in London, that place more venerable than many a court, and you will see representatives of all the nations assembled there for the profit of mankind. There the Jew, the Mohametan, and the Christian deal with one another as if they were of the same religion, and reserve the name of infidel for those who go bankrupt. There the Presbyterian trusts the Anabaptist, and the Church of England man accepts the promise of the Quaker.[174]

Could this be the modern myth of salvation – a world united by a market that is regulated by territorial sovereigns? Can the sovereign lawmaker join with other 'nations assembled' to totalise the boundaries of the confessional subject and replace the fallen boundaries within and between the Old World religions to create a subject of order? The answer to this question was about to be found in the assembly of nations brought together in the aftermath of the religious wars of the Reformation at the Peace of Westphalia in 1648. This assembly is to be the focus of Chapter Five. Chapter Four, however, focuses on the fragments of that peace, the formative nation states themselves.

---

172 Grbich, 2005, p 131.   173 Keenan, 1993, pp 152, 171.
174 Voltaire, 1961, p 26.

Chapter 4

'The sovereignty of man lieth hid in knowledge'

This chapter explores the precarious nature of the newly emerging sovereign state during the seventeenth and eighteenth centuries. It analyses how the state is constituted by the discourses of salvation that materialise from the legal, economic and scientific narratives of the time. Particular attention is paid to how the construction of these narratives relied heavily on the myth of a savage past, upon which the Old World grounded its birth into modernity. Even today, reliance on Freud's theories on totem and taboo, Marx's primitive accumulation, Hegel's spirit, Locke's social contract, Hobbe's state of nature: all of these myths fetishise the New World as the primitive Other. The savage nature of the New World thus provides the Old World with its origin.[1] The aim of this chapter is to look beyond these myths of worldly origins to the processes that hold these divisionary realities in place.

This excursion into narratives of origin begins with a reading of Francis Bacon's utopian fantasy, *New Atlantis*, published posthumously in 1627. This text is an early example of how the idea of nation and national development was already being constructed in the seventeenth century. This chapter draws on later texts from the Renaissance and Enlightenment periods of European history, particularly those of John Locke, in order to explore further the boundaries of nation and its subjects and their role in the genealogy of development. The events described in this chapter demonstrate how the irrational, formless, shape-shifting individual of the Renaissance was disciplined and stabilised by the direction of state governance to which total loyalty was owed. Both fear of the irrational self and faith in the rational behaviour of the sovereign spun the coin upon which the merchants of global capitalism relied.

The New Atlantis

Bacon's dream of a New Atlantis is set in the time of discovery foretold by the biblical book of Daniel toward the end of time when many 'shall pass to and

---

1 See Beard and Pahuja, 2003.

fro, and knowledge shall be increased'.[2] Bacon's story is narrated by a member of a crew of explorers sailing from Peru to China and Japan. They become lost and prepare for death but discover instead the kingdom of Bensalem – the New Atlantis. This island kingdom is located beyond the classical Pillars of Hercules (promontories of the Strait of Gibraltar), the ancient limits of navigation and knowledge in the southern oceans 'between life and death; for we are beyond both the old world and the new'.[3] In this sense Bensalem represents a land of redemption. It is a space containing past and future: Augustine's time outside of space. This time is national and it is measured by its position along a temporal path stretching from the savagery of the New into the idealistic fantasy of the Old World as a 'transcendent exemplarity'.[4] Without the savage or the ideal, the fantasy of Bensalem could not exist.

The crew are taken in by the citizens of Bensalem and instructed in their customs and society before being asked to return to Europe to report on what they have learnt. They are told that the history of Bensalem dates back to the time of the Exodus, around 1400 BC, when a Peruvian crew of explorers discovered the island. In this way, God's own means of salvation – Christ – is written out of the narration.

At the time of Bensalem's supposed discovery, the world comprised many great seafaring kingdoms. The crew is told that what they know as North America had then been known as Atlantis. Atlantis had been densely populated – a proud kingdom in 'arms, shipping and riches', as were Mexico (Tyrambel) and Peru (Coya).[5] 'But the Divine Revenge overtook not long after those proud enterprises emerged. For within less than the space of one hundred years, the great Atlantis was utterly lost and destroyed' by a great flood.[6] Unredeemed, Atlantis had not been granted salvation but, instead, had been returned to primitive savagery.

> So as marvel you not at the thin population of America, nor at the rudeness of the people; for you must account your inhabitants of America as young people; younger a thousand years, at the least, than the rest of the world; for that there was so much time between the universal flood and their particular inundation. For the poor remnant of human seed which remained in their mountains peopled again the country again slowly, by little and little; and being simple and savage people, (not like Noah and his sons, which was the chief family of the earth), they were not able to leave letters, arts, civility to their posterity.[7]

---

2   *Daniel* 12:4.   3 Bacon, 1974, p 219   4 Fitzpatrick, 2001, p 128.
5   Bacon, 1974, p 226. This anticipates Locke's famous statement: '[I]n the beginning all the world was America' (Locke 1960, section 49). See also, Hegel's comment that America was 'the land of the future, where, in the ages that lie before us, the burden of the World's History shall reveal itself' (Hegel, 1956, p 86).
6   Bacon, 1974, pp 226–27.   7 Ibid, p 227.

The survival of Bacon's Bensalem from Divine revenge was owed to its 'original' lawgiver, King Solamona, who reigned 300 years before Christ. He was esteemed both for his good will and because he was 'wholly bent to make his kingdom and people happy' by instituting a new system of laws that were based around the movement of peoples onto and away from the island.[8] King Solamona instituted his laws of isolation believing:

> the happy and flourishing estate wherein this land then was, so as it might be a thousand ways altered to the worse, but scarce any one way to the better; thought nothing wanted to his noble and heroical intentions, but only (as far as human foresight might reach) to give perpetuity to that which was in his time so happily established. Therefore amongst his other fundamental laws of this kingdom, he did ordain the interdicts and prohibition which we have touching the entrance of strangers.[9]

In this passage Bacon gives to Bensalem the keys to bind and to lose – for if this is the land of salvation then not everyone can enter. In Bensalem, the keys of salvation are not kept by God and His Church but by the territorial sovereign. The isolationist policies adopted by Bensalem resulted in it losing contact with the rest of the world and remaining unaffected by the collapse of the ancient civilisations and the chaos of the religious wars of the Reformation and the early industrial revolution. It had escaped into its own future. It was a future based on a process of 'constant purification and social normalisation' both within and outside itself.[10] For as Bacon sought to exemplify, Bensalem was caught in a process of development (a concept not yet coined), which might just as easily return it to a savage past as allow it to progress into an ideal Christian paradise. Now in a space of time the trick was to remain there, lest it fall back to nature.

So while it was to the crew's relief that the Bensalems had 'languages and were . . . full of humanity',[11] conversely, the Bensalem officials did not welcome the European crew, who were initially allowed onto the island for three days only as detainees in quarantine at the Strangers' House.[12] This stay was permitted only after the Bensalems had been assured that the crew were Christian and an oath had been taken that they were 'no pirates, nor have shed blood lawfully nor unlawfully within forty days past'.[13] Violence had well and truly been handed over to the prerogative of the state. Indeed, the containment of violence was very much a part of this crystallisation of sovereignty

---

8 Ibid, p 228.   9 Ibid, p 228.   10 Foucault, 1995, p 67.
11 Bacon, 1974, p 216.
12 The coincidental similarities in the story of New Atlantis and that of the author's island home, Australia, are striking.
13 Bacon, 1974, p 217. For a contemporary example of such exclusion, see the UN Convention relating to the status of refugees, Arts 1F and 33.

and an international law of nations. As Foucault has argued in his own telling of the origins of modern society, the outlawing of private warfare during the Classical period and its transformation into a national prerogative, 'cleansed' civil society of warlike relations, creating in the process a strange, new discourse in which society itself was produced from the marginalised relations of war.[14] This led Grotius to write, in 1625, that only a state may 'commit some act of aggression, or injustice'; 'a band of pirates or robbers' cannot nor could they ever become a state, 'although they may preserve among themselves that degree of subordination, which is absolutely necessary to the subsistence of all society'.[15] He continued:

> For with the latter, the commission of crime is the *sole* bond of union, whereas the former, though not always free from blame, but occasionally deviating from the laws of nature, which in many cases have been in a great measure obliterated, still regulate their conduct by the treaties, which they have made, and certain customs that have been established, being united among themselves for the mutual support of lawful rights, and connected with foreign states by known rules of standing polity.[16]

So too, in the utopian fantasy of Bensalem, violence and antagonism were eliminated and repressed into the guise of sovereign lawmaking. Indeed, violence was never mentioned in the text except implicitly in relation to the prohibition of strangers and, more particularly, of pirates. But the laws of exclusion are never stable. Hence, after the third day had passed, the Governor of the Strangers' House, who was by vocation a Christian priest, visited the crew to advise them that:

> The state hath given you licence to stay on land for the space of six weeks: and let it not trouble you if your occasions ask further time, for the law in this point is not precise.[17]

---

14 Foucault, 1995, p 66.   15 Grotius, 1814, Book III, Chapter 3.2.

16 Ibid. See also, Sir William Blackstone's definition of piracy in his *Commentaries on the Laws of England* written in 1783 in which he states that piracy is:

> an offence against the universal laws of society; a pirate being, according to Sir Edward Coke, *hostis humani generis*. As therefore he has renounced all the benefits of society and government, and has reduced himself afresh to the savage state of nature, by declaring war against all mankind, all mankind must declare war against him: so that every community has a right, by the rule of self-defence, to inflict that punishment upon him, which every individual would in a state of nature have been otherwise entitled to do, for any invasion of his person or personal property (Blackstone, 1978, p 71).

17 Bacon, 1974, p 220.

Through its strict 'interdicts and prohibitions' Bensalem was given all the trappings of an independent and sovereign nation state. Besalem's *raison d'être* – its *raison d'etat* – was to keep its people happy and ultimately preserve their survival into salvation. Here and now, in the lead up to the Peace of Westphalia in 1648, nation was being imagined and signified.[18] Nation was thus exchanged for the body of Christ as the medium between salvation and sin. The Bensalem kingdom had a common language, a defined territory, a history and a secular scientific technology that eclipsed the conflict of religion. It concerned itself with the nature and purposes of society and its govern-ance, the relationship between the individual and the community and their welfare and quality of life.[19] The sovereign state defined itself as an entity aware of what must be governed and what must be expelled, and like the confes-sional subject, it sought thereby to arrive at a greater knowledge of itself, in order that it might direct and shape that reality in its own interests, namely the production of wealth and an increase in strength vis à vis other states. The nation state was located within a confessional discourse of salvation. Like the medieval Christian Church before it, the state had assumed the brokerage of its subjects' redemption. This brokerage was inscribed onto the subject though a multitude of physical and mnemontechnic disciplinary practices based on the violence of law and the narratives of national belonging that coded the flow of desire to accord with that of the collective body politic.

If the promise of nation was to be redeemed then, like the confessional subject, the state was required to increase its knowledge of itself; knowledge based on the conceptualisation and alienation of the *polis* from bare life as the means to eternal preservation.[20] Is this not the same abstraction of sin from the medieval confessional subject? Is this not also the same abstraction of labour from the bodies subject to the circulation of economic exchange? Thomas Lupton had already been telling tales of the perfect nation in a work called: *Siuqila: Too Good to be True* published in 1580.[21] Lupton's work narrated the travels of a Christian man called Siuqila, a man who meets a variety of peoples in his travels including a man called Omen in a country called Mauqsun. Weary of the 'wickedness, naughtinesse, falsehode, and other great enormities of his owne Countrie', Siuqila asks Omen about the customs of Mauqsun. Owen then tells Siuqila of the 'commendable customs, the plaine meaning and true dealing, the Lordes liberalities, the Ladies great courtesis, the husbands fidelities, the wiues obedience, the maydens modestie, the masters

---

18 The Peace of Westphalia is usually relied upon as the mythical origins of international law. It refers to the series of peace treaties signed during 1648 by representatives of France, the Holy Roman Empire, Netherlands, Portugal, Spain, Sweden, Switzerland, and the Papacy follow-ing the Thirty Years' War in Europe. It marks the beginning of a system of sovereign states with equal rights upon which modern international law is said to be based. The Peace of Westphalia of 1648 is referred to below and discussed in greater detail in Chapter Five.

19 Jones, 1970, p 214.   20 See Agamben, 1998, p 48.   21 Sherman, 1997, p 111.

sobrietie, the seruants diligence, the Magistrates affabilities, the Judges equi-
tie, the commons amitie, the preferring of publique commoditie, the generall
hospitalitie, the exceeding mercie, the wonderfull charitie, and the constant
Christianitie [of the Mauqsunians]'.[22]

Lupton's text bears strong similarities to the medieval Penitentials cited in
Chapter Two in which vocations are established and the moral conduct of each
vocation was also constructed and regulated.[23] It also illustrates the space of
becoming, referred to by Montaigne. In the utopian texts of both Bacon
and Lupton, the vocations of both nation and citizen were determined. In
Luptons's text, the economy was regulated through plain and true dealings
and public ownership, the lawgivers are affable and equitable, and wives,
husbands, servants, indeed everyone keeps to their station.

As William H Sherman writes of Elizabethan England, terms such as 'the
commonwealth' were not merely 'an idea but an ideology and an ideal' that
advocated 'the maintenance of an ordered society through cooperative striving
of every particular member, in his or her ordained capacity, for the common
good'.[24]

Bacon's *New Atlantis* was, in effect, an anatomical investigation of an
anticipated body politic – a model precursor to manuals such as those produced by contemporary organisations today such as the United Nations, the
International Monetary Fund (IMF) and the World Bank and, as such, it is
relevant to a genealogy of development conceptually and in practice.[25] In like
manner to Bacon's fantasy, the texts of today's development agencies pre-
sume that a body politic is dependent on a society comprising natural vocations and processes (economic, demographic, etc.) that can be harnessed for
the rational art of governing a population. In this sense, they are products of
utopian dreams made possible by the subjectification of the nation state into
a space of discursive sovereignty. Nationalism can be seen to represent the
same need for verbalisation, for signifying in human terms that which would
otherwise remain unknown of the truth about oneself.

From this perspective, stories such as the *New Atlantis* produced a particular
kind of national state in which its members might achieve maximum freedom, the fundamental of rights and duties and the pursuit of wealth.[26] These
stories are closely associated with the originary myth of the social contract,

---

22 Cited in Sherman, 1997, p 112.
23 The text was a great success at the time such that Lupton wrote a second part in 1581, entitled
    *The Second part and knitting vp of the Boke entituled Too good to be true herein is continued the
    discourse of the wonderfull Lawes, commendable customes, & strange manners of the people of
    Mauqsun.*
24 Sherman, 1997, p 106.
25 The texts of development agencies such as the IMF and the World Bank are discussed in
    Chapter Six, below. See also, Ferguson, 1965, p xi.
26 Gordon, 1991, pp 2–3.

whereby human development – the preservation of life for the individual on its way to salvation – is provided by the state to those who pass as its citizens by means of assimilation and sacrifice. The state thus usurped the place of the Church and its status as the confessor to its unredeemed flock. Those peoples who stray from the flock, those who are presumed to be without faith nor understanding, the pagans, savages, natives, witches, vagrant masterless men, independent or lesbian women and underdeveloped peoples, those surviving at the axis of evil and those living outside the rule of law are not only represented as primitive, stagnant and incapable of economic growth, but also as anarchic, troublemaking, mad, unlawful citizens – stateless, both in the sense of being without nation and without form.[27] They remain a manifestation of sin located in a savage space without law or stabilised boundaries.

Those without a vocation in this concept of nation came to represent tragic excess – subjects outside the ordered body politic and yet constitutive of it, existing, as Marx wrote, as 'residuum', a 'congealed mass' or 'coagulated jelly'.[28] In order to be received into the body politic – to seek God's glory – the subject had to fall into a certain frame of mind that had little to do with embodiment. It had much and more to do with 'the possession of requisite mental capacities' – a belief that only served to strengthen the foundations of the mythical thesis that a social contract was based on free will and 'sound mind'.[29] A frame or space of mind carved out in a manner not unlike that of the medieval confessional subject, but one which began to look outwards to what it was *not* rather than to what it was in the eyes of God. In addition, bio-political discourses, including those appearing in subsequent centuries, would function to segregate, eliminate and normalise society on biological and racist grounds.[30] Once told, these originary myths of sovereignty explained not only why states were formed, but also why a return to the lost primordial unity was impossible. These myths were what kept anarchy at bay.

In anticipation of these processes, the fictional Bensalem represented the nation cleaved together through juridical doctrines of exclusion and historical narratives of a Christian heritage that denied 'other collectivising features, other systems of irreducible "differences" '.[31] These laws were 'fundamental' to protect Bensalem's Christian race within its pure state. The unknown visitor and the wayward stranger were considered infectious: a threat to the homogeneity and cohesion of the state, which itself was constructed not unlike a scientific laboratory where no infection of difference was allowed to contaminate an ideal set of conditions. 'In the laboratory Nature can at last be

27 Beard, 2001.   28 Pye, 2000, p 147.   29 Mykitiuk, 1994, p 74.
30 Foucault, 1995, p 67.   31 Balibar, 1991, p 60.

fixed in place; here the scientist can transform as well as isolate and uncover his subjects.'[32]

For the nation to be itself it had to be racially and culturally pure. It had to isolate the pagans, the sinners and the weak both within and beyond its body in order to eliminate, expel or repel them. It had to be able to identify itself and that which was governable within it. A failure to do so would result in its own expulsion or elimination into New World savagery until its parts were taken up and christened into the Word of another. The narratives of nation and its subjects worked to ensure their realisation; their baptism into a reality. To do so, the narrative unified the state by means of an 'historic mission' and a series of related 'ideal signifiers'. The first and foremost signifier was 'the very *name* of the nation or "fatherland" ', in this case, Bensalem, a combination of Hebrew words (*ben, shalem*) meaning 'son or offspring of peace, safety and completeness'. Onto these signifiers was transferred the same 'sense of the sacred and the affects of love, respect, sacrifice and fear which [had] cemented religious communities' but which instead ends up tending to replace religion forcing it also to become 'nationalised'.[33] The name was thus reminiscent of the power of the *ius patrium*, the sovereign power of the father over his family and the related hagiographic epithet 'father of the people', which 'provides a kind of genealogical myth of sovereign power: the magistrate's *imperium* was nothing but the father's *vitae necisque potestas* extended to all citizens'.[34]

The same can be said then of human genealogy, which also worked to constitute the cohesion of nation. The citizens of Bensalem traced their heritage through a Christian history based on patriarchal bloodlines. The Feast of the Family, described in detail in the story, was a custom granted to any man, who lived to see thirty persons descended of his body alive together and all above three years old.

During the feast, family members were able to discuss with the father all disputes, distress, or vice or seek from him his advice. The governor assisted to 'put in execution by his public authority the decrees and order' of the father. A familial 'ethnicity' was thereby produced that was politically sanctioned by the force of law. Indeed, as Agamben observes, it is this successor of the father's *vitae necisque potestas* that founds the juridico-political life of the subject because 'a life that may be killed, which is politicised through its

---

32   Boesky, 1997, pp 138, 145. Bacon's *New Atlantis*, his representation of the ideal commonwealth, was appended to his *Sylva Sylvarum, or a Naturall Historie in Ten Centuries* (London, 1627), an anthology of experiments in which nature is mastered and 'perfected': 'Birds and beasts of strange colours' can be invented by experiments done to feathers and skin (II 379.); impure or salty water can be made pure through percolation; growing cycles of plants can be speeded up or slowed down, and plants can be moulded into curious shapes (II 52). The *Sylva Sylvarum* was part of Bacon's unfinished *Instauratio Magna*.

33   Balibar, 1991, p 95.   34   Agamben, 1998, pp 88–89.

very capacity to be killed' is what enforces the law and brings into being political life.[35] As Orford would point out, this masculine birth of time requires the mother to disappear.[36] Hence, the bountiful father in Bensalem was heralded with privileges as a 'well-beloved friend and creditor' for they say 'the king is debtor to no man, but for propagation of his subjects'.[37] The mother of the descendants, in contrast, 'from whose body the whole lineage is descended' was placed during the Feast of the Family in a loft to the right of his chair, with a private door and glassed window, 'where she sitteth but is not seen'.[38] Since the Feast of the Family inscribed onto the citizens of Bensalem a sense of belonging in relation to a bloodline, it hid the role and labour of the mother, interpolating the citizen 'as an individual, in the name of the collective whose name one bears'. The mother, in turn, is cast back into an unfathomable position, an abstraction herself, while life, bloodlines, families were bound into the Christian heritage of Bensalem increasing the 'naturalisation of belonging and the sublimation of the ideal nation' as 'two aspects of the same process'.[39]

In this transformation the very underpinning of law's power is transformed as it becomes less a force of coercion and rather a force of persuasion and normalisation used to regulate behaviour.[40] As Foucault has observed, the power of the sovereign to take life or let live,

> presents itself as the counterpart of a power that exerts a positive influence on life, that endeavours to administer, optimise, and multiply it, subjecting it to precise controls and comprehensive regulations.[41]

Because family life had now become the locus of power and law, it is life that is protected by that power as a fundamental right of each person.[42] The sovereign right to kill becomes an 'excess' 'that does away with life in the name of securing it'.[43] This value put on life is in turn absorbed in the constant

---

35 Ibid, p 89.　　36 Orford, 2005.　　37 Bacon, 1974, p 233.　　38 Ibid, p 232.

39 Balibar, 1991, p 96.

40 Foucault has argued that the West has, from the 18th century to the present, created so many technologies of power that are foreign to the concept of law that it fears the effects and proliferation of those technologies and therefore attempts to recode them into forms of law. Foucault, 1998b, p 109.

41 Foucault, 1998b, p 137.　　42 Ibid, p 145.

43 Ibid, pp 142–43. Describing events in the 18th century, Foucault states:

> Western man was gradually learning what it meant to be a living species in a living world, to have a body, conditions of existence, probabilities of life, and individual and collective welfare, forces that could be modified, and a space in which they could be distributed in an optimal manner. . . . Power would no longer be dealing simply with legal subjects over whom the ultimate dominion was death, but with living beings, and the mastery it would be able to exercise over them would have to be applied at the level of life itself; it was the taking charge of life, more than the threat of death, that gave

negotiation of an immanent economy of exchange, where life is valued as labour – as the means to its own end.

The power of the sovereign to take life or let live made Bensalem a nation forever 'in doubt and in danger; the fact that the "false" is too visible will never guarantee that the "true" is visible enough'.[44] Accordingly, the narrator (per Bacon) urged the crew to remain well behaved:

> Let us look up to God, and every man reform his own ways. Besides we are come here amongst a Christian people, full of piety and humanity: let us not bring that confusion of face upon ourselves, as to show our vices or unworthiness before them. Yet there is more. For they have by commandment (though in the form of courtesy) cloistered us here within these walls for three days: who knoweth whether it be not to take some taste of our manners and conditions? And if they find them bad, to banish us straightaways; if good, to give us further time. For these men that they have given us for attendance may withal have an eye upon us.[45]

By conforming their behaviour to that of obedient and civilised Christian subjects, these new citizens-in-waiting were granted permission to 'stay on the island for the space of six weeks' on the condition that they remained within a mile and a half of the city walls.[46] The citizen of the emerging nation state was made-to-measure or cast away. The sublimation and idealisation of Christian citizenry, 'the privileged figure of which is aesthetic' thereby 'culminated in the description and valorisation of a certain type of man, demonstrating the human ideal, both in terms of body and of mind. . . . This ideal connects up with the first man (non-degenerate) and the man of the future (the superman)'.[47]

The politics of nation

The narrative of Bensalem sought to teach its readers that until savagery and ignorance were exorcised from the world such primitive conditions must be lawfully repelled. Bensalem had to sustain its enlightenment and its soundness of mind. To do so required the creation of pure territories and rational subjects – a practice of exclusion, which today has become a field of domestic law on immigration existing in a fundamentally constitutive relation to the law of nations. From this perspective, migration law is arguably a confessional practice of the lawful body politic. Those people who fall outside national

power its access even to the body.' Michel Foucault, 'Faire vivre et laisser mourir: la naissance du racisme' (February 1991) *Les Temps Modernes* 37, p 52 cited in Stoler, 1995, p 84.

44 Balibar, 1991, p 60.   45 Bacon, 1974, p 219.   46 Bacon, 1974, p 221.
47 Balibar in Balibar and Wallerstein, 1991, pp 37, 58.

laws – outside of nation – fall into view as they are marked out and inscribed by the international law on refugees and asylum seekers. In this way the law both expels them as it binds them. They are delivered over to their own 'separateness' and, at the same time, consigned to the justice of the law that abandons them without mercy, 'at once excluded and included, removed and at the same time captured'.[48]

This befits the contemporary attempt by Henkin et al. to limit and justify the discipline of international law by arguing that:

> [it] is a conceptually distinct and self-contained system of law, independent of the national systems with which it interacts. *It deals with relations which individual states do not effectively govern* [emphasis added].[49]

During the consolidation of the state system, sovereignty came to describe the will inherent in the nation state as a rational member of an international society. These sovereign individuals decide upon and control what is and what is not governable, what is national and what is international.[50] Sovereignty thus marks the threshold between inside and outside, order and chaos, savagery and civilisation that creates and defines the space in which the juridico-political order can have validity.[51] Anything outside this order is posited as beyond (legal) justice, as the sinfulness of the outlaw. These outlaws are not 'exempted from historical analysis'; they are an effect of the jurisprudence of international law and the nation state that it constitutes.[52]

In these narratives it is the New World and its state of nature that provides 'the unlocalisable a permanent and visible localisation'.[53] Today, as the narrative of globalisation weakens the divide between Old World and New World, these so-called 'outlaws' are left with no space at all.[54] This is the structure of exception that Agamben takes from Schmitt's conception of sovereignty in his text, *Politische Theologie*.[55] Schmitt states there:

> The exception is that which cannot be subsumed; it defies general codification, but it simultaneously reveals a specifically juridical formal element: the decision in absolute purity. The exception appears in its absolute form when it is a question of creating a situation in which juridical rules can be valid. Every general rule demands a regular, everyday frame of life to

---

48 Agamben, 1998, p 110.
49 Henkin et al., 1993, p xviii. The author thanks David Kennedy for bringing this text to her attention during his seminar on international law in Canberra in June 2001.
50 See Anghie, 1999.   51 Agamben, 1998, p 19.   52 See Eliade, 1965, p 98.
53 Agamben, 1998, p 20.
54 It is noteworthy that those who seek asylum in Australia are called 'unlawful citizens' prior to their recognition in legal terms as refugees.
55 Schmitt cited in Agamben, 1998, p 15.

which it can be factually applied and which is submitted to regulations. The rule requires a homogenous medium. This factual regularity is not merely an 'external presupposition' that the jurist can ignore; it belongs rather, to the rule's immanent validity. There is no rule that is applicable to chaos.[56]

It is the sovereign who decides the limits of its own totality – the order of its realm – and who situates the law just as the essence of the Old World, its very possibility, depends on its authority to create and maintain a stable identity. The uncolonised regions of the New World act as a limit to Old World law 'in the form of the rule's suspension' but nonetheless form part of that law in so far as they also are constituted by it.[57] The New World is not the savage anarchy that knows no law; that awaits *logos*, but the world that results from its suspension. In this way the New World narratives gave logical and chronological priority to the notion of society as a kind of anarchical condition out of which the territorial state emerges as a gradual locus of power based on a division between international and internal governance; between the unnamed as that which is ungovernable and the named, which is. This is the story of international law: the rise of the state from the fragmentation of the Christian Roman Empire, which creates an ordering of the international – one in which a society of individual states compete for territory, wealth and resources as they sift out the savage from within – this is the myth of mercantilism – the Peace of Westphalia.

On this premise the Old World founds its own hegemony and sovereignty over the New. It is the Old World that claims the right to name its origin. It must therefore stand outside the order it names and remain still within it. In consequence, each act of colonisation arguably involves the naming of the New World (wherever it may be) – a taking of the outside – as well as the constitution of *nomos*, that is, the taking of land and the determination of a juridical and territorial ordering.[58]

This jurisprudential origin, located in the state of nature, is well represented in the foundational texts of international law. Francisco de Vitoria's (1480–1552) well known texts are an early example of the separation of the Old World from the New World. His assertion of European sovereignty over the New World was based on his ability to declare the state of nature in which the indigenous peoples were living subject to particular laws. It was no longer that chaotic and indescribable state into which Columbus had ventured and God had forsaken. It is to these laws that the Spaniards turned in defence 'to avail themselves of the rights of war' when any violation was committed by the indigenous peoples as the Spanish appropriated their gold and their souls.[59]

---

56 Ibid, p 16.   57 Agamben, 1998, p 18.   58 Schmitt, 1974, p 48.
59 de Vitoria, 1917, section II, 153e.

In other words, the indigenous peoples were drawn into the realm of law only to be named outlaws in a state of 'legitimate' war. In this way, having learned from the earlier experiences of explorers such as Columbus, the Spaniards were able to move into the doubt-ridden New World without removing themselves from the symbolic jurisdiction of their sovereign monarchs and their rule of law.

Fransisco Suarez (1514–1617), Hugo Grotius (1583–1645), and Samuel Pufendorf (1632–94), fathers of international law, were handed down this story on the right to legitimate violence in the New World's state of nature. By the seventeenth century, entire political treatises were being based upon its foundation. Being natural, these laws were carried by all people. As a result, John Locke (1632–1704) declared that the state of nature is not a Hobbesian 'absence of restraint', but rather a Christian form of freedom where each person is a subject and arbiter of law because:

> [the] Execution of the Law of Nature is in that State, put into every Man's hands, whereby every one has a right to punish the transgressors of that Law to such a Degree, as may hinder its Violation . . . each being, where there is no other, Judge for himself, and Executioner, which is, as I have shew'd it, the perfect *State of Nature*.[60]

Here we find traces of Balibar's citizen, who, 'at least virtually, "makes the Law", i.e. constitutes it, or declares it to be valid'.[61]

It follows, argued Locke, that those who place themselves outside these laws, whether in civil society[62] or natural society, place themselves outside human society and into a state of war – risking incoherence and ultimately, death.[63] It is here that the concept of the 'collapsed state' arguably arises as that unredeemed space of debt – the mark of sin and in modern times, lawlessness and war.[64] War is now represented as the scene of savagery that threatens the very existence of states. The state of war is any situation in which there has been a transgression of the law of nature because a transgression 'threatens to take away everything else', including preservation.[65] It is a right that extends beyond the natural right to kill a transgressor[66] to a right by all humankind to kill a common murderer in the name of preservation based on the underlying threat of the re-emergence of savage anarchy;[67] but the laws of war are themselves an appropriation of anarchy and freedom, allowing no man to return to lawlessness without punishment. Each state is allowed only to 'progress'

---

60 Locke, 1960, sections 7 and 57. See Tully, 1993, p 24.   61 Balibar, 1994, pp 10–11.

62 In contrast, those 'who are united into one Body, and have a common establish'd Law and Judicature to appeal to, with authority to decide Controversies between them, and punish Offenders, are in *Civil Society* one with another' (Locke, 1960, section 87).

63 Locke, 1960, section 16.   64 See Chapter Six, below.   65 Locke, 1960, section 17.

66 Ibid, sections 19 and 176.   67 Ibid, section 11.

into a 'developed' state. Even in war there is, ostensibly, law, just as in the perfect state of nature there is law within each individual. Thus, each individual is subject to the sovereign lawmaker, who can ensure freedom only through obedience.

In contrast to the unredeemed state of nature, political society is argued to form when the violent forces of war are repossessed by the state to preserve and regulate the lives and property of subjects, to execute laws with legitimate violence, and to wage wars to preserve the community, including colonies abroad, against other states.[68] In this sense sovereignty can be understood as political society united in the cause of self-preservation within a Westphalian Peace.[69] Each state is bound to govern what it can, acting as a promise to its parts to redeem itself against transgressions of the natural law in order that it might reach salvation.

In contrast, those people clinging to the lawless flow of New World imaginings remain unformed – stateless. Although subject to natural law, they remain unredeemed; each person an outlaw, carrying the germ of civilisation inside himself in a system of individual self-government. Hence, the only means of relating to 'these peoples', who were without an overarching sovereign, without nation, was, claimed Locke, to deal with and punish them on an individual basis.[70]

Locke believed that the indigenous people had no need of nation because they lived with 'few Trespasses, and few Offenders', 'few controversies' over property and therefore 'no need of many laws to decide them'.[71] The kings were no more than the generals of armies, who, 'although they command absolutely in war', in peacetime and in internal affairs 'exercise very little dominion, and have but a very moderate Sovereignty, the Resolution of Peace and War, being ordinarily either in the People or in a Council'.[72]

The imperial politics of the Old World was thus based on a perception of New World life as without politics or society. New World peoples lived in this state of nature and would remain there for they confined 'their desires within the narrow bounds of each mans smal propertie'.[73] They had no temptation to 'enlarge their Possessions of Land, or contest for wider extent of Ground' because they lacked money and a large population to activate the desire to possess more than they needed.[74] Locke summed this up in *The Third Letter concerning Toleration*:

---

68 Ibid, sections 3, 131, 135 and 171.
69 This argument continues to be advocated by international lawyers today. E.g., see Franck, (2001), where Franck argues that the US military action against the Taliban and Al Qaeda in Afghanistan is lawful under the United Nations Charter pursuant to the doctrine of self-preservation.
70 Locke, 1960, section 41.   71 Ibid, section 107.
72 Ibid, sections 108, 87 and 144–48.   73 Ibid, sections 10 and 107.
74 Ibid, sections 10 and 107.

> Let me ask you, Whether it be not possible that men, to whom the rivers and woods afforded the spontaneous provisions of life, and so with no private possessions of land, had no inlarged desires after riches or power, should live in one society, make one people of one language under one Chieftain, who shall have no other power to command them in time of common war against their common enemies, without municipal laws, judges, or a person with superiority established amongst them, but ended all their private differences, if any arose, by the extemporary determination of their neighbours, or of arbitrators chosen by the parties.[75]

Locke thus accords the luxury of the state of nature to the 'spontaneous provisions of life', the scarcity of which would require the arbitration of a sovereign lawmaker. Without scarcity, a fluid, natural society lived without knowledge of desire. Human labour lay dormant, waiting its alienation from the person. Until that time, each individual existed within a spontaneous, natural system of individual labour that knew no communal concept of property. For the sake of preservation, each person had exclusive rights over their labour and its product – fruit and venison[76] and corn[77] – to the extent that it did not spoil and there was enough and as good left in common for others even after European settlers had appropriated land for themselves. There was no need to seek out consent.

> Let him plant in some inland, vacant places of America, we shall find that the Possessions he could make himself upon the measure we have given, would not be very large, nor, even to this day, prejudice the rest of Mankind, or give them reason to complain, or think themselves injured by this Incroachment.[78]

Thus, according to Locke, the savage lived free from desire where appropriation without consent continued until money – the ultimate signifier and magical form and object of faith – is introduced. By introducing money, infinite time is also brought into the state of nature and man is then no longer bound to keep only that which would not spoil.

> Where there is not something both lasting and scarce, and so valuable to be hoarded up, there Men will not be apt to enlarge their *Possessions of Land*, were it never so rich, never so free for them to take. For I ask, What would a Man value Ten Thousand, or an Hundred Thousand Acres of excellent *Land*, ready cultivated, and well stocked too with Cattle, in the

---

75 John Locke, *The Third Letter Concerning Toleration* [1692] cited in Tully, 1993, p 152.
76 Locke, 1960, section 26.   77 Ibid, section 48.
78 Ibid, section 36. This argument is used later by Hegel when writing during the 1820s and 30s about the peoples of Africa. See Hegel, 1956, p 86.

middle of the in-land Parts of *America*, where he had no hopes of Commerce with other Parts of the World, to draw *Money* to him by the Sale of the Product? It would not be worth the inclosing. . . . Find out something that hath the *Use and Value of Money* amongst his Neighbours, you shall see the same Man will begin presently to *enlarge* his *Possessions*.[79]

Forgotten here are the centuries of trade that had taken place between indigenous peoples within North and South America and more recently with the Old World. The debt of the New World was set to be redeemed. As an anonymous commentator observes in his memorandum on the East India Company:

But some nations having departed from the ancient simplicity of living contented with productions of their own countries and having by navigation and trade, raised themselves to wealth, power and increase of inhabitants; it thereupon grew necessary for other nations to fall into like methods, lest otherwise they should have been a prey, as well as a derision to them whom trade hath rendered mighty and opulent.[80]

Fortunately, it had been 'well knowen' since at least 1583, according to Sir Peckham Knight, 'the chiefe adventurer, and furtherer of Sir Humfrey Gilberts voyage to Newfound Land':

that all Savages, aswell those that dwell in the South, as those that dwell in the North, so soone as they shall begin but a little to taste of civility, will take marvelous delight in any garment, be it never so simple; as a shirt, a blew, yellow, red or greene cotton cassocke, a cap, or such like, and will take incredible paines for such a trifle.[81]

That is at least once their minds are made sound, and thus readily 'reduced to civility in manners and garments'. For Hakluyt acknowledged in a *Pamphlet for the Virginia Enterprise by Richard Hakluyt, Lawyer, 1585* that:

If the people be content to live naked, and to content themselves with few things of meere necessity, then traffick is not. For then in vaine seemeth our voyages, unless this nature be altered as by conquest and other means it may be, but not on a sudden.[82]

---

79 Emphasis in the original. Locke, 1960, sections 48–49.
80 CK, *Some Seasonable and Modest Thoughts Partly Occasioned by, and partly concerning the East Indian Company* (1696) cited in Harper, 1939, p 233.
81 Cited in Hakluyt, 1904, p 111.   82 Hakluyt, 1935, p 332.

These narratives of modes of production and the forms of life that come with the predominance of rational industry over 'primitive accumulation' created and legitimised material connections amongst territory, wealth and power that were essential for state formation and the proclaimed redemption that the state would provide. The conclusion drawn by Enlightenment scholars, from these narratives of the New World, was that political society must by necessity come into being in order that representative government and positive laws could regulate labour, appropriate property and distribute their products.[83]

As Nicholas Barbon wrote in his *A Discourse of Trade*, 'Trade is now become necessary to Preserve Governments, as it is useful to make them Rich'.[84] Just as the labourers of the Old World were being drawn into the new division of labour, so too, the peoples of the New World were drawn into the desires and objectives of the imperial 'desire of seeking . . . Gods glorie'.[85] Indigenous peoples were forced to assimilate or risked being seen as a threat to the preservation and very existence of law and nation. The New World peoples became 'an appropriated category' of history that was naturalised as a convenient and violent illustration of an unworkable society.[86] Modern reason was yet to be revealed to these peoples of the New World with the expectation that they too could learn to see themselves as 'masters of nature and, hence, as masters of their own fate'.[87]

Only 'there' where savagery existed was chaos said to reign. The ironic effect produced was that the peoples of the Old World could look across the seas of contemporaneousness and feel nostalgia at the 'inevitable' fall of a world. Certainly the indigenous peoples of the New World:

> may appear to some to be the most wretched people upon the earth: but in reality they are far more happier than we Europeans: being wholly unacquainted not only with the superfluous but the necessary Conveniences so much sought after in Europe, they are happy in not knowing the use of them. They live in a Tranquillity which is not disturbed by the Inequality of Condition: the Earth and sea of their own accord furnishes them with all things necessary for life; they covet not magnificent houses, Household stuff &ca they live in a warm and fine Climate and enjoy a very wholesome Air: so that they have very little need of Clothing and this they seem to be fully sensible of for many to whome we gave Cloth &ca to, left it carelessly upon the Sea beach and in the woods as a thing they had no manner of use for. In short they seem'd to set not value on anything we gave them nor would they ever part with any thing of their own for any one article we could offer them this in my opinion argues

83 Locke, 1960, sections 30, 38, 50 and 129.   84 Barbon, 1690, p 2.
85 Hakluyt, 1850.   86 Juteau-Lee, 1995, pp 1, 5.   87 Nandy, 1983, p ix.

that they think themselves provided with all the necessarys of Life and that they have no superfluities.[88]

'All they seem'd to want', wrote Cook, 'was for us to be gone'.[89]

Like their traditional lands,[90] the New World peoples who did not enter into economic circulation were of no use to the Old World, either as consumers or labourers, and became like valueless wares: 'The Value of all Wares arise from their Use; Things of no Use, have no Value, as the English Phrase is, *They are good for nothing*'.[91]

Good for nothing, that is, except perhaps the labour of their bodies.[92] Already, in 1680, William Petyt had argued that 'sufficient stores of treasure cannot otherwise be got than by the industry of the people' and thus the labourer was to be considered the source of national wealth.

> It is evident that national power is not chimerical but is founded on people and treasure; and that according to the different conditions of these its true pillars, it immediately grows more vigorous or languid; that sufficient stores of treasure cannot be got than by the industry of the people. . . . People are, therefore, the chiefest, most fundamental and precious commodity, out of which may be derived all sorts of manufactures, navigation, riches, conquests and solid dominion. This capital material being of itself raw and indigested is committed into the supreme authority in whose prudence and disposition it is to improve, manage and fashion it to more or less advantage.[93]

As Locke argues, it is the 'Industrious and Rational' who draw from nature the 'greatest conveniences of life' for the benefit of all.[94] Pollexfen agreed that '[o]ur moveable riches had their original and must have their increase from labor and industry of our people' concluding that '[t]he employment and

---

88 Beaglehole, 1969, p 399. See Beckett, 1994; and Walker, 1952.   89 Ibid, p 306.
90 As Locke wrote, 'Land that is left wholly to Nature, that hath no improvement of Pasturage, Tillage, or planting, is called, as indeed it is, Waste; and we shall find the benefit of it amount to little more than nothing.' Locke, 1960, section 42.
91 Emphasis in the original. Barbon, 1690, p 13.
92 A principle argument for restricting the trade of the colonies by the Navigation Acts was based on the belief that the colonies had taken a proportion of the labouring power of the mother country and thus its wealth. Colonial governments were therefore required to repay this advantage by providing employment for an equivalent number of labourers at home through the strict control of commerce. See Furniss, 1965, p 5.
93 Petyt, 1680, p 238. In seeking to explain the wealth of the Flemings, Daniel Defoe argues in his *A General History of Trade, and especially consider'd as it respects British commerce*: 'A native produce in any country will by consequence bring a trade to that country. But it is the labor and industry of the people that alone brings wealth and makes that trade profitable to the nation' (Defoe, 1713, Book II, p 30).
94 Locke, 1960, sections 34, 37, 41, 42, 43, 45 and 48.

good management of our people must be the way to get riches'.[95] Here we see the materialist predication of the subject in the 'irreducible possibility that the subject be more than adequate – super-adequate – to itself'.[96]

The 'varying degrees of increasing integration of world markets of goods, services, capital and labour',[97] which continues to promote the restructuring of a peoples' economy and resources for the benefit of global capitalism, had begun. It was assumed to be the only way to achieve a higher quality of life for the people of any particular nation. No person was exempt from these universalising forces of nation, law, labour and commerce. European settlers thus owed the home country the cost of their labour, which they had removed to the colonies with them. The mercantilist laws of the period demanded that labour in the colonies furnish employment for those still in the imperial home country by exporting raw material to that country alone. Meanwhile, back in the homeland, the least well off were advised by the new doctrines that they had indeed 'benefited from the "improvements" accruing from a "more rational" use of land'.[98] The New World was again used as evidence of justifying the exploitation of labour for each person's benefit.

> There cannot be a clearer demonstration of any thing, than several Nations of the *Americans* are of this, who are rich in Land, and poor in all the Comforts of Life; whom Nature having furnished as liberally as any other people, with the materials of Plenty, i.e. a fruitful Soil, apt to produce in abundance, what might serve for food, rayment, and delight; yet for want of improving it by labour, have not one hundredth part of the Conveniences we enjoy: And a King of a large fruitful Territory there feeds, lodges, and is clad worse than a day Labourer in *England*.[99]

Everywhere, the absence of savagery and the presence of enclosed territory and industrialisation marked the 'beginning of history', which ultimately conditioned the possibility of the ideal man within the ideal nation state.[100]

The body politic comprised a population subject to a power that penetrated into the subjectivity of each person. Here begins the collection of statistics and knowledge aimed at improving the labour power of the nation – a

---

95 Pollexfen, 1700, pp 43, 158.   96 Spivak, 1996, p 109.

97 *An Agenda for Development*. Ad hoc Open-Ended Working Group, 16 June 1997, para 6.

98 Hulme, 1990, pp 16, 27. By the time of Adam Smith's writing, the narrative of progress and the fear of a return to savagery is naturalised to the extent that one may argue:

> Among civilised and thriving nations, . . . a workman, even of the lowest and poorest order, if he is frugal and industrious, may enjoy a greater share of the necessaries and conveniences of life than it is possible for any savage to acquire (Smith, 1993, p 9).

99 Emphasis in the original. Locke, 1960, section 41.   100 Hegel, 1956, p 176.

power that was to be disciplined, educated and cared for by the mercantile strategies of the state.[101]

Discursive practices of national development began to shape the distinction between economic growth and pure subsistence, market principles and reciprocity and exchange, and industrialisation and hunting and gathering, thereby legitimating particular ways of managing the health of the nation, its redemption and its eventual salvation. The result is a 'normalising' society based on a culture that 'rejects something that it will designate for itself as Exterior'.[102] The creation of the 'internal enemy' and 'the dangerous individual' was framed in 'a theory of social defence'.

This was the promise of nationhood – the regulation, through political society, of labour, trade and property in order to preserve and strengthen the state and so return its citizens to a time redeemed of doubt and desire; to a state of fulfilment. This was the promise of nation that drove imperial endeavours into the unredeemed regions of the New World. Yet, in that drive toward totality, each nation entered into a competitive relationship with its rivals. In the attempt to draw the borders of a new competitive body politic – a body made flesh – the state expelled that which was of no significance by throwing it into a state of otherness. Nation was a state that required fortitude against other states in a contest for military and commercial rivalry over the conquest, colonisation and exploitation of the New World.[103]

This is the same context of rivalry in which the fantasy of Bensalem, the New Atlantis, was to have been read. In telling the story of a New Atlantis, Bacon warned of the precarious nature of the great seafaring nations of his time. His story is set within a threatening temporal framework of loss and regeneration in which countries were at risk of falling back into savagery and rude immaturity. Here the signifiers of Christianity, race and scientific technology govern who is civilised/superior/master and who is savage/inferior/slave, creating a dichotomous boundary between them.

When Bacon argues in his essay, *Of Plantations*, that the savages of the New World must be encouraged to learn from the Old World of Britain of a condition better than their own, he is also assuming that there is a lesson to be learnt by Britain of its own identity.[104]

> If you plant where savages are, do not only entertain them with trifles and gingles; but use them justly and graciously, with sufficient guard nevertheless: and do not win their favour by helping them to invade their enemies, but for their defence it is not amiss. And send oft of them over

---

101 Locke, 1960, sections 30, 41, 42 and 43. Tully, 1993, p 85.
102 This quote is from the French edition of Michel Foucault's *Madness and Civilization* cited in English in Stoler, 1995, p 34.
103 See Shennan, 1974, Chapter 5.
104 Bacon, 1968c, p 32. See Martin, 1992 and Sessions, 1996.

to the country that plants, that they may see a better condition than their own, and commend it when they return.[105]

This was the task given to the narrator of the *New Atlantis* by the Governor of Bensalem: to return home and publish what he had learned 'for the good of other nations; for we here are in God's bosom, a land unknown'.[106] Such had been the aim of Bacon's narrative. During the decade in which Bacon was promoted from Solicitor General in 1607 to Lord Chancellor in 1618, he continually urged King James to plot out 'a new way for the understanding, a way . . . untried and unknown', articulating a desire for dominion over nature connected, overtly and covertly, to imperial aggrandisement.[107] This narrative continues to weave itself through modernity in the promise of development – a place unknown from whence we are asked to see a better condition than our own, and commend it when we return.

The science of nation

This section analyses the role of science and technology in Bacon's dream of the perfect state. In Bacon's fantasy of a New Atlantis, the original lawmaker King Solamona was presented as an admirer of the biblical King Solomon, who was said to have written a natural history of 'all that is green from the cedar to the moss, . . . and also of all that liveth and moveth'.[108] God had granted King Solomon dominion over nature and 'a mighty empire in Gold'. In a similar fashion, the governance of Bensalem was left to scientist-priests such that Bensalem became dedicated to the scrutiny of nature because, according to Bacon, the greatest instauration was humankind's restoration of dominion over nature.[109]

The emergence of scientific methodology thus incorporated nature into the subjectification of man. Since sin was no longer understood as creation itself but rather objectified conceptually, nature, too, had been freed from sin and abstracted into an object of human knowledge. Nature, like humankind, could be studied and improved upon by scientist-priests, whose work would determine humanity's dominion over God's creation. As a consequence, the relation of the individual to God was further undermined as God's inscription failed to limit the possibilities open to humanity and its salvation. Instead, the Christian religion was colonised by scientist-priests, who claimed the means to go only God knows where.

Bacon's techno-Christian heritage is narrated as the principal source of the

---

105 Bacon, 1968c, p 459.   106 Bacon, 1974, p 247.   107 Bacon, 1968d.
108 *Kings* 4:33.
109 Their foundation, Salomon's House, or the College of Six Days' Works, has in its posses-
     sion some parts of King Solomon's work, namely the Natural History. Bacon, 1974, p 229.

nation's redemption. It is not Christ who descends to earth in this story of redemption. Instead, about 'twenty years after the ascension of our Saviour' 'a small ark or chest containing a book and a letter' appeared out of a pillar of light rising from the sea to the heaven and was presented to a wise man from Salomon's House 'sometimes called the College of Six Days' Work'. The book contained all the canonical books of the Old and New Testament and some other books of the New Testament 'which were not at that time written but were nevertheless in the Book', including King Solomon's natural history. The miraculous contents of the ark could be read by all: 'Hebrews, Persians, and Indians, besides the natives' as if written in their own language. Thus was the land 'saved from infidelity'. The national cohesion of Bensalem was set to be worshipped as a god-given heritage, the citizens redeemed by the contents of the Christian ark, which promised the means to Solomon's 'mighty Empire of Gold'. The etymological histories of Grotius, Bodin and Lafitau, discussed in Chapter Three, which sought to assuage the perceived danger to piety and the fear born of superstition, with faith in a single, universal language, were thus developed by Bacon into a universal Christian-scientific language that could be understood by all.

The role of technology and science acted not only as a signifying theme within Bacon's fantasy but also as the methodological approach to the telling of it. Bensalem was indeed a Solomonian work-in-progress. As Boesky writes, Bensalem may be considered as an attempt by Bacon to heed his own call in *De Augmentis* for the ordered and directed experiment, which he explained as a 'quest or search' that allegorises the 'text's desire to find something: an ending, meaning, or meanings'.[110] For Bacon 'this search always repeats or reinvents an earlier search; it is (literally and thematically) a *research*'.[111]

Bensalem can thus be seen as an experiment of reformation based on nationhood. In the original edition of the *New Atlantis,* the story ended with Bacon's catalogue, *Magnalia Naturae*, which lists the principal goals of the College of Six Days' Works where the scientist-priests undertook their research. The *Magnalia Naturae* is set out only in fragments: 'Making of new species, . . . Instruments of destruction, as of war and poison . . . Impressions of the air and raising tempests' as well as the 'prolongation of life'.[112] The scientist-priests in Bacon's New Atlantis followed the same course of inquiry as any of the reformers of the seventeenth century, who asked:

> What Magique . . . doe wee find in all or any of his enterprizes, or what methode of Wisdome, or of knowledge, or of power, or of acquiring

110 Boesky, 1997.   111 Ibid.

112 *Magnalia Naturae* in Bacon, 1974, p 249. Likewise Robert's *Map of Commerce* of 1638 provides a substantial guide to the economic resources of every continent. In 1639 Plattes issued *A Discovery of Infinite Treasure*, which contained a series of proposals for agri-cultural reform as well as a companion guide on mining and metallurgy, *A Discovery of Subterraneal Treasure* (Webster, 1975, p 356).

wealth, which is still allowable to the progress and industry of Gods deare people?[113]

The preservation of nation was thus entwined in the exploitation of nature as well as, and by means of, human labour and know-how.

The value of things, of commodities, no longer lay only in goods themselves but conceivably in the means of their production. Knowledge was thus the ultimate value in Bacon's fantasy – the key to redemption. In contrast to the primitive quest of the shipwrecked crew for gold and spice, the Bensalem scientists searched for knowledge and light:

> But thus you see we maintain a trade, not for gold, silver, or jewels; nor for silks; nor for spices; nor any other commodity of matter; but only for God's first creature, which was *Light*: to have *light* (I say) of the growth of all parts of the world.[114]

Bacon, anticipating the utilitarian idea that belittled the importance of foreign trade, argued that national wealth could be increased by industrious exploitation of the nation's resources. The mercantilist belief that a nation's wealth was to be measured by its comparative supply of precious metals was joined by Bacon's drive toward self-sufficiency and dominance based on knowledge.[115]

The Baconian view was that local conditions and natural resources placed no limitations on national development. As Caroline Merchant argues, nature for Bacon had to be 'bound into service', made 'a slave' and 'put in constraint'.[116] The 'secrets' of nature were described as 'holes and corners', which man must not scruple 'entering and penetrating'.[117] Bacon continually exhorted his English readers to possess nature, to 'search out her secrets' and to 'storm her castles'.[118] Nature, woman, labourer and colony became

---

113 Letters from John Beale to Hartlib, 15 September 1657, cited in Webster, 1975, p 328.
114 Emphasis in the original. Bacon, 1974, p 230.
115 Money metals were thought to signify national wealth and the amount of national wealth was proportionate to the supply of such metals. Any import of metals therefore increased national wealth and export caused a decrease in wealth. In a country with no indigenous metals, foreign trade was the only means to gain wealth. The interchange of goods for goods (barter) could not create wealth – a surplus in the exchange was required to make a profit. This basic theory was revised over time by merchants who argued for the need to export precious metal to cover the purchase of goods that could be processed and finally disposed of for greater profit. The ultimate aim remained the importation of precious metal. See, for example, Mun, 1989. See also, Furniss, 1965.
116 Merchant, 1980, p 169.   117 Ibid.
118 In 1623, in the *Advancement of Learning*, Bacon urged the English to turn 'with united forces against the Nature of Things, to storm out and occupy her castles and strongholds, and extend the bounds of human empire, as far as God Almighty in his goodness may permit' (Bacon, 1974, p 372 cited in Merchant, 1980, p 169).

resources that were to be stripped and exploited, if necessary by force. The 'remoter and more hidden parts of nature' became an obsession for Bacon, who in his impatience with the 'deplorably narrow limits of man's dominion over the universe' used increasingly violent imagery.[119] Bacon's scientific inquiries assumed that by mastering nature, it could no longer threaten perception as a wonder but only as a subject of representation.[120] The 'researches' of imperialist colonisation formed part of this practice of classification – of naming – beginning in the early modern period to deal with the symbolic ordering of everything that was 'thinkable' both in the past and in the present, whether 'biological', 'natural' or 'social'.[121] The aim was to secure meaning and form, which were no longer held together by divine order.[122] It is not surprising to read of the increasing collections of curiosities during this period, as the *curieux* pried into secrets and enjoyed 'a special relationship with totality' as if the things of the world 'were being shored against a more extravagant emptiness than the lack that propels the acquisitive bourgeois subject'.[123] A lack, perhaps, that re-emerged in the crisis of the Old World discovery of the New World and the betrayal of God's promise. Citing Krzysztof Pomian, Pye explains that:

> the collector of curiosities is one who dissatisfied with a knowledge of the common and normal, seek[s] greater knowledge of the singular, and accordingly searches among natural and artistic artefacts for rare, and exceptional objects, objects supposed to have a special link with totality as they constitute the source of additional information without which the knowledge as a whole, or one or other of its domains, would remain incomplete.[124]

Richard Sennett has described this 'purification urge' toward ordering the world according to clearly articulated categories permitting of no ambiguity and dissonance as the 'desire to be all-powerful, to control the meanings of experience before encounter so as not to be overwhelmed'.[125] In terms of international relations, this purification urge was one that linked back into the purification of 'nation', as well as into the competitive relations of the mercantilist era. Hence, in an ideal world – in the story of a New Atlantis – when the crew tried to reciprocate some of their own knowledge, they were met with indifference because the Bensalems already had knowledge of Europe through their system of secret intelligence. Indeed, they knew more than the crew themselves. As Bensalem was large and fertile it had no need to trade in goods, but because it was thought that science could not develop without exchange, Bensalem had regulated trips to Europe through a system

119 Bacon, 1968a, pp 18, 57.   120 Judovitz, 1988, p 193.
121 Guillaumin, 1995, pp 67–68.   122 Ibid, p 68.   123 Pye, 2000, p 138.
124 Pye, 2000, p 133. Pye cites Pomian, 1990, pp 56–57.   125 Sennett, 1970, p 116.

of intellectual espionage sending missions every 12 years to collect knowledge of the affairs and state of countries, and 'especially of the sciences, arts, manufactures, and inventions of all the world'. Carefully chosen spies, called 'Merchants of Light' or 'Lamps' remained 'in-country' for 12 years returning on the next ship. In this sense Bensalem practised the very model of a modern cultural imperialism: a nation with no blood on its collective hands controlling the flow of unwanted labour while maintaining a healthy import of knowledge in a scenario of aggressive competition.

Bacon took the discovery of the New World by Europeans as the basis for all intelligent efforts to obtain new knowledge. In a way similar to the religious dissention of the Reformation, Bacon sought the meaning of the Word beyond the text. Bacon's was a work of discovery, rather than the scholastic art of reading a canonised Word. Observation and experimentation had become the essential mode of obtaining important knowledge; and the knowledge that awaited discovery did not lie within the existing resources of western culture, within the canon, but beyond in the unnamed, just as the New World had lain outside the known.[126]

Moreover, the modern scientific separation of mind from body legitimised the location of knowledge in the territorial sovereign rather than the person of the labourer.[127] In this process, the labour of bodies was disconnected from the land in the same way that science was disconnecting humankind from nature. Thus, corporate bodies, be they national or private, came to possess intellect by turning knowledge into private property and property into money.[128]

Concomitant with the development of these laws of property was the unspoken division of labour from the means of production, and the deterioration of artisanship and specialisation. In this way modernity moved toward a world in which labour was exploited everywhere while the knowledge and value that labour produced was kept in the treasuries of merchants and monarchs – the means and ends of salvation. Hence, the 'desire to be all powerful' that drove Bacon's modern man to expand the 'deplorable limits' of his dominion resulted in an economic and cultural imperialism over each and every means to such expansion.

Thus, while religion remained the chief source of the Old World's sense of superiority, technology and science in the Baconian age played a leading role in shaping Old World perceptions of the New. These 'purifiers' in turn were used to determine what could and could not be contained within the idea of nation; what could redeem and preserve and what would only lead to a return

---

126 Grafton, Shelford and Siraisi, 1992, p 198.
127 Although once taken from the self-employed labourer, the struggle for the property rights to this knowledge would occur between the nation state and the global corporation.
128 See, for example, Shiva, 2000.

to savage anarchy. Science and technology were increasingly regarded as significant measures of the overall maturity and superiority attained by Old World cultures as time and invention became bound together as signifiers of progress.[129] Never again would man need to return to his dependence on a transcendent Other.

As a consequence, the new science of modernity would enable the colour of one's skin or indeed the fashion of one's clothing to be classified and transformed into the expression of a specific nature and provided a place along the historical continuum of progress in the search for redemption.[130] Difference and novelty were no longer overwhelming wonders but undiscovered objects of knowledge. The new, universal language of science was used to inscribe goods and people with their own physical individuality such that the 'nature of the appropriated and/or their physical characteristics are seen as causing their behaviour, or at least their subordinate position'.[131] Indeed, by the end of the seventeenth century such knowledge would be used to classify and thus justify the annexation of a whole labour force into slavery according to intellectual, epistemological and geographical criteria.[132]

As Balibar writes, all of these practices operated to naturalise socially constructed histories by capturing the inevitable change over time of human experience in a secure form through the projection of historical and social differences onto an imaginary nature.[133] Out of these practices of naturalisation, discursive regimes of truth would emerge based on the concepts of race, culture, ethnicity, development and a capitalist economics. These concepts represented 'the ideal synthesis of transformation and fixity, of repetition and destiny'.[134] As Balibar has also noted, the 'discovery' of such concepts, which is endlessly rehearsed, 'is that of a humanity eternally leaving animality behind and eternally threatened with falling into the grasp of animality'.[135] Notably, all of these signifiers are attached to 'a "heritage", and "ancestry", a "rootedness", an original state of nature, all signifiers of the imaginary face-to-face relation between man and his origins' – humanity and its salvation.[136]

Bensalem is a figurative example of a First World nation. It existed 'ahead of and outside of time, claiming its authority in antiquity, enshrining European inventors in its museum yet at the same time dedicating itself to newer inventions in its College of Six Days' Works'.[137] Bensalem was like any nation 'unresolved in-between the universal and the particular and always "becoming" other than what it is'.[138] This is evidenced most starkly by William Rawley's addendum to Bacon's text: *'The rest was not perfected'*. There was no 'end' no *'finis'*, which is reminiscent of the vast collections of curiosities

129 Adas, 1989, p 3.   130 See Guillaumin, 1995.   131 Juteau-Lee, 1995, p 16.
132 See Guillaumin, 1995, p 67.   133 Balibar, 1991, p 56.   134 Ibid, p 57.
135 Ibid.   136 Ibid.   137 Boesky, 1997, p 151.   138 Fitzpatrick, 2001, p 112.

during the period.[139] The text was left infinite refusing closure as it progressed from the discovery of the New World, which framed the temporality and identity of the Bensalem fantasy. The rite of first contact by the European crew is thus disrupted and replaced by 'an uncanny sense of belatedness'.[140] This sense of belatedness is evident in the daily lives of the Bensalems as they rush to and from the crew with a strange sense of exigency and distraction.[141] What emerges is:

> a society that has become the theatre of an uncontrollable adventure, so that what is instituted never becomes established, the known remains undermined by the unknown, the present proves to be indefinable, covering many different social times which are staggered in relation to one another within simultaneity – or definable only in terms of some fictitious future; an adventure such that the quest for identity cannot be separated from the experience of division. This society is *historical society par excellence.*[142]

This is the future that haunts the modern western world today of a fantastic, imaginary space held out to us by investors – the moment that never actually arrives – the day of redemption and so, salvation. Citizen, labourer, merchant are all subjects of God's redemption and nation's promise, determined by 'perpetually gambling on [their] own wish-fulfilments'. 'What one owned was promises, and not merely the functioning but the intelligibility of society depended on the success of a program of reification'.[143] The Old World still struggles to remain the sovereign, theoretical subject of all histories, including those emerging from the New World in India, China or some other heart of darkness – all variations on a master narrative.[144]

The struggle to remain sovereign invests itself in the promise of development – modernity's discourse of salvation. Development is a process that

---

139 Bacon, 1974, p 247. Hakluyt examines at least two curiosity cabinets and compares them to his own collection of travel narratives: 'in the course of this history often mention is made of many beastes, birds, fishes, serpents, plants, fruits, hearbes, rootes, apparell, armour, boates, and such other rare and strange curiosities, which wise men take great pleasure to reade of'. 'So as the commodities already knowen, besides many yet unknowen are these, and that in great quantitie' (Hakluyt, 1907, p 12).

140 Boesky, 1997, p 148.

141 An anxiety reminiscent of the dread felt by Salman Rushdie's Indian character, Saleem Sinai, in the novel *Midnight's Children*, who experiences the post-independence era of India's nationhood as filled with a desire to fulfil the historical burden of expectation attendant on nation. In Sinai's words, 'I must work fast, faster than Scheherazade, if I am to end up meaning – yes, meaning – something. I admit it: above all things, I fear absurdity' (Rushdie, 1995, p 9 cited in Gandhi, 1998, p 5).

142 Emphasis added. Lefort, 1986, p 305.

143 Agnew, 1986, pp 157–58 citing Pocock, 1976, p 99.   144 Chakrabarty, 1992.

will, in the twentieth century, encompass all those activities which, from time to time, fall within the purview of statecraft to justify the state's very hold over its population – the *raison d'être* of state-centred accountability for production, welfare, education, healthcare and so forth. Taken from its historical perspective, the promise of development cannot be considered an adequate methodology for analysing the institutions of the state, its economy, its human and natural resources and/or its political framework. This is because development discourse is not external to the state or any other of the objects within its domain of knowledge but constitutive of them. Development is constructed in association with the construction and maintenance of the current system of nation states and their governance internationally and domestically, which is supported in turn by established hierarchies of power, based around western narratives of sovereignty and law, science and technology and capitalist economics and their link to redemption and salvation: nation's promise.[145] Accordingly, the development discourse is a code for reinforcing, expanding, reducing, globalising or transforming the exercise of state power and the state system itself.[146]

Like their Bensalem predecessors, development practitioners and their theories demand:

> [that states] take on or withdraw from their functions, act in new and different ways, form new relations with other bodies and other States, divide, compose and assemble themselves differently, and position themselves in certain networks and relays.[147]

The state is seen as an impartial instrument – a laboratory – which requires particular specifications: good governance for implementing plans, the right economy for engineering growth.[148] The assumed impartiality of the state apparatus refutes its very political nature as well as other interests arising from imperialism, gender differences, ethnicity, class or race. A lack of development, by definition, is the result of government failure to mould its population properly; either its bureaucracy is corrupt or has planned poorly or lacks training, or its people have not been given the capacity to develop; for example they do not want to work, they prefer to commit crime, or they have problems with alcohol – the state has become infected.[149] The outcome is a failed state. The art of development, therefore, is not simply the task of government, it is the means to legitimate government. Those who sit in the House of Six Days' Works and who control the discursive power of development

---

145 See Anghie, 1999.   146 Ferguson, 1997, pp 223, 232.
147 Dean, 1996, pp 209, 211.   148 Ferguson, 1997, p 226.
149 These commonly held views of indigenous people in Australia are discussed in Aboriginal and Torres Strait Islander Commission 1988.

control the construction of politically legitimate intervention and exclusion. The story used to narrate the development of nation is one of trial, torture, death and resurrection – of the victory of light over darkness, which portrays suffering as necessary human experience and experiment.

The labour of nation

By the turn of the seventeenth century the labour abstracted from the industrious poor had become the wealth of the nation. The direction and maintenance of the labouring classes had necessarily increased the riches of the world. 'For the earth is grateful and repays their labour not only with enough but with an abundance'.[150] The emerging territorial nation state provided the ideal laboratory to administer the improvement of humankind, and imperialism rationalised the savage. In his *Two Treatises*, Locke outlined his strategy of mercantilism on the basis of his belief in the disciplinary power of individual governance.

> This shews, how much numbers of men are to be preferred to largenesse of dominions, and that the increase of lands and the right of imploying of them is the great art of government. Any Prince who shall be so wise and godlike as by established laws of liberty to secure protection and incouragement to the honest industry of mankind against oppression of power and narrowness of Party will quickly be too hard for his neighbours.[151]

The exploitation of labour was 'the great art of government'. For although man's original sin had caused him to 'change his pleasure into labour, and his ease into industry',[152] penitent labour would enable degenerate man to redeem himself from the savagery of sin into a more civilised human condition.[153] Christian-based providence relied on labour and industry as Daniel had prophesied: 'In the sweat of thy face shalt thou eat bread, till thou return unto the ground'.[154] In this way the form of man could change, like his pleasure, his labour, his condition. Man's labour was thus linked to the promise

---

150 Hay, 1751, p 19.
151 Locke, 1960, Chapter 5, section 42. Locke was secretary to the politically influential Earl of Shaftesbury, and a member of two Boards of Trade: 1673–74 and 1696–1700. The Trade Boards were inquisitorial bodies responsible for the regulation of the mercantile system including national and international trade, manufacturing, the employment of the poor, commercial exploitation and administration of the colonies and the navy. The Boards reported to the king or the Privy Council, not Parliament.
152 Pettus, *Volatiles from the History of Adam and Eve* (1674, p 153) cited in Webster, 1975, p 325.
153 Webster, 1975, p 325.   154 *Genesis*, 3:19; Milton, 1909, Chapter X, lines 205–6.

of nation and its desire to rest in peace in the Sabbath of eternal life. Just as Bacon had foretold of the exploitation of nature to the benefit of humanity, so too had he envisaged the salvation of humanity through the merger of its labour with the arts and sciences:

> For man by the fall fell at the same time from his state of innocency and from his dominion over creation. Both of these losses however can even in this life be in some part repaired; the former by religion and faith, the latter by arts and sciences. For creation was not by the curse made altogether and for ever a rebel, but in virtue of that charter, 'In the sweat of thy face shalt thou eat bread', it is now by various labours (Not certainly by disputations or idle magical ceremonies), subdued to the supplying of man with bread; that is, to the uses of human life.[155]

This reparation of man was no less than the Reasonable Man born of the exploitation of nature and his own labour. When Francis Bacon suggested that poverty might be reduced or prevented if the resources of the community, including its labour, were rationally used, he was not only developing a Puritan idea but also laying the foundations for the concept of development and a new symbolic mercantile order founded on capitalist relations and the nation state that were later taken up by reformers such as John Locke.

Locke's premise was that the individual was 'only as white paper or wax, to be moulded or fashioned as one pleases'.[156] This included the 'art of conducting men right in society' and international relations, 'supporting a community amongst its neighbours'.[157] The object was to shape all people into reasonable men who could balance the weight of evidence in order to arrive at the correct conclusion and thus seek faith in the sovereign state through understanding. Locke argued that the very nature of understanding was to conclude on 'the more probable side' such that 'a man who has weighed them, can scarce refuse his assent to the side on which the greater probability appears'.[158] This was not because the exercise of one's judgement was related to truth but because the science of weighing the evidence and the 'force' of the argument caused assent.[159] The scepticism felt by Montaigne was thus repressed by the law of reason. Locke argued:

> those things which come from convention are rightly distinguished from things natural, for things natural, since they are always the same, could

155   Bacon, 1855, Book II, aphorism 52.
156   Locke, 1996, section 216; and see also, section 2.
157   Locke, 1996, section 400; and Locke, *Draft Letter to the Countess of Peterborough* [1697] in Axtell, 1968, pp 392, 396.
158   Locke, 1975, Book 4, Chapter 20.15; and see generally, Book 4, Chapter 4.
159   Ibid, Book 4, Chapter 16.1 and Chapter 20.1.

be easily brought together into a science. But those things that come from institutions, since they both often change and vary from place to place, lie outside science. . . . For when many men, in different times and different places affirm the same thing as certain, this ought to be referred back to a universal cause, which can be none other than a dictate of reason itself and our common nature, since nothing is capable of instilling the same principles in the minds of men, or of compelling them to the same judgement.[160]

It is no wonder then that the fictional Bensalems' revered ancient King Solamona, feared strangers who might allow 'novelties, and commixture of manners'[161] to dilute the Bensalem symbolic order and ruin it as had already occurred in Atlantis where only 'a poor remnant of human seed' had been left.[162] The confessional subject was now to be made pure through the confession of the 'dictates of reason' and the 'common nature' of man. In developing this gift of reasoning, the rewards and punishments were praise and disgrace as well as corporeal punishment when necessary. Humanity was to be 'compelled' by the 'same judgment' made subject to the same 'purification urge' driving the construction of nation. Locke's assumption of knowledge as probable rather than definite relied on a single humanity under a universal rule of law as the touchstone of truth, which lent credit to any Reasonable Man trading in the emerging imperialism of a global political economy.[163] Individuals needed only to be educated to speak in the language of reason. Montaigne's doubt has become Locke's redemption.

The practical effects of instilling the 'dictate of reason and our common nature' into human subjectivity can be seen in Locke's *The Conduct of the Understanding* and *Some Thoughts Concerning Education*. Here, the shifting form of humanity was the foundation upon which Locke developed a disciplinary regime whereby individuals were moulded through punishment and reward such as praise and blame by teachers and mentors, the workhouse system, and the threat of eternal damnation.[164] The space of the confessional self was to be re-moulded anew by the belief in humanity's ability to use and control subjectivity.

As Locke would argue, although man had no innate disposition to moral conduct he did have empirically verifiable motives to pleasure and pain.[165]

---

160   Locke, 1990, p 107 citing Grotius Prolegomena 30 xii.   161   Bacon, 1974, p 228.

162   Ibid, p 227.

163   The conscience is seen as an 'inner tribunal' while the Royal Society employed probable forms of reasoning such as 'evidence', 'probability' and 'testimony' from the inquisitorial methods of justice that spread throughout Europe from 1215.

164   See Locke, 1996.   165   Locke, 1975, Book 2, Chapter 28.5.

> Morally Good and Evil then, is only the Conformity or Disagreement of our voluntary Actions to some Law, whereby Good or Evil is drawn on us, from the Will and Power of the Law-maker; which Good and Evil, Pleasure or Pain, attending our observance, or breach of the law, by the Decree of the Law-maker is that we call Reward and Punishment.[166]

Happiness and misery are the two extremes that move desire to 'operate and influence all our actions, without ceasing'.[167] While many of our actions, such as hunger, are implanted by the will of God, others such as the desire for 'Honour, Power or Riches' are produced by custom and education.[168]

Locke acknowledged the existence of a confessional subject shaped through techniques used previously by the Church to legitimate its domination, but which had ultimately been undermined during the Reformation.[169] Locke acknowledged that God tolerated many kinds of faith and that the penal disciplines of an overarching universal church were no longer a legitimate source of force. Instead, Locke identified three sources of 'rectitude or obliquity': divine law, civil law and the law of opinion or reputation.[170] The first of these laws concerns the procurement of happiness in the afterlife. The remaining two kinds of law discipline the actions of individuals in political society. The second draws power from 'the force of the Commonwealth, engaged to protect the lives, liberties and possessions of those who live according to its laws, and has power to take away life, liberty or goods, from him who disobeys'.[171] The third draws power from the panoptic nature of the community and the force of praise and blame, honour and dishonour:

> He therefore that would govern the world well, had need consider rather what fashions he makes, than what laws; and to bring any thing into use he need only give it reputation.[172]

Using penitential techniques, old habits of thought and behaviour were to be deconstructed and new habits of toleration, industriousness, and military preparedness put in their place.[173] Tully gives the example of Locke's *Some*

---

166 Ibid.   167 Ibid, Book 2, Chapter 21.42.   168 Ibid, Book 1, Chapter 21.45
169 See Tully, 1993, p 210.   170 Locke, 1975, Book 2, Chapter 28.7.
171 Locke, 1975, Book 2, Chapter 28.10 and Shennan, 1974.
172 'Credit, disgrace' Bodleian, MS Locke f. 3, ff 381–82, December 1678 cited in Tully, 1993, p 212.

> Thus the measure of what is everywhere called and esteemed Vertue and Vice is this approbation or dislike, praise or blame, which by a secret and tacit consent establishes itself in the several Societies, tribes and Clubs of men in the world; whereby several actions come to find credit or Disgrace among them, according to the Judgement, Maxims or Fashions of that place (Locke, 1975, Book 2, Chapter 28.7).

173 Locke, 1996, Dedication and sections 1–2, 52, 54, 64, 216.

Thoughts Concerning Education, where Locke argued that to inscribe the will of God onto a young man's mind it was necessary to tell the pupil that God hears, sees and governs all and rewards those who obey.[174] Then by continual use and practice it becomes both habitual and pleasurable, so that 'reason and consideration at first recommends, and begins their trial, and use finds, or custom makes them pleasant'.[175] Once habits are secured, the disciplined subject cannot bear the reproach with which they are punished for unconventional behaviour. In this sense, Locke's theories develop the practice of *exagoreusis*. Like the confessional subject, the Lockean subject was to be given a greater awareness of their own 'sinfulness' so that they might remedy the self accordingly.[176] In correcting himself, the gentleman brought himself into line with society's requirements of him. The result sought in this case, was of course, not unity with Christ but unity with nation.[177] In this way, those who failed to perform according to the dictates of nation were cast out – marked by criminality, deportation or other forms of mnemonic 'forgetting', thus combining the practices of *exagoreusis* and *exomologesis*.

As James Tully observes in his work on John Locke's political philosophy, the application of these disciplinary techniques in churches, workhouses, and educational institutions would render individuals 'subject to law' and made them fit for the rights and duties laid out by the mercantile state.[178] These practices did not only apply to gentlemen. According to the logic of mercantilism, the exploitation of labour for the purpose of enriching the nation also required the discipline of labouring bodies. For 'the bodies of men are without doubt the most valuable treasure of the country' but only 'if they are well employed in honest labor and useful arts'.[179] Wealth 'does not offer itself up to the idle and indolent, nor indeed to all who seek it, since some we see toil to no avail'.[180] Tully provides the example of Locke's *Report of the Board of Trade*, which was Locke's proposal to reform the English system of about 200 workhouses or poorhouses 'for setting on work and employing the poor of his kingdom, and making them useful to the publike and thereby easing others of that burthen'.[181] The report bears remarkable similarities to the contemporary reports of the World Bank in which the poor are represented as a burden to civilised society, living off the labour of others. As Tully explains, the cause of their poverty was, according to Locke, 'the relaxation of discipline and corruption of manners'.[182] The solution to their poverty was to use the poorhouses to correct and reform the poor by instilling habits of

---

174   Ibid, section 136 cited in Tully, 1993, p 223. See also, the examination of Jeremy Bentham's plans for a 'panopticon' penitentiary, in Foucault, 1991, pp 201–02.

175   Locke, 1996, section 2.10.6.

176   See Connolly, 1995, p 20. See also, Chapter Two, above.   177   Braswell, 1983, p 22.

178   Tully, 1993, p 67. See Tully, 1993, p 65.   179   Davenant, 1699, p 9.

180   Locke, 1990, p 135.   181   Tully, 1993, p 64.   182   Ibid.

'virtue and industry' through a system of severe corporal punishments and simple but useful and repetitive work.[183]

Through his work, Locke produced a model of power deployed around the confessional subject, the sovereign nation and global commerce and its correlative imperialism. National authorities relied upon disciplinary techniques such as those of Locke to secure their domination and declare their legitimacy as sacred and innate.[184] Just as what God said was argued to be true by virtue of it being His Word, likewise, true sovereignty could be recognised because Truth was the Word of the most powerful:[185]

> His power being known to have no equal, always will, and always may be, safely depended on, to show its superiority in indicating his authority, and maintaining every truth that he hath revealed. So that the marks of a superior power accompanying it, always have, and always will be, visible and sure guide to divine Revelation; by which men may conduct themselves in their examining of revealed religions, and be satisfied which they ought to receive as coming from God.[186]

Hence, the weight of evidence leaned toward the more powerful rationality of sovereign power and imperialism.

If, as Foucault has argued, human life has become increasingly subject to the mechanisms of political power through the 'processes of subjectivisation' whereby the individual constitutes itself as subject in relation to external disciplinary practices, then this is because the confessional had provided the means to do so. As Agamben writes:

> the spaces, the liberties, and the rights won by individuals in their conflicts with central powers always simultaneously prepared a tacit but increasing inscription of individual's lives within the state order, thus offering a new and more dreadful foundation for the very sovereign power from which they wanted to liberate themselves.[187]

This offering of the body is, arguably, akin to the Christian submission of the self to God, who always keeps His promise. The concept of development, the idea that the individual is owed the means 'to one's body, to health, to happiness, to the satisfaction of needs and, beyond all the oppressions or "alienation", the "right" to rediscover what one is and all that one can be,

---

183   Tully, 1993, p 225 discussing Locke, 1975, Book 1, Chapter 3.22–7.
184   Locke, 1975, Book 1, Chapter 3.22–7. Tully, 1993, p 225.
185   Locke, 1958b, p 92; and, Locke, 1975, Book 4, Chapter 18.10.
186   Locke, 'A Discourse of Miracles' in Locke, 1958a; Locke, 1975, Book 4, Chapter 19.15; Book 4, Chapter 16.13.
187   Agamben, 1998, p 121.

this "right" ... [is] the political response to all these new procedures of power'.[188]

The Christian disciplinary practices of *exomologesis* and *exagoreusis* had arguably survived – the former inscribing onto the individual the collective memory of a national sovereignty and a civilised society; the latter producing the individual subjectivity that made such an inscription possible by presenting it as a pure form of individual freedom. 'What manner of subjection is this?' Origen would recognise it as 'that state in which we should desire to be subject to Him, even as the Apostles are, and all the saints who have followed Christ'.[189] Thus, obedient subjection makes those who obey it into the members of a single body just as the nation state is willed into being by the national citizen, who desires salvation. One might call this desire the sovereign's will.

188 Foucault, 1998b.
189 This quote from Origen is taken from Tellenbach (1940, p 3) and is cited, above, in Chapter Two.

Chapter 5

The Peace of Westphalia: words, writings and outrageous actions

The divisiveness of civilisation

Previous chapters have sought to demonstrate how the First World and a particular form of individual subjectivity can be traced back to the crisis experienced by the embodiment of the medieval Christian Church in western Europe upon its discovery of the New World. This crisis can arguably be said to have produced a dramatic shift in the perception by western Europe of its own identity such that it was able to assume for itself the authority to discharge the debt that had been preventing it, the Christian world, from achieving salvation. In assuming this new identity the Old World positioned itself in the divine space of a future-perfect present, while casting the New World into the fallen state of unredeemed sin. In this way, Old World peoples were able to assert themselves as the chosen ones, complete and fully redeemed, while constructing New World peoples as underdeveloped. The Old World continued to secure this ostensibly superior identity by violently colonising the New World in a way that fetishised the New World as the source of Old World desires. The constitution of the New World existed necessarily as a space that resisted complete incorporation into the Christian body such that it remained marked as a space of savagery and barbarism. By imagining the New World in this way, the Old World was able to assure itself that a totalising embodiment of a united Christian world was not impossible but still partly unredeemed. This hope of global redemption had become the new object of faith but not one that was taken seriously because to do so would require the sacrifice by the Old World of its unique identity of assumed superiority. The Old World becomes, in effect, a 'unity somehow prematurely stopped'.[1]

Expressed in classic metaphoric terms, the Old World stands, then, in the position of a romantic figure, with a 'longing for unattainable fulfilment; a sense of incompleteness and decay; a disintegrated ego and a melancholy

---

[1] Janowitz, 1985, pp 26–27.

born of diasparactive existence'.[2] The romantic ideals of the civilising mission, 'the white man's burden', and the contemporary discourses of development can all be understood as symptoms of a world grieving for a romanticised consummation that it will never find.[3] It is a world 'laboring through the illusion of self-serving words to keep accountability, self-awareness and the pain of unrequited love at bay'.[4] The Old World was haunted by its 'capacity for faith, hope, for longing', a world seeking a promised future that was always distant, 'but made ever present to [it] by the quality of the love that "groans" for it'.[5] This groaning imperialism was so violent and tyrannical by the early twentieth century that virtually all of the territories of Asia, Africa and the Pacific were controlled by the major nations of the Old World.

The Old World nations themselves rested in the Peace of Westphalia of 1648, which was embraced as the origin of a civilised rule of law governing the Christian 'family of nations' in 'a Christian and Universal Peace'. This civilised peace reinforced the unity of the Old World, by proclaiming itself as the space of lawfulness. It was a peace that must be:

> observ'd and cultivated with such a Sincerity and Zeal, that each Party shall endeavour to procure the Benefit, Honour and Advantage of the other; that thus on all sides they may see this Peace and Friendship in the Roman Empire, and the Kingdom of France flourish, by entertaining a good and faithful Neighbourhood'.[6]

The covenant between God and man was now subsumed by the covenant amongst nations. The Peace of Westphalia created a body of civilisation comprising a European community of sovereign states. A body made possible through the recognition that its members existed only in the Other – with each sovereign part possessing equal legal standing and a guaranteed independence. The identity of this new family of sovereigns was thus dependent on principles and a vision that were of a higher unifying purpose than just the states themselves. The parties to the Peace of Westphalia had agreed:

> That there shall be on the one side and the other a perpetual Oblivion, Amnesty, or Pardon of all that has been committed since the beginning of these Troubles, in what place, or what manner soever the Hostilitys have been practis'd, in such a manner, that no body, under any pretext whatsoever, shall practice any Acts of Hostility, entertain any Enmity, or cause any Trouble to each other; neither as to Persons, Effects and Securitys, neither of themselves or by others, neither privately nor openly, neither directly nor indirectly, neither under the colour of Right, nor by

2 Hamelman, September 2001.   3 Ibid.   4 Ibid.   5 Brown, 1987.
6 Treaty of Westphalia, 1648, Article 1.

the way of Deed, either within or without the extent of the Empire, notwithstanding all Covenants made before to the contrary: That they shall not act, or permit to be acted, any wrong or injury to any what-soever; but that all that has pass'd on the one side, and the other, as well before as during the War, in Words, Writings, and Outrageous Actions, in Violences, Hostilitys, Damages and Expences, without any respect to Persons or Things, shall be entirely abolish'd in such a manner that all that might be demanded of, or pretended to, by each other on that behalf, shall be bury'd in eternal Oblivion.[7]

The Old World was thus freed from the eternal oblivion of the unredeemed realm of nature, the wars of doubt and the uncivilised world of savages and barbarians. Peace acted not only as the overarching principle of com-munity but also required the permanent forgetting of the past: 'a perpetual Oblivion, Amnesty, or Pardon of all that has been committed since the beginning'. Yet, the creation of order left the Old World with an obscure sense of an origin forgotten; of having been broken off from a greater whole. This lack was to be represented by the uncivilised realm of the New World in which peoples have yet to be redeemed from the eternal oblivion of troubles.

The correlation between state sovereignty and an overarching peace would become the hallmark concern for international lawyers in the following centuries. Peace (and war) became the realm of international law – the law of civilised nations. In the centuries following the Peace of Westphalia, the sovereign nation states of the Old World captured a sense of control over their own identities by claiming themselves as supreme authorities bound only by custom and consent: the law was theirs. By 1758, Vattel, in his *Law of Nations* was questioning whether the will of these sovereign bodies could be made subject to any overarching international law.[8] A century later the pre-dominant Austinian view of law was 'a species of commands' that flow from 'a determinate source', namely a sovereign power. This led jurists to argue that despite the lack of any overarching global sovereign, international law did exist, 'at least certainly among the greater part, and those the most civil-ised'.[9] This law of nations had been handed down from the future-perfect present of a Westphalian Peace just as the Decalogue had been given from Him who was, by custom and consent, the law.

To analyse the effects of these events more closely, this chapter explores three imaginary spheres of humanity that were prevalent in the nineteenth century, when jurisprudence about the nature of international law was argu-ably at its most intense. These three spheres are referred to as: the civilised,

7 Treaty of Westphalia, 1648, Article II.   8   See de Vattel, 1916.
9 Wheaton, 1836, p 43. See also, Westlake, 1894 and Lawrence, 1895.

the barbarous and the savage. The first sphere is that of a Westphalian Peace – the civilised community of sovereign states in Europe, as well as those colonial dependencies that were settled by people of European birth or descent including North and South America, Australia and New Zealand. The second – the barbarous – included Turkey in Europe and the old historical states of Asia that had not become European dependencies, such as Persia, China, Siam and Japan. The rest of the world was given meaning under the third signifier of savagery.[10] These three signifying realms are used here in their active sense as verbs; as signifiers that identify the subject and secure its objectification – to civilise; to barbarise; and, to savage.

The civilising

To civilise: 'to make civil, bring out of a savage state; elevate in social and individual life; enlighten; refine.'[11]

During the long nineteenth century leading up to the First World War, scholars of international law began to turn their attention away from the nature of Old World sovereignty to the justification of the consequent legal order created by the universalising force of Old World law and its interdependence with the concept of nation.[12] As Antony Anghie has argued, the positivism of the nineteenth century marks a shift in the nature of the jurisprudence of international law such that treaties and custom replace natural law as the exclusive and primary source of international law.[13] The Old World, which had assumed the place of the Father, now commanded the law in so far as it was the law. The idea that the Old World might somehow be subject to the laws of nature was therefore irreverent and profane. While peace remained the conceptual frame upon which the law was stretched, international law was now understood as positive in nature rather than natural; scientific and man-given rather than inherent in humanity. The result: man could giveth and he could taketh sovereignty away. The christening of the New World by the Old World continued.

The positivists of the nineteenth century, such as Westlake, argued that international society, like national society, formed a global polis, a society:

the members of which claim from each other the observance of certain lines of conduct, capable of being expressed in general terms as rules and hold themselves justified in mutually compelling such observance, by force if necessary; also that in such society the lines of conduct in question are observed with more or less regularity, either as the result of

10 Lorimer, 1883, pp 101–02.   11 *The Macquarie Dictionary*, 1989.
12 See generally Anghie, 1999.   13 Ibid, p 2 and generally.

compulsion or in accordance with the sentiments which would support compulsion in case of need.[14]

This definition of lawful society is not that different from the society of civilised nations described by Grotius, in so far as he argued that only states could legitimately 'commit some act of aggression' but a 'band of pirates or robbers' could not.[15] Grotius also recognised that although states might deviate from the laws of nature, they would still:

> regulate their conduct by the treaties, which they have made, and certain customs that have been established, being united among themselves for the mutual support of lawful rights, and connected with foreign states by known rules of standing polity.[16]

Nonetheless, the positivists sought to distinguish the nature of positive international law from the natural laws of divine origin. This is the same distinction drawn by Christianity between the Old Law, contained principally in the Decalogue, and the New Law, which was revealed by Jesus Christ and contained in the New Testament. In this sense, the positivism of international law can be seen as yet another shift away from divine justice to a justice dealt out by human reason alone – from an inscription of debt to its negotiation.

The Christian distinction is exemplified in the arguments put forward by Slater, a contemporary theologian. Slater writes that 'because the code of morality which we have in the Old Testament was inspired by God and imposed by Him on His people, it follows that there is nothing in it that is immoral or wrong', however, imperfect it is compared with the 'higher morality of the Gospel'.[17]

> it contained nothing that is blameworthy. It was suited to the low stage of civilization to which the Israelites had at the time attained; the severe punishments which it prescribed for transgressors were necessary to bend the stiff necks of a rude people; the temporal rewards held out to those who observed the law were adapted to an unspiritual and carnal race. Christ came not to destroy it but to fulfil and perfect it. Christ is the author of the New Law. He claimed and exercised supreme legislative authority in spiritual matters from the beginning of His public life until His Ascension into heaven. In Him the Old Law had its fulfilment and attained its chief purpose.[18]

14 Westlake, 1894, p 2 cited in Anghie, 1999, p 16.
15 Grotius, 1814. See Chapter 4, above.   16 Ibid.   17 Slater, 1999.   18 Ibid.

Leaving to one side the anti-Semitic assumptions of Slater's remarks, the hermeneutic significance to be drawn from Slater's argument is that the law of Moses had had for its object the formation and preservation of a particular people for the worship of the one true God. Once Christ came to found the new kingdom, the law was no longer to be confined to a single nation, but was to apply to all the nations of the earth.

This Christian justification for the abrogation of one system of laws for another is analogous and is perhaps itself informed by the imperial narrative of the positivist jurists who argued against the existence of a natural international law in support of the positing of laws by Christian nations once the Old World had identified itself. The objective is the same – the attainment of Westphalian 'Christian and Universal Peace'. 'By the death of Christ on the Cross the New Covenant was sealed, and the Old was abrogated'. And when 'the Gospel had been duly promulgated the civil and ceremonial precepts of the Law of Moses became not only useless, but false and superstitious, and thus forbidden'.[19] Just as Christ had come to repay the debt of humanity with his suffering, so too, those peoples who entered into a sovereign state of Christian peace (nation) could redeem themselves by turning away from their eternal oblivion and rest in the Peace of Westphalian unity. Once redeemed, justice would be served, and the sacrifice of those peoples of the New World who had 'suffered weariness, hunger, thirst, scourging and death' could be explained, as Anselm had explained Christ's own sacrifice.[20] Like Christ, the positivists came 'not to destroy the law but to fulfil it'; and as Christ had insisted that the law be one of charity towards God and man, the lawmakers posited laws of civilisation to bring peace to the world. It is written: 'God is love' (*John* 4:16). As Slater writes:

> As was suited to a law of love which replaced the Mosaic Law of fear, Christ wished to attract men to obey His precepts out of motives of charity and filial obedience, rather than compel submission by threats of punishment. . . . He was not content with a bare observance of the law, He boldly proposed to His disciples the infinite goodness and holiness of God for their model, and urged them to be perfect as their heavenly Father is perfect.[21]

In like manner, the positivists of international law sought to incorporate the peoples of the New World into their precepts of Westphalian Peace 'out of motives of charity and filial obedience', rather than by violent compulsion. In other words, the positivists sought to construct from the territories of the New World, which were already marked by practices of imperial *exomologesis*,

19 Ibid.   20 Anselm, 1998b, Chapter I.3. See Chapter Two, above.
21 Slater, 1999, p 18.

a series of obedient confessional subjects of international law, which would look up to the Old World as a place of 'infinite goodness and holiness . . . for their model'.[22]

> For such as were specially called, and who were not content to observe the commandments merely, He proposed counsels of consummate perfection. By observing these His specially chosen followers, not only conquered their vices, but destroyed the roots of them, by constantly denying their natural propensities to honours, riches, and earthly pleasures.[23]

This would become the basis for Kipling's call to 'take up the white man's burden'.[24] By 'destroying their roots' and overcoming 'their natural propensities' to a lesser good, savage peoples could be admitted into the body of civilised nations – into a universal peace. Thus, the rule of law and the power of positive international law became a means to bring the New World into the fold of civilisation. National sovereignty became the new covenant between the New World and the Old. The nineteenth century was thus a period of the coming of, and redemption through, law. The New World was made to recover from its Fall and seek instead the freedom of subjective obedience to Old World authority, an authority rooted in national sovereignty. Previously subjected to the 'universal' laws of nature through practices of fear and violence, the New World was now brought peace by an Old World, positioned beyond the Fall. The peoples of the New World were to remain unredeemed and without the love of the Father until such time as they were either inscribed by the violence of a coloniser's law or christened as an equal sovereign into the realm of civilisation and peace.

By the late eighteenth century, JJ Moser, in his texts, *The First Basic Notions of the Present European Law of Nations* (1778) and *The Most Recent European Law of Nations* (1779), referred to the peculiar circumstances of trade relations with Asian sovereigns to whom he said the European law of nations was not applicable. He continued to argue, however, that they be governed by the natural and universal law of nations, which 'did not allow European Powers to occupy the land of extra-European nations under the pretext of religion or otherwise'.[25] Likewise, JHG von Justi (1779) strongly criticised the activities of the various European East India companies engaged in aggressive trade as being unlawful, pursuant to the law of nations.[26] In spite of taking cognisance of the development of world trade on the basis of a universal framework of the law of nations, in his *Precis du droit des gens*

22 Ibid.   23 Ibid.
24 This is a reference to Rudyard Kipling's famous poem, *The White Man's Burden*, written in 1899 in response to the American takeover of the Philippines after the Spanish-American war.
25 Cited in Alexandrowicz, 1955, p 509.   26 Alexandrowicz, 1955, p 510.

(1789), GF de Martens denied the existence of a universal positive law of nations, which he believed was confined only to European countries. Though he admitted the existence of civilised nations outside Europe, Martens was reluctant to call the law applicable to European-Asian relations the law of civilised nations.[27] So, while a multilateral trading system had existed for centuries, the international law regulating trade and the positive law of treaties was being confined to a few civilised countries in Europe that were redeemed beyond the Fall.

> Is there a uniform law of nations? There certainly is not the same one for all the nations and states of the world. The public law, with slight exceptions, has always been, and still is, limited to the civilised and Christian people of Europe or to those of European origin.[28]

The world was now divided into two – the lawful and the outlaw. In this way the Old World could both assume its own identity while keeping the New World as that part of the unity 'somehow prematurely stopped'.[29]

It is worth citing a rather lengthy paragraph from the work of Bhabha on these seemingly conflicting descriptions within the emerging colonial discourse:

> what is being dramatized is a separation – *between* races, cultures, histories, *within* histories – a separation between *before* and *after* that repeats obsessively the mythical moment of disjunction. Despite the structural similarities with the play of need and desire in primal fantasies, the colonial fantasy does not try to cover up that moment of separation. It is more ambivalent. On the one hand, it proposes a teleology – under certain conditions of colonial domination and control the native is progressively reformable. On the other, however, it effectively displays the 'separation', makes it more visible. It is the visibility of this separation which, in denying the colonized capacities of self-government, independence, western modes of civility, lends authority to the official version and mission of colonial power. Colonial fantasy is the continual dramatization of emergence – of difference, freedom – as the beginning of a history which is repetitively denied. Such a denial is the clearly voiced demand of colonial discourse as the legitimisation of a form of rule that is facilitated by the racist fetish.[30]

The peoples of the New World were acknowledged to have some form of law, but it seemed, on Old World inspection, to be like its peoples: savage and

27 Ibid, p 514   28 Wheaton, 1836, p 15.   29 Janowitz, 1985, pp 26–27.
30 Bhabha, 1986, pp 170–71.

unruly such that it would not be able to bring peace, maintain order and regulate trade. The territories of the New World existed in pre-Westphalian times. Without the law of civilised nations the New World could not redeem itself and would face the same fate as Bacon's New Atlantis. International lawyers were thus compelled to turn their ordering processes to the outlaw. They did so using the racist discourses developing in the social and natural sciences of the late eighteenth century. Thus, the 'scientific method' of inter-national law continued the Christian desire to name in a way that made 'definitions stick'.[31] In effect, the savage entered into law and humanity when it had altered itself to such an extent that it was no longer recognisable as anything but a subject of international law. As Anghie writes, 'Sovereignty, in the case of non-European societies, did not arise "naturally" but had to be bestowed'.[32]

The New World was repeatedly called by a name not of its choosing; all former, heterogeneous identifications within the New World were prohibited except that one exteroceptive image of itself that was offered to it by the Old World.[33] The effect resembled the second birth of each Christian into the Church through baptism. The New World was born again into the Old. As a consequence, writes Anghie, positivist jurists were able to 'recast entirely the basis of relations between civilised and uncivilised by framing the project as though the colonial encounter was about to occur, as opposed to already having taken place'.[34]

The Old World was now re-performing its discovery of the New World, but this time it would not be lost for words; there would be no cause for wonder. The Old World wished a return to the source of its authority in order that it might cut its own ambiguous unity with God and His laws of nature and assume instead its mastery of law by reason. The Old World sought its own origins, its own lost original experience of creation. The New World func-tioned for the Old as the point from which the Old World could 'see itself in a likeable, idealised form, as worthy of love': the redeemed world of civilisation, the world of the Gospel, loving, righteous, compelling – a world subject to 'the supposedly naïve gaze' of the New World, which stares back at the Old, fascinated.[35] In other words, the Old World represented itself as the world that the New World wanted to join; and yet, always lingering in the dark heart of the Old World was the fear that the New World would not answer the call and refuse to be named. Instead, at a more material level, the New World might begin to authorise its own world, one in which the narratives of First World redemption no longer rendered the international relations of power, profit and labour legitimate and meaningful while marking others as meaningless. From the perspective of the Old World, the New World was

31 Bauman, 1991, p 9.   32 Anghie, 1999, p 72.   33 Stavrakakis, 1999.
34 Anghie, 1999, p 34.   35 Zizek, 1993, p 200.

allowed to exist but only on the condition that it accepted the laws of the Old World.

The shift to positivism during the nineteenth century allowed the Old World to insist upon the form of law into which the New World could 'evolve' by positing Old World laws as civilised, and therefore the next stage in the progression of New World states.

What were previously taken as natural laws provided by God or built into a natural order were sanctioned as part of the contingent but nonetheless settled custom or conventions constituting civilised, Christian identity.[36] In the same way that Locke sought to rely on the 'reason' of English custom and convention to educate gentlemen, jurists sought to form and educate the subjects of international law using the 'customary' nature of that law. As Angie notes, the originary myth of a state of nature was thus transposed onto an original set of fundamental principles.[37] Those unable to draw upon these principles – those states that had not undergone the disciplinary training of the Enlightenment – were likely to remain in the savagery of the New World. This was the very threat of 'eternal oblivion' held out by the Peace of Westphalia as an incentive to those who might otherwise seek another path of redemption by way of a different society. By 1908 Oppenheim argued that 'we are no longer justified in teaching a law of nature and a "natural" law of nations'.[38] International law had become 'the body of rules [both customary and positive] prevailing between states'.[39]

The same foundational notions of religion, ethnicity and family used in nation-building were adopted by international lawyers to conceive of the peace inherent in the realm of international relations.[40] International society was confined to the Christian community, bound by Christian law, which was 'the justification of, or legal title to, the domination of non-Christian peoples'.[41] Lawrence would go so far as to argue that European states had belonged to a family of nations 'since time immemorial'. 'Many of them existed before the real majority of rules came into being'. Anything like a ceremony of initiation would have been wholly inapplicable to their case'.[42] These European states existed instead in a time outside space, representative of that 'model of wholeness, of fulfilment, or pure presence' and set against the space of a New World, which caused 'the imperfect fragmentation of such a whole'.[43] Europeans states were the lawmakers – masters; sovereigns.

The disciplined polities of scientific, political, economic and technical technologies that the sixteenth and seventeenth century theorists and state-builders had constructed were now not only governable subjects of international law but the authors of the 'New Law'.[44] These states *were* the law:

36 Widder, 2002, p 2.   37 Anghie, 1999, p 21.   38 Oppenheim, 1908, p 328.
39 Westlake, 1894, p 1   40 Anghie, 1999, p 17.   41 Roling, 1960, p 29.
42 Lawrence, 1895 and Wheaton, 1836, p 84.
43 Spence, 1996, p 24. See Chapter Two, above.   44 See Slater, 1999.

> Without society no law, without law no society. When we assert that there is such a thing as international law, we assert that there is a society of states: when we recognise that there is a society of states, we recognise that there is international law.[45]

The law of man thus grounds the signification of the Old World.[46] By extracting the New World from itself, by outlawing the New World, the Old World performed again its own conceptual redemption. The construction of this redemption is based on the incarnation of the Word – the natural law – into the positive law of civilisation. What was once divine had become worldly; law was no longer a mystery but an observable system of relations posited as an immanent system of knowledge. This knowledge represented the will of civilised nations as the negotiable signifier of truth made possible by language. Language, and the human mastery of it, continued to assume the power of inscription. Behind the text, material exploitation and violent imperialism drove the international division of labour onwards.

If the New World was to be represented by language then it had to accept this law in order to emerge from its 'natural order'. 'It is a discretion', wrote Oppenheim in his treatise of international law in 1905, 'and not international law, according to which the family of nations deal with such states as still remain outside that family'.[47] Man was no longer willing to observe and contemplate some law that nature was willing to yield, but began instead to prescribe conditions and to provoke natural processes.[48] The positivists were in effect, 'making nature' on the premise that 'though one cannot know truth as something given and disclosed, man can at least know what he makes himself'.[49]

According to the positivists, the relations between states could be made subject to the scientific gaze; they could be understood by reference to certain 'fundamental principles'.[50] While international law formed part of the human as opposed to natural sciences, jurists, such as Westlake, sought to argue that international law still possessed a place amongst the sciences[51] – a place that provided it with the credentials of 'rigor, consistency and precision', thereby removing international law from the imaginary chaos of 'a shapeless mass of undigested and sometimes inconsistent rules'.[52] Once acquired, the laws could be used to re-mould and re-animate the New World.[53]

The Baconian practice of classifying and observing separate parts of the whole could thus be applied to international law in an effort to develop a

45 Westlake, 1894, p 3.   46 Stavrakakis, 1999, p 32.
47 Oppenheim, 1905, Vol. I, 34.   48 Arendt, 1998, p 231.   49 Ibid, p 282.
50 Anghie, 1999, p 20.   51 Westlake, 1894, p vi. See also, Korhonen, 1996.
52 Cited in Anghie, 1999, p 18.   53 Lacan, 1993, p 9 and Stavrakakis, 1999, p 19.

coherent and overarching order. In the same way that the medieval Church claimed for itself the powers of absolution to bind and to lose, so too the positivists claimed the power to either bind states within a Westphalian Peace or lose them into eternal oblivion.[54] Lawrence regarded the science of international law:

> not as an instrument for the discovery and interpretation of a transcendental rule of right binding upon states as moral beings whether they observe it or not in practice, but as a science whose chief business it is to find out by observation the rules actually followed by states in their mutual intercourse, and to classify and arrange these rules by referring them to certain fundamental principles on which they are based.[55]

Here, the existence of the nation state is taken for granted. Only the civilised powers had the capacity and reason to observe law and the violent military force to enforce, or not, that law. Therefore, only the customs emerging from their own practice could be considered part of international law.[56]

These processes of lawmaking were not natural but violent manifestations of force. The United States of America entered the scene as an imperial power in relation to the Philippines following the war with Spain of 1898. In 1898 Kaiser Wilhelm II introduced a new law for the German navy, aimed at both challenging Britain's naval supremacy and expanding the market available to German exports through a new *Weltpolitik*. Japan was able to claim itself as a great power by military victories over China in 1895 and Russia in 1905. From 1867 Japan had already begun to strengthen its membership of the society of civilised states by adopting European methods of industrialisation, a process catalysed by the Commander of US naval forces in the China Seas, Commodore Matthew Perry, who sailed into Edo Bay in 1854. He insisted on landing and demanded of the Japanese Government, with the utmost courtesy and show of arms, that it engage in commercial relations with the USA and western powers. The story reads like a reversal of Bacon's tale of the New Atlantis, in which a crew sails out from a New Atlantis into the world of ungovernable spaces:

> On the arrival of the Commodore, his suite of officers formed a double line along the landing-place, and as he passed up between, they fell into order behind him. The procession was then formed and took up its march toward the house of reception, the route to which was pointed out by Kayama Yezaiman and his interpreter, who preceded the party. The marines led the way, and the sailors following, the Commodore was duly

---

54 *Matthew* 16:19. See also, *Matthew* 18:18 and *John* 20:22–23.
55 See Lawrence, 1895, p 1.   56 See Westlake, 1894, p 3.

escorted up the beach. The United States' flag and the broad pennant were borne by two athletic seamen, who had been selected from the crews of the squadron on account of their stalwart proportions. Two boys, dressed for the ceremony, preceded the Commodore, bearing in an envelope of scarlet cloth the boxes which contained his credentials and the President's letter. These documents, of folio size, were beautifully written on vellum, and not folded, but bound in blue silk velvet. Each seal, attached by cords of interwoven gold and silk with pendent gold tassels, was encased in a circular box six inches in diameter and three in depth, wrought of pure gold. Each of the documents, together with its seal, was placed in a box of rosewood about a foot long, with lock, hinges, and mountings all of gold. On either side of the Commodore marched a tall, well-formed Negro, who, armed to the teeth, acted as his personal guard. These blacks, selected for the occasion, were two of the best-looking fellows of their color that the squadron could furnish. All this, of course, was but for effect.[57]

There was to be no more savagery, but a civilisation known as humanity. The nature of trade and commerce was such 'that it was unnatural for governments to close their countries to the free flow of trade'.[58] From this perspective, closure was an act of aggression, whereas the ability to trade was an inevitable mark of evolutionary progress – of civilisation illuminating the remaining hearts of darkness.

The merger of juridical concepts of sovereignty with those of materialist circulation secured the boundaries of an ever-expanding Westphalian Peace against the threat of eternal oblivion. Under the new imperialism, Europeans were by no means content to purchase only what indigenous merchants wished to sell. European merchants moved into 'unindustrialised', 'backward' territories and invested capital in them, establishing mines, plantations, docks, warehouses, factories, refineries, railroads, taking over the resources of the territory and transforming large sections of the local population into wage employees, if not slaves. The practice of lending money to corrupt or unstable rulers to enable them to hold power begins here, centuries before the technique was adopted by organisations such as the International Monetary Fund or the World Bank.[59] The authority of money thus stamped its sign of legitimacy onto the ruler – the circulation of money venturing to join, in a complicit deal, its own sovereign realm with the juridical sovereignty of the state.

The centuries-old Asian custom of permitting foreign traders living in their countries to apply their own laws in their disputes and dealings among

---

57 Cited at www.fordham.edu/halsall/mod/1854Perry-japan1.html.
58 Panikkar, 1954, p 123.   59 See Orford, 1997 and Orford, 2003.

themselves, degenerated into treaties forcibly imposed on the Asian states not yet colonised in a show of legalised custom.[60] As Alexandrowicz observes:

> Asian states who for centuries had been considered members of the family of nations found themselves in an ad hoc-created legal vacuum which reduced them from the status of international personality to the status of candidates competing for such personality.[61]

The law relating to state responsibility – expropriation of alien property and rules relating to compensation, protection of nationals in foreign countries and the right of intervention for the protection of nations – were developed during this period of expansion to protect European interest and nationals.[62] As Westlake argued:

> When people of European race come into contact with American or African tribes, the prime necessity is a government under the protection of which the former may carry on the complex life to which they have been accustomed in their homes . . .[63]

It was asserted that:

> The inflow of the white race cannot be stopped where there is land to cultivate, ore to be mined, commerce to be developed, sport to enjoy, curiosity to be satisfied.[64]

The forces constituting the Great Powers, their military strength and access to international trade and commerce through the control of the seas and waterways, were marked out as signifiers of both a civilised peace and its means.[65]

Asian and African territories were declared wholly uncivilised by European powers because they could not provide European foreigners with the same

---

60 Anghie, 1999, pp 52–53.
61 Alexandrowicz, 1955, p 318. By 1900 the major ports of China were under the control of the British, French, German and Portuguese. The USA, fearing that China would be divided, as Africa was, into exclusive spheres, declared its own 'open door' policy in China to protect commercial interests. Supported by Britain, China would remain territorially intact and independent, but forced to give the imperial powers special concessions or 'spheres of influence' and permit merchants of all nations to trade without discrimination. See Moon, 1927, p 445.
62 Anand, 1987, p 26.   63 Westlake, 1894, p 141.   64 Ibid.
65 Prior to the Congress of Westphalia, both Britain and Russia had specified that certain matters were not to be raised, particularly questions concerning the freedom of the seas and the colonisation of the New World. In 1818 the number of Great Powers had been increased to include France. Palmer and Colton, 1965, pp 412–13.

protection and standards of law and order to which they were ostensibly accustomed in their own countries. If any people tried to keep civilisation out, 'international law had to treat such nations as uncivilised'.[66] If a country, such as China, did not desire a role in the international trade system 'she must be made to do so, in the interests of peace, prosperity and progress'.[67] After King Leopold II of the Belgians annexed the Congo from the rest of the African continent in 1876–77, ostensibly to introduce civilisation, the French, Germans, Portuguese and British followed soon after. Within less than two decades the entire continent was partitioned by European powers at the 1884–85 conferences in Berlin.[68] The resulting agreement provided that the parties were to 'protect and favour all religious, scientific, or charitable institutions and undertakings … which aim at instructing the natives and bringing home to them the blessings of civilization'.[69] 'Christian missionaries, scientists, and explorers, with their followers, property, and collections' were also to be 'the objects of especial protection'.[70] In his opening address to the Berlin Conference, German Chancellor Otto von Bismarck noted that 'all the governments invited, share the wish to bring the natives of Africa within that pale of civilisation by opening up the interior of the continent to commerce'.[71] African peoples played no part in the conference. The central theme was trade in the Congo basin and the Congo and Niger Rivers. It was agreed that any party taking possession of land in Africa was required to notify all other members (none of whom were native to Africa) of this possession and to exercise its authority in its possessions so as to protect existing rights within the territory.[72]

Through the narrative of a state of nature, the New World had provided the Old with its civilised identity by founding itself in the orginary myth and negation of New World savagery. Now, having identified and named itself, the Old World sought to maintain its international rule of law. To cross into the uncivilised anarchy of the New World had become a matter of stepping outside of law.[73] Underlying this Old World totality were the sovereign states. Just as sovereignty marked the threshold between inside and outside, order and chaos, the society of nation states marked the borders of a civilised Old World.[74] Recognition of national sovereignty occurred when 'a state is

---

66 Westlake, 1894, pp 92–101.   67 See Panikkar, 1954, pp 120–38 and 166–99.

68 The Conference met at Berlin from November 1884 to February 1885 and resulted in the The Berlin Act of 26 February 1885 Annex 1 to Protocol No 8, Protocols and the General Act of the West African Conference. The Act divided Africa into 'spheres of influence' and established the Congo basin as the Congo Free State under the sovereignty of King Leopold II of the Belgians in his personal capacity as chief financial backer of the private International Congo Association.

69 The Berlin Act 1885 Par VI.   70 Ibid.

71 The Berlin Act 1885, Protocol No 1, Meeting of November 15, 1884.

72 The Berlin Act 1885.   73 Anghie, 1999, p 24.   74 Agamben, 1998, p 19.

brought by increasing civilisation within the realm of law'.[75] International society 'exercises the right of admitting outside states to parts of its international law without necessarily admitting them to the whole of it'.[76] It was a difficult task, and 'no general rule can be laid down'.[77] The task of defining relations between the civilised and the uncivilised was no less than an exercise in representation – the exercising of the power to signify meaning. As Oppenheim was forced to acknowledge, 'no other explanation of [the fact that these non-sovereign entities engaged in sovereign behaviour] can be given except that these not-full Sovereign States are in some way or another International Persons and subjects of International Law'.[78] These 'non-sovereign' entities were cast in similar ways to the savages portrayed by Locke (see Chapter Four), who held within them the potential of civility. It was, therefore, not possible to say whether the New World is outside or inside the juridical order, inside or outside the Body of Christ, the body politic, the body of humanity. Outside and inside become 'indistinguishable'.[79]

By recreating the origins and realm of civilisation, the jurists of the Old World had marked out the unredeemed subjects of international law. Only through reform could an uncivilised state meet international obligations and maintain diplomatic channels understood and acknowledged by European states. To be heard, the barbaric state was required:

> to reform radically its legal and political systems to the extent that they reflected European standards as a whole. . . . In the domestic sphere, then, the non-European state was required to guarantee basic rights relating to dignity, property, and freedom of travel, commerce, and religion, and it had to possess a court system that comprised codes, published laws, and legal guarantees'.[80]

In this way the sovereign realm of exchange merged together with political sovereignty to form what it meant to be modern, progressive, dignified and redeemable.

Somewhat ironically, nationalism became the mode through which colonised peoples sought to maintain an identifiable consciousness and self-representation. In doing so, they began to fulfil Hegel's fantasy of an enlightened world where 'international conversations and transactions can only be conducted between nations and their real or potential representatives'.[81] Hegel equated humanity – humankind – to a process of historical emergence from darkness into light. Hegel declared that in sub-Saharan Africa:

---

75 Hall, 1884, p 184. See Anghie, 1999, pp 43–48.   76 Westlake, 1894, p 82.
77 Lawrence, 1895, p 59.   78 Oppenheim, 1912, p 110.   79 Agamben, 1998, p 29.
80 Anghie, 1999, p 53.   81 Gandhi, 1998, p 105.

history is in fact out of the question. Life there consists of a succession of contingent happenings and surprises. No aim of state exists whose development could be followed and there is no subjectivity, but merely a series of subjects who destroy one another.[82]

History as a symbolic ordering of modernity enabled meaning to be given to an immature human spirit that developed into its own totality, into a civil society as promised by nationhood.[83] It is a future-perfect present outside of space – a world comprising those European and New World powers of the emerging West.

> our epoch is a birth-time, and a period of transition. The spirit of man has broken with the old order of things. . . . The spirit of the time, growing slowly and quietly ripe for the new form it is to assume, disintegrates one fragment after another of the structure of the previous world.[84]

Hence, we learn from a section entitled 'Roosevelt and the Modern Age' in the 1997 edition of the *Encyclopedia of U.S. Foreign Relations* that:

> In 1898 the world order created by the Spanish Roman Catholic rule in the late-fifteenth century ended dramatically when the President of the United States forcibly removed the last vestige of Spanish Roman Catholic hegemony in Latin America and Asia.[85]

It would seem, however, that US President Theodore Roosevelt did not view this as in any way severing the overall expansion of the Old (Christian) World into the New. The existence of the New World was still closely bound up with the spread of Christianity, with the rights of Christians over pagans and the rights of pagans against Christians. So begins the 'opening of a new century and a new modern age'.[86] To Roosevelt:

> The object lesson of expansion is that peace must be brought about in the world's waste spaces. . . . Peace cannot be had until the civilised nations have expanded in some shape over the barbarous nations. . . . It is our duty toward the people living in barbarism to see that they are freed

---

82 Hegel is referring to sub-Saharan Africa because he considered North Africa to have 'history' as a consequence of its occupation or colonisation by Asian or European peoples, and Egypt to be geographically a part of Asia. Hegel, 1956, pp 91–93.

83 Hegel, 1956, pp 91–93.   84 Hegel, 1910, p 10.

85 Jentleson and Paterson, 1997, Vol IV, 31. Theodore Roosevelt was President of the United States from 1901 to 1909.

86 Jentleson and Paterson, 1997, Vol IV, 31.

from their chains, and we can free them only by destroying barbarism itself. . . . Exactly as it is the duty of civilised power scrupulously to respect the rights of weaker civilised powers . . . so it is its duty to put down savagery and barbarism.[87]

The implication of Roosevelt's call is that savagery and barbarism cannot be equated with peace because of their threat to civilised nations. Roosevelt locates the threat within the barbarous nations themselves in so far as they are chained down by their own savagery, which must be destroyed before these nations can be redeemed and reborn into peace – as had been the USA.

Despite its Eurocentric origins, the nation state was recognised by colonised peoples as a concept from which they had been excluded and they actively sought to adopt it as their own to become, in effect, a confessional subject of international law. As Said concedes:

> Along with armed resistance in places as diverse as nineteenth century Algeria, Ireland and Indonesia, there also went considerable efforts in cultural resistance almost everywhere, the assertions of nationalist identities, and, in the political realm, the creation of associations and parties whose common goal was self-determination and national independence.[88]

The anti-colonial nationalisms that began to emerge from around 1890 became 'an allusive, cross-cultural, intertextual, or interdiscursive phenomenon, strung across borders of different descriptions as well as staked out within geopolitical boundaries'.[89] The same threatening yet necessary negotiation between the subject and the confessor had begun. Nationalism was both the subjectification of colonised peoples into a western legally recognised international personality as well as a threat to that obedience in so far as the governance of those states was never entirely within the mastery of the Old World. By subjecting themselves to a form set out for them by the

---

87   Beale, 1956, p 34. Roosevelt firmly believed that 'the so-called white races' are 'the group of peoples living in Europe, who undoubtedly have a certain kinship of blood, who profess the Christian religions, and trace back their culture to Greece and Rome' (Beale, 1956, p 27).
88   Said, 1993, p xii. The Anglo-Boer War of 1899–1990 inaugurated for Britain a decade of imperial crisis including the anti-imperial resistance flowing from South Africa, Ireland, Bengal and Egypt (Boehmer, 2002, p 4). The rise to power of the Young Turks in 1908 and the Chinese Revolution of 1911 continued attempts by threatened peoples to save themselves from colonisation through modernisation into nationalism. In India a National Congress met for the first time in 1886 and the Muslim League held its first conference in 1907. By 1914 considerable effort had been made to give Indians a share in government and administration.
89   Boehmer, 2002, p 3.

imperial powers, anti-colonial nations took on their own consciousness with the means to become the creator of their own progress.

Indeed, the threat to peace did not in fact lie in the heart of darkness, but in the Old World itself. It was imperial rivalry that would lead eventually to the 1914–18 World War. This was 'the war to end all wars' and when it had come to an end, US President Woodrow Wilson declared that 'the world must be made safe for democracy'.[90] Wilson's call for democracy further institutional-ised the power of law into a confirmed system of sovereign states that inscribed onto the subjects of international law a memory of belonging.[91] The sacred totality promised by the incorporation of two worlds thus con-tinued into the inter-war era. In British Prime Minister Lloyd George's words, the duty of the Allied Forces was, 'not to soil the triumph of right by indulging in the angry passions of the moment but to consecrate the sacrifice of millions to the permanent redemption of the human race from the scourge and agony of war'.[92] The call to peace continued together with the redemp-tion of humanity. The civilised, the barbarians and the savages were to live together in a world subject to:

> A free, open-minded and absolutely impartial adjustment of all colonial claims, based upon strict observance of the principle that . . . the interests of the population concerned must have equal weight with the claims of the government whose title is to be determined.[93]

In President Woodrow Wilson's vision of a League of Nations, the Peace of Westphalia blossomed into global form. Now, New World powers had the potential to be made equal before the law of nations, possessed with the machinery for the peaceful settlement of disputes. Yet, as Anand points out, the imperial interests were what mattered and these were to be determined by the European powers. The wishes of the people were irrele-vant.[94] The outcome was a modified form of imperial rule in the form of a mandate system that did not apply to the colonies of the victorious powers.[95]

Article 22 of the League Covenant referred to the inhabitants of the colonies taken from the Central Powers as 'peoples not yet able to stand by themselves under the strenuous conditions of the modern world', and provided that the

90 Lefort, 1988, p 17.   91 Ibid.

92 Six treaties of settlement made up the final settlement between 1919 and 1923, The Treaty of Versailles 1919, Treaty of Neuilly 1919, Treaty of St Germaine 1920, Treaty of Trianon 1920, Treaty of Sevres 1920, Treaty of Lausanne 1923.

93 The 5th of President Wilson's Fourteen Points.   94 Anand, 1987, p 31.

95 Stavrianos, 1966, p 454.

[t]utelage of such peoples should be entrusted to advanced nations who by reason of their resources, can best undertake this responsibility . . . and that this tutelage should be exercised by them as Mandatories on behalf of the League.[96]

Article 22 thereby also provided the Old World with its secure position as a superior world. The other world was apparently still lacking – still gazing naively up at the Old World from the origin. Since the turn of the nineteenth century, the concept of holding territories as Old World protectorates had been a common legal tool of Old World powers used to exercise economic control over a state without taking on the responsibility of administration and governance. As Anghie notes, the protectorate corresponded with 'a growing appreciation for the uses of the "informal Empire" and the realisation that an important distinction could be made between economic and political control'.[97] This was the new Wilsonian 'democracy'.

There were to be three types of mandate territories: A, B, and C. Category A territories were mostly in the Middle East. These territories were expected to become independent in the short term. Category B territories (most of the German colonies) and C territories (colonies with a small population) were thought to need 'mandatory' administrations for the long term. The Covenant of the League of Nations maintained an imperial relationship between the Old and the New Worlds. The Old World clung to what it had. When Mussolini invaded Ethiopia in 1935 in revenge for the defeat Italy had suffered in 1896, the illusion of peace was again shattered and the Old World fell into its countless pieces.[98]

The barbarous

To barbarise: 'to make barbarous or crude; to corrupt.'[99]

This section breaks down further the constructed binary relationship between the Old and the New Worlds. The aim is to show the Old World as the source of barbarism, to show its own history as no more than a history of imperialism over itself as its attempts to transpose itself into a 'family of nations'. Despite the imaginings of Old World jurists in the nineteenth and twentieth centuries with respect to the ostensible superiority of the Old World in relation to the New, the Old World itself was a heterogeneous mass of rivalry and conflict. It remained in doubt. As Elleke Boehmer states, during the period of High Imperialism from 1880 to 1920:

---

96 The Covenant of the League of Nations, 1925, Article 22.
97 Anghie, 1999, p 57. See Gallagher and Robinson, 1953, p 1.
98 In 1896 Italy invaded Ethiopia (then known as Abyssinia) and was defeated. Apart from Liberia, Abyssinia was the only African nation to have maintained its independence.
99 *The Macquarie Dictionary*, 1989.

the metropolis witnessed a rising social and political radicalism, galvanised at crucial points by campaigns for Irish Home Rule, by women's struggle for self-representation, and by the international spread of socialist and Marxist ideas, formalised within the (Europe-centred) Second International (1889–1914).[100]

The governmental framework of nations in Europe was similarly heterogeneous comprising autocracies, parliaments, republics and monarchies. In 1861 Italy was formed from a number of kingdoms, duchies and other political bodies, as was the German Empire in 1870–71.[101] What governments did have in common were the disciplinary techniques to administer their subjective fragments as a whole body. What they had was Westphalian sovereignty. Within Europe and those parts of the New World that had been settled by Europeans, the uncivilised were to be expelled, reformed or killed. Governments moved their administration from the traditional areas of law and order, foreign policy, administration and taxation to education, health, employment and morality, gaining control of the latter three responsibilities from the Church. The issuing of passports also began to develop 'to erect and sustain boundaries between nationals and non-nationals both at their physical borders and among people within those borders.[102] States thus monopolised 'the legitimate means of movement' in order to 'embrace' their citizens and extract from them the resources they needed to reproduce themselves over time, thereby securing the juridico-materialist merger.[103] Everywhere in Europe nation states systematically compiled statistics on births, deaths, marriages and employment, poverty, household structure and family budgets. Even those in rural and remote areas began to feel the gaze of central governments and the promise of nation. 'In the civilised world, no one [was to be] without a relationship to the state'.[104] This 'primary inscription of life in the state order' – this citizenship – 'names the new status of life as origin and ground of sovereignty and, therefore, literally identifies ... the members of the sovereign'.[105] Hence, the doubt raised by Montaigne's discussion of an individual's identity in Chapter Three ('We are Christians by the same title that we are Perigordians or Germans') becomes a political problem of inclusion in, or exclusion from, nation.[106]

Within nations, ethnic and linguistic minorities were marginalised and prevented from playing a greater role in public life, and treated as amoral, immoral, peripheral, barbaric, uncivilised. As Michael Ignatieff argues, nationalism 'does not simply "express" a pre-existent identity: it constitutes one. It divides/separates/re-classifies difference. It does so by abstracting from

100   Boehmer, 2002, p 4.   101   Phillips, 1996, p 7.   102   Torpey, 2000.
103   Ibid, pp 1–2.   104   Stoler, 2000, p 35.   105   Agamben, 1998, p 129.
106   Montaigne, 1958, Book II, Essay 12, 325.

real life. It is a fiction, an invented identity, a form of Narcissism'.[107] This is the same purpose behind Bacon's writing of the New Atlantis explored in Chapter Four. Nationalism 'turns neighbours into strangers, turns the permeable boundaries of identity into impassable frontiers'.[108]

Social theorists, such as Joseph de Gobineau and Houston Stewart Chamberlain popularised the idea of distinct Nordic-Aryan, Slavic and Semitic races in Europe, lending scientific credibility to the traditional concepts of Northern and Southern European stereotypes. The Italian anthropologist Cesare Lombroso wrote in 1871 that only 'white people', who had achieved 'the most perfect symmetry of bodily form' recognised 'the human right to life, respect for old age, women and the weak' and had created 'true nationalism'.[109] The Celtic populations in Wales, Scotland and Ireland, the Bretons, Basques and Occitans in France and the Basques and Catalans in Spain were disempowered and unrepresented in nation-building enterprises.[110]

In other cases, minority peoples were simply forced to go elsewhere. The Poles in the eastern regions of Germany were thus forcibly removed across the border into Russia in the 1880s and 1890s.[111] Jews and Roma/Gypsies were left without a place within any European nation. Jews were described as contrary to the nation-state; a 'cosmopolitan' people who lacked a sense of patriotism.[112] In fact, a Jewish nationalist movement would arise but its people would not be granted territory to settle in Europe. Likewise, itinerant Sinti and Roma Gypsies claimed no particular homeland and were compared to savages who steal children, practice cannibalism and generally create trouble.[113] The Old World responded with international legal agreements so that by 1906 Germany had bilateral treaties 'to combat the Gypsy nuisance' with Austria-Hungary, Belgium, Denmark, France, Italy, Luxembourg, Netherlands, Russia and Switzerland.[114] Gypsies thus became the nineteenth century equivalent of Grotius's pirates and robbers who could never form together into a sovereign state, 'although they may preserve among themselves that degree of subordination, which is absolutely necessary to the subsistence of all society'.[115] This paradoxical tendency of the nation to exclude as it unifies continues today as nations attempt to exclude from their frame of fantasy ungovernable, multilayered and polyphonic networks of people and discourses using the confessional laws of immigration to mark out and inscribe peoples into a realm of their own 'separateness'. This is nationalism; the solidification of sovereignty and self-representation; fragmented bodies within a fragmented unfinished whole. The Old World was attempting, despite all appearances, to conceive of itself as one body set against a fetishised world of savages from which it had itself

---

107 Ignatieff, 1995, p 14.   108 Ibid, p 19.   109 Cited in Phillips, 1996, p 8.
110 Phillips, 1996, p 16.   111 Ibid, p 9.   112 Ibid, p 12.   113 Ibid.
114 Ibid.   115 Grotius, 1814, Chapter 3.

evolved. Surely, this was not *barbarism* – the creation of a world where white man could arrive and walk in freedom, trade without tariff, and seek justice without interference?

> As for the industrial competition, the Chinaman and the Hindoo may drive certain kinds of white traders from the tropics; but more than this they cannot do. They can never change the status of the white laborer in his own home, for the latter can always protect himself, and as soon as he is seriously menaced, always will protect himself, by protective tariffs and stringent immigration laws.[116]

The western subject of modernity, defined by their race and their own labour power, was protected and predicated by their citizenry, that is, by nation. It is no wonder that interracial union caused such fear in the colonies in so far as it 'called into question the very criteria by which Europeanness could be identified, citizenship should be accorded and nationality assigned'.[117] The Baconian fantasy of nation had reached the new modern age, a point acknowledged by President Theodore Roosevelt in his call to expand peace and civility into 'the world's waste spaces', as well as to contain the savagery of the New World through protective trading and migration. Indeed, America had become the New Atlantis – a new world made old – an old world reborn into new life:

> [w]here immigrants, or the sons of immigrants, do not heartily and in good faith throw in their lot with us, but cling to the speech, the customs, the way of life, and the habits of thought of the Old World which they have left, they thereby harm both themselves and us. If they remain alien elements, unassimilated, and with interests separate from ours, they are mere obstructions to the current of our national life, and moreover, can get no good from it themselves. In fact, though we ourselves also suffer from their perversity, it is they who really suffer most.[118]

Just like in Bacon's fantasy, there is no mention here of women, or more specifically, the mothers of citizens. The mother sits where she is not to be seen, or 'she' is the country from whence the migrants have come. The sons of immigrants, however, are those called to maintain the cohesion of nation by confessing away their sinful origins and become instead one with the USA.

> It is an immense benefit to the European immigrant to change him into an American citizen. . . . The immigrant cannot possibly remain what he

116 Roosevelt, 1894b, pp 245–46.   117 Stoler, 2000, p 20.
118 Roosevelt, April 1894b, p 26.

was, or continue to be a member of the Old World society. If he tries to maintain his language, in a few generations it becomes a barbarous jargon; if he tries to maintain his old customs and ways of life, in a few generations he becomes an uncouth boor. He has cut himself off from the Old World and cannot retain his connection with it; and if he wishes ever to amount to anything he must throw himself heart and soul, and without reservation, into the new life to which he has come.[119]

Modern imperialism was thus a process of nation-building that included the assimilation of infectious 'alien elements' into the current of life as the Old is reborn into each new world nation that it conquers.

The problem is so to adjust the relations between two races of different ethnic type that the rights of neither be abridged nor jeoparded; that the backward race be trained so that it may enter into the possession of true freedom, while the forward race is enabled to preserve unharmed the high civilization wrought out by its forefathers. The working out of this problem must necessarily be slow; it is not possible in offhand fashion to obtain or to confer the priceless boons of freedom, industrial efficiency, political capacity, and domestic morality. Nor is it only necessary to train the colored man; it is quite necessary to train the white man, for on his shoulders rests a well-nigh unparalleled sociological responsibility. It is a problem demanding the best thought, the utmost patience, the most earnest effort, the broadest charity, of the statesman, the student, the philanthropist; of the leaders of thought in every department of our national life.[120]

Was this not the same 'problem' that was being 'worked out' at an international level since the beginning of the nineteenth century in the Concert of Europe?[121] Acting mainly through congresses, the Great Powers (Austria,

---

119 Ibid.   120 Roosevelt, 1905, p 464.
121 The Concert of Europe was formally constituted in the Quadruple Alliance of 20 November 1815. Its members were those powers that had defeated Napoleon and its objective was the protection of the newly won order. In this respect the Concert bears a strong resemblance to the Peace of Westphalia. British Foreign Secretary, Castlereagh thus argued in Parliament in May 1815 that:

> Much will undoubtedly be effected for the future repose of Europe by these Territorial Arrangements, which will furnish a more effectual barrier than has before existed against the ambition of France. But in order to render this Security as complete as possible, it seems necessary, at the point of a general Pacification, to form a Treaty to which all the principle Powers of Europe should be parties, fixed and recognized, and they should all bind themselves mutually to protect and support each other, against any attempt to infringe them – It should re-establish a general and comprehensive system of Public Law in Europe, and Provide, as far as possible, for repressing future attempts

Russia, Prussia and Great Britain) would decide the fate of the small countries, intervene in their affairs, define boundaries, exercise guardianship over states weaker than themselves, formulate rules, render judgments in controversies and enforce their decisions.

Territories and empires that had been pulled together by marriage, conquest and annexation, but with little or no attention to the wishes of the populations within them, were now granted national status by the Great Powers.[122] The Congress of Vienna claimed a right 'to issue or deny a certificate of birth to states and governments irrespective of their existence'.[123] Lord Palmerston, then a rising politician and later British Foreign Secretary, described the Congress of Vienna from September 1814 to June 1815 thus:

> The smaller sovereigns, Princes and states, had no representatives in the deciding congress, and no voice in the decisions in which their future destiny was determined. They were all obliged to yield to overruling power, and to submit to decisions which were the result, as the case might be, of justice or expediency, of generosity or of partiality, of regard to the welfare of nations, or of concession to personal solicitations.[124]

The citizens of international society were thus also placed under surveillance, given 'certificates of birth', and diplomatic 'passports' indicating a legal personality rooted in nation. Here, too, at the international level, the education, health, employment and morality of each state is assumed by the Great Powers for the welfare of all. Each member was to be measured against a background of savagery such that the Revolution of Naples led Austrian Chancellor Metternich to write:

> A nation half-barbaric, in absolute ignorance, of boundless superstition, hot-blooded as Africans, a nation that can neither read nor write, whose last word is the dagger, such a nation offers fine material for constitutional principles![125]

The Old World states were required, instead, to act as Christ had done; as a model to the unredeemed. The Christian nature of the Old World had been

to disturb the general Tranquillity, and above all, for restraining any projects of Aggrandizement and Calamities inflicted upon Europe since the disastrous era of the French Revolution. (Albrecht-Carrie, 1970, p 33).

122   Hence, nationalist revolts in the Balkans during the 1870s against Ottoman control and a war between Russia and Turkey were settled by a Great Power Agreement in the Treaty of Berlin of 1878. The Agreement recognised three new states, Romania, Serbia, and Montenegro, while Bulgaria was given autonomy within the Ottoman Empire.
123   Lord Palmerston cited in Anand, 1987, p 13.   124   Ibid.
125   Letter to Weinzirl 7 July 1820 cited in Schroeder, 1962, p 33.

transposed into a family of civilised nations in which the welfare of the smaller states was determined by the greater powers for the sake of peace.

The admission of Turkey into the folds of civilised nations in 1856 demonstrated that in order to maintain a European balance of power, the Great Powers of Europe were no longer concerned with signifiers of religion but with those of civilisation (not natural law but positivism). Thus 'civilised society' was recognised in national rather than religious (but nonetheless Christian) qualities. Hence, in a state visit to the Ottoman Empire, Kaiser Wilhelm II of Germany saw no reason not to declare himself protector of the world's Muslims[126] (given their territorial hold in the balance of power), and in 1917 Britain would see no reason not to answer the Jewish question with the creation of a national homeland in a land without people for a people without land. Now, trapped in the overdetermined narratives of post-colonial imperialism, peoples fight desperately for statehood leaving the genealogy of that state system unquestioned. As Leela Gandhi argues:

> Clearly, the nationalist work of psychological and cultural rehabilitation is a crucial and historically expedient phase in the liberation of a people consigned ... to barbarism, degradation and bestiality by the harsh rhetoric of the colonial civilising mission. Nonetheless, aggressive asseverations of cultural identity frequently come in the way of wider international solidarities.[127]

The broader framework of nationalism and international law thus inhibits a more subtle and sophisticated reading of the respective struggles for self-determination in the international community. The war over territorial statehood seems to be the only option for either party if they wish to be heard – if they wish to speak a language that will bring them representation.

The savage

To savage: 'to assail violently; maul.'[128]
During the nineteenth and early twentieth centuries, the savages of the New World comprised those peoples considered unable to possess sovereignty over their land and its resources. So savage were they that they had no capacity to exist in a lawful society. Jurists of international law introduced these people into international society as savages entitled to mere 'human recognition' and, by the end of the Imperial era, they became known instead as subjects of 'Category C mandate territories'. The changes were nominal; the peoples themselves were to remain subject to the international personality of the

---

126 Phillips, 1996, p 49.   127 Gandhi, 1998, p 123.
128 *The Macquarie Dictionary*, 1989.

power that had invaded their lands.[129] By absorbing these territories and their peoples into its civilised body, the Old World sought to govern them in the same way that it had governed its own peoples. The indigenous peoples were to be transformed into normalised and proper governable citizens or left as exceptions to humanity – as outlaws of nation.

The fantasy of the 'white man's burden' had the Old World believing that perhaps, with the appropriate techniques, indigenous peoples might be moulded like wax into the form of the white labourer of the Old World, improved upon and developed to fit the needs of the mercantile state, although their resistance was to indicate otherwise.

In the first issue of *The Australasian Anthropological Journal*, 10 August 1896, Australasia is described as having 'numerous kinds of men representing several ancient races'.[130] These representatives are not the newly arrived Europeans – these people had for many centuries been classified, catalogued, regulated, studied and individualised as part of the species of white men.

The ancient races of which we read are 'the various tribes of blacks in Australia' that have descended from three or four races of the black species of men: the Negritos or dwarf blacks of Africa and other islands of the Pacific; the harsh skinned, mop haired Papuas of India and the New Hebrides; and, the primitive Dravidians of the hills and forests of India.[131]

> after the three races of blacks referred to above had made their way into Asia and its islands, which were then united to the mainland, they there fished, hunted, and lived upon the products of the chase, and the forest, without agriculture, or domesticated animals and have so continued to hunt and exist, . . . up to the present: for it must be always remembered that it has been well established that a black of himself, while of pure race, or unless crossed with a higher type or race, or with people of a different kind of head and brain from that of the blacks, never invents any improvements, but remains the same hunter of the stone age type as his ancestors were.[132]

Represented here is the pure savage, the unmoulded wax form. These savages were the debt of humanity and, like the peoples of the Old Testament, an 'uncivilised and rude race'. 'Higher' races – like Christ – had come to mould

---

129 Anghie, 1999, pp 49–51.   130 'Introductory', 10 August 1896, p 3.
131 The woolly haired, thick lipped, flat nosed negroes of western Africa do not form part of the 'ethnological elements of the Australasian blacks' 'Introductory' 10 August 1896, pp 3, 5 and 14.
132 The work continues, 'from the earliest findings, these so-called "permanent varieties" have remained the same, unchanged in appearance, and are as different in every way, as are the numerous species of animals.' 'Introductory', 10 August 1896, p 5.

their sinfulness into a truer form of humanity, at least to the extent made possible by the rudeness of their minds:

> If taught by a higher race, he keeps what he learns but does not improve upon it or invent any advance by himself. . . . Therefore, . . . the three black races of Australia are in the same state as they were in the Stone Ages.[133]

These savage peoples are signified by their passivity and timelessness, existing within a concrete evolutionary hierarchy of human races. Already the emerging field of evolutionary biology that had become popular with Charles Darwin's work, *The Origin of the Species by Natural Selection* had introduced the idea that:

> [n]ew and improved varieties will inevitably supplant and exterminate the older, less improved and intermediate varieties . . . And as natural selection works solely by and for the good of each being, all corporeal and mental endowments will tend to progress towards perfection. . . . Thus, from the war of nature, from famine and death, the most exalted object, which we are capable of conceiving namely, the production of higher animals directly follows.[134]

The most exalted object – progress towards perfection – was thus introduced into humanity by means of a second coming of a higher kind, whose perfection supplants and exterminates the older and intermediate. Emerging from the fantasies of origin were manifestations of sin so marked as to be unredeemable and inevitably finite. Entire parts of humanity were to be written off. This was the form of white man's forgiveness of itself – humanity's confession. Many of the 'savages' were no longer to be seen as wax forms to be moulded into civilised man. Their minds and bodies were unable to be improved and were therefore ungovernable and of no value. Instead indigenous peoples were to be regarded as ancient forms of little use to contemporary circumstances. The evolutionary theories that came to supplant the Enlightenment ideas of the eighteenth century gave colonial settlers reason to abandon their attempts at embracing New World peoples as infantile wards and allowed them in many cases to regard the New World

---

133 'Introductory', 10 August 1896, p 5.
134 Williams, 1988; and Hirschman, 1981. The science of evolution was already taking shape in the work of 1809 by Frenchman Jean Lamark, *Philosophie Zoologique*. This book called into question the biblical version of creation. Later, Charles Lyell, who published *Principles of Geology* between 1830 and 1833, based his theories on *Philosophie Zoologique* and examined the increasing body of evidence that forces of a geological nature were responsible for changes and creation in the world.

peoples instead as superseded branches of humanity destined to become extinct.

The Old World filled the present and the future just as the New World lay in a forgotten past. Old World colonists, merchants and slave traders were of a different world and a future time. Thus, it was not so much a matter of conquest but one of the progress of time that caused the 'disappearance' of indigenous peoples and their cultures from disputed land; an invisible hand that directed the merchants toward prosperity and an evolved form of eugenics that justified the writing-off of other people's bodies and their labour.

In 1852 an Australian historian by the name of John West had written:

> The right of wandering hordes to engross vast regions – forever to retain exclusive property in the soil, and which would feed millions where hundreds are scattered – can never be maintained. . . . The assumption of sovereignty over a savage people is justified by necessity – that law, which gives to strength the control of weakness. It prevails everywhere: it may be either malignant or benevolent, but it is irresistible.[135]

Locke's state of nature meets Darwin's theory on evolution.[136] Race and technology signify the 'means of introducing . . . a fundamental division between those who must live and those who must die', as well as those who could be oppressed and exploited through the hierarchisation and partition of society.[137]

While race marks the very surface of humanity, technology acts as evidence of the proclaimed biological classifications of the fit and superior.[138] The theory of natural selection in its anthropological form gave European culture a self-fulfilling belief in itself as the pinnacle of all creation. The Old World invasion into virtually all of the world's territories was proof of one's natural

---

135 West, [1852], 1971, cited in Attwood, 1996, p xi.
136 These sorts of conclusions continue to be drawn today:

> The old way of life survived [before 1788]. But that way of life was doomed, even if the Papuans, the Javanese or the Maoris had been the first outsiders to settle in Australia . . . What happened to the Aborigines after 1788 had probably happened a few thousand years earlier to all our ancestors . . . All over the world, the relatively simple way of life of hunters and gathers was wrecked by the coming of people who domesticated plants and animals . . . Everywhere, groups of people lost their vast sweeps of land . . . Such a form of land use was bound to be overthrown or undermined. The world's history [i.e., progress] has depended heavily on the eclipse of this old and wasteful economic way of life . . . There is no way it could be preserved. The miracle is that it survived until 1788 and later' (cited in Attwood, 1996, p 110).

137 Balibar and Wallerstein, 1991, p 39. Foucault, February 1991, p 52, cited in Stoler, 1995, p 84.
138 Stoler, 1995, p 84.

right to possess it. It was not a far step to speed up the processes of nature. This is Hegel's 'path of history', allowing many to believe that the genocide and the extinction of New World peoples is a mark of progress. As a continuing belief it justifies the strict application of land rights legislation, economic sovereignty and the sceptical governmental regulation of indigenous affairs and self-determination. The Old World colonisation of the New was simply a step into the future. Race and culture now become marks of difference used to mask the violent outcome of religion, politics and commerce. Hugh Morgan, an historian of the late 1990s, has written of the indigenous peoples in Australia:

> Guilt industry people have great difficulty in accepting, or recognising, that [A]boriginal culture was so much less powerful than the culture of Europeans, that there was never any possibility in its survival. They also cannot understand that this statement has nothing to do with individual morality. Human nature is the same regardless of race . . . The necessity of choice forces us, in the end, to accept that cultures are not equal, that some cultures will expand and grow . . . The indisputable fact . . . is that throughout human history many cultures have died out because they were not strong enough to survive in competition with more powerful cultures.[139]

The colonisation of the New World recognises the genocide of indigenous societies by European settlers as the history of progress. Here, progress means the development of each nation through the sacrifice and/or redemption of peoples by means of violent invasion, genocide, rape, slaughter, racism, unjust laws, exclusion and disease. The progress of development is thus immutable – not a result of choice or individual morality but the inevitable coming of perfection.

'We', the people of the Old World are the future/progression, while, 'they', the people of the past, are the bygone/backward. The Old World has been consigned to a past (but not history) far from the peoples of today. Indigenous culture is portrayed as passive – incapable of innovation and deliberate development. Mercantilism thus merged with law and begot genocide. The law of the mercantile state, which had so carefully nursed the disciplinary powers of education and custom, turned to the evolutionary and economic 'sciences' to justify its inability to incorporate each individual into the body of nation. In the new centres of civilisation, the indigenous peoples were savaged so that the state was able to represent itself on the world stage as civilised. The colonial nations struggled to develop themselves in a competitive global environment. The clash between settler and savage and, later,

---

139 Morgan, 1993, cited in Markus, 1996, p 92.

citizen against non-citizen, is justified as a legitimate process of national development. The well-being of the colony must come first. The citizenry is equated to the state while the indigenous/non-citizen is left as tragic excess. The result is an extraordinary act of violence as the settler state gathers 'strength wherever it can be found for the ordeal of development', which is in turn a means to come to terms with the feelings of lack, of loss, of fragmentation.[140] Past and ongoing opposition by indigenous peoples to colonisation is ignored. Instead, the original inhabitants of the land are located in the temporal space left behind by the Old World when it entered into modernity. These mythical representations of indigenous peoples as a bygone people without the ability to 'develop' deny the strength and resistance of the indigenous polity and counter any suggestion that indigenous peoples are in fact modern, that the 'old way of life' has survived and re-formed, that it is not 'doomed', and that indigenous peoples are 'fighting back'.

Instead, the 'old ways' of indigenous peoples are rarely viewed as useful (progressive) except to those who seek to find ways out of modernity: authors of New Age literature, environmentalists within the sustainable development movement and the tourism industry, who have all gained from their 'regression' into aboriginal ways of knowing. The 'old ways' present a knowledge of the past from which we can pick and choose discarded ways of knowing or where we 'moderns' might find our lost spiritualism, while the current economic and industrial power wielded against great odds by indigenous peoples is overlooked.

Most of the knowledge and skills taken from indigenous peoples goes unacknowledged in so far as it is incorporated into the great initiative and ingenuity accorded to the early colonial settlers and explorers. As a consequence, indigenous knowledge is not credited as having repositioned non-indigenous systems of knowledge, although it is increasingly being appropriated as a source of future knowledge. The effect of viewing indigenous and non-indigenous histories as dichotomous – the 'traditional' and the 'modern' – presents the two communities as mutually exclusive, the only way of effecting change being through the replacement of the one by the other. Here the historical recognition of the colonial encounter serves only to found the beginnings of history – the fantastic origin of modernity. Indigenous resources are thus incorporated into the performance of nationalism, whereby colonial societies

> propel themselves forward to a certain sort of goal . . . by a certain sort of regression – by looking inwards, drawing more deeply upon their indigenous resources, resurrecting past folk-heroes and myths about themselves and so on.[141]

140 Nairn, 1977, p 348.   141 Ibid.

The contemporary lives of indigenous peoples living in territories still under the control of settled peoples remain for the most part erased by the violence of the Word. Like the subsequent immigrants arriving from the Third World into the First World, they are expected to assimilate, to exist silently under the significant culture not of their own making. It is really irrelevant whether the migration was chosen freely or not, once part of that nation, the migrant becomes subject to a course chosen by others.

Indigenous peoples today are not considered part of the Third World proclaimed at the Bandung Conference.[142] Nor are they directly subject to International Monetary Fund or World Bank conditionality; nor the security concerns of a transposed white man's burden hidden in the dark heart of international development agencies such as the United Nations Development Program or the many non-governmental organisations that continue to intervene in these countries as if across some tangible border between East and West, South and North, developed and undeveloped.[143] This is not to say, however, that the indigenous peoples in the West are not for the most part still considered in some ways inferior or underdeveloped, or that they are not subject to developmentalist theories of the civilising mission. Nor have these indigenous peoples ceased to seek a personality recognised by international law.[144] Certainly, indigenous peoples are finding some recognition at the international level, and, indeed, their movement continues to challenge the nationalist structures of international law. Their attempts to gain recognition and self-determination are opposed in large part by the belief that they already exist in the 'perfect' nation state. They have no where to go that is not already national. The governance of the colonising power is seen merely to be fulfilling its duty as a subject of civilisation, the very duty, of the Old World – to transform the New – to complete humankind's history, nation by nation.

The 'civilised', the 'barbaric' and the 'savage' worlds continue to exist in the constitution of the universalising, globalising force of Old World law. The illusion within this Rooseveltian call to civilisation is that following the annihilation of the threat of savagery and barbarism, the Old World of peace and civility will triumph and arrive at a universal identity with itself – it will reach the end of history.

---

142 In 1955 the Bandung Conference in Indonesia brought together 29 states from Asia and Africa.

143 See Orford, 2003.

144 This has led to debates, in both the International Labour Organisation (ILO) and the United Nations Working Group on Indigenous Populations, on whether or not to allow the reference to indigenous peoples as 'peoples' or 'populations'. The ILO uses both words, the Working Group uses the latter word only on the basis that the term 'peoples' strengthens the arguments for self-determination and territorial independence by the indigenous peoples. See Iorns, 1992, pp 202 and 212.

By placing itself at the end of history, the Old World of the civilised West also positioned itself as the model to be imitated by a figurative New World. The meaning of the West itself became figurative of 'prophecies of something that has always been, but which will remain veiled for men until the day when they behold the Saviour *revelata facie*, with the senses as well as in spirit'.[145] The Old World thus assumed an identity that was not only the 'tentative form of something eternal and timeless' but also one that represented itself as a form that 'always has been and always will be'. The civilised West had imagined itself as 'both tentative fragmentary reality, and veiled eternal reality'.[146] The Old World became the true reality – the developed world – while the undeveloped world remained a prefiguration of reality that had to recur fully within the national form moulded for it by the Old World. As the uncivilised spheres of barbarism and savagery were interpreted and integrated into the eternal plan of salvation, the more real they became.

Still, during the period of High Imperialism the world was yet to speak using the discourse of development and underdevelopment. The stage, however, had been set. President Truman was preparing to enter that stage and declare the world subject to the new discourse. The consequences of this discourse will be the focus of the sixth and final chapter of this genealogy.

145 Auerbach, 1984, pp 59–60.   146 Ibid.

Chapter 6

The art of development

This chapter begins by focusing on a sense of crisis experienced by the Old World which took place following the Second World War. However, the horrors of that war and the corresponding failure of the rule of law are not the subjects of this chapter's investigation of crisis. It should be clear from Chapter Five that the barbarism and savagery of the Second World War were no less than the horrendous intensification of the violent deployment of national power by European states in the preceding centuries. The sense of crisis focused on here is the fear of Marxism and its political manifestation in communism.

The alternative narratives of salvation inherent in the discourses of communism during the Cold War era threatened and exposed the 'invisible hand' of capitalism since much of the threat of socialist revolution was taking place in the newly independent nations of the Third World. The very identity of the Old World both as the promise and final stages of an ideal civilisation were under threat. Communist theories brought into question the claim by the Old World – as represented by the United States of America – that it possessed the keys of absolution. This communist challenge distracted the gaze of the New World and intensified the sense of redundancy felt by the imperial powers in their relation to the newly independent colonies. It was therefore essential for the Old World both to defeat the threat inherent in the 'false philosophy' of communism, as well as to maintain the 'newly independent' world as its binary limit. Success in both of these aims was necessary if existing relations of power at both the international and the national level were to be protected. Hence, President Truman issued a declaration in his inaugural address to Congress on 20 January 1949.

The declaration contained two themes. The first declaration was a declaration of war against communism, which was said to represent 'a regime with contrary aims and a totally different concept of life'. The second concerned the apparent duty of the 'developed' world to intervene in the 'underdeveloped' regions in order to improve them.[1] This chapter is concerned with the consequential events of the latter declaration.[2]

In making his declaration, President Truman, as the leader of the often-called 'free world', was essentially marking out underdeveloped regions of the world in order that they continue to acknowledge their indebtedness to the promise of capitalist development. Truman's address represented the origin of a new purposive existence for the Old, now developed, World. The event of his address was the awaited Second Coming. The prophecies that a New Atlantis would rise from a state of savagery had been realised.[3] Hegel had predicted it: the USA was 'the land of the future, where in the ages that lie before us, the burden of the World's History shall reveal itself'.[4]

From this perspective, the USA undertook to restore Old World identity by building 'an even stronger structure of international order and justice'.[5] This was the 'lot' of the USA; 'to experience, and in large measure to bring about, a major turning point in the long history of the human race'[6] – to fulfil the desire of peace on earth.

> The supreme need of our time is for men to learn to live together in peace and harmony. . . . In this time of doubt, they look to the United States as never before for good will, strength, and wise leadership. It is fitting, there-fore, that we . . . declare our aims to all peoples. . . . Above all else, our people desire, and are determined to work for, peace on earth – a just and lasting peace – based on genuine agreement freely arrived at by equals.[7]

In this statement, Truman expressed the post-world war promise of develop-ment in terms of a new peace desired by *its* people, and open only to their *equals*. The post-war era was thus a restructuring of imperialism and a call to make equal what was new. In this 'time of doubt' President Truman outlined his Four Point programme 'for peace and freedom', comprising:

(1) the support of the United Nations and its related agencies 'to strengthen their authority and increase their effectiveness';
(2) the creation and administration of world economic recovery, especially of Europe under the Marshall Plan;
(3) the formation of collective defence arrangements; and
(4) a programme of technical assistance for underdeveloped areas.[8]

---

1 Truman, 20 January 1949.
2 For a post-Cold War perspective, see the works of Orford, which provide a detailed analysis of the interrelated topics of the Cold War and First World intervention in the Third World; Orford, 1997; Orford, 1996a and b; Orford, 2003.
3 '[I]n the beginning all the world was America' Locke, 1960, Section 49.
4 Hegel, 1956, p 86.   5 Truman, 20 January 1949.   6 Ibid.   7 Ibid.
8 Ibid.

The second and fourth points of the programme divided the world in such a way as to maintain an ongoing difference between the Old and New Worlds as two distinct 'projects'. In this way, the underdeveloped regions of the New World were opposed to Europe's own post-war poverty, which was instead represented as the sins of a prodigal son. The aim of the European programme was 'to invigorate and strengthen democracy in Europe, so that the free people of that continent [could] resume their rightful place in the forefront of civilization' and 'contribute once more to the security and welfare of the world'.[9]

At the same moment that the Old World was revealed in all its developed glory, the *underdeveloped* world was christened into being, together with the discursive foundations of a new deployment of power:

> More than half the people of the world are living in conditions approaching *misery*. Their food is inadequate. They are *victims* of disease. Their economic life is *primitive* and *stagnant*. *Their* poverty is a handicap and a threat both to them and to more prosperous areas. For the first time in history, *humanity* possesses the knowledge and the skill to relieve the suffering of *these people*. All countries, including our own, will greatly benefit from a constructive program for the better use of the world's *human* and *natural* resources. Experience shows that our *commerce with other countries expands as they progress industrially and economically.* Greater *production is the key to prosperity and peace.* And the key to greater production is a wider and more *vigorous application of modern scientific and technical knowledge.*[10]

The existing construction of the binary relationship between the Old World and the New World made sense of Truman's assertion that for the first time in history, '*humanity* possesses the knowledge and the skill to relieve the suffering of *these people*' as if 'these people' were not yet 'redeemed' and somehow not yet a part of what it was to be human. The developed world was thus made to represent the promise of development and all that it might embody because '[a]t least half of the peoples of the World are living, by no fault of their own, under such poor and inadequate conditions that *they* cannot, out of their own scanty resources, achieve decent standards of living'.[11]

Dependent on both 'human' and 'natural' resources and 'modern scientific and technical knowledge', the Four Point Program responded to Bacon's call to humanity to restore its dominion over nature. The inner logic of economic growth and technological advance incorporated developing nations into a

9 Ibid.   10 Emphasis added. Truman, 20 January 1949.
11 Emphasis added. UN Economic and Social Council First Year, Official Records, Second Session, p 227, cited in De Senarclens, 1997, p 191.

universal historical trajectory. The individual people living in the 'under-developed regions' were seen not as people but as an economic and technical problem of incorporation.[12]

The assumption of a First World burden would not have been possible without the preceding centuries of imperial aggrandisement both within and beyond the boundaries of the Old World. Already the 'miserable poverty' and 'stagnant primitivism' of more than half the world's people had been assumed by the narratives of New World deficiency, which had for centuries enabled the Old World to maintain its own identity as one of civilisation and peace. The 'underdeveloped' regions of the world were thus imbued with untransformed, backward and vulnerable powerlessness; regions with a low dependency on creativity and innovation akin to Bacon's description of the indigenous Americans, 'the poor remnant of human seed . . . being simple and savage people, . . . they were not able to leave letters, arts, civility to their prosperity'.[13]

These disempowering discourses calmed the fears and fed the desires of the Old World by erasing the revolutionary potential of 'more than half the world's people', as well as their current exploitation and oppression. In line with the changing and potentially destructive international topography of a new world order, the 'civilised' nations of the Old World were only too willing to replace the older divisions between the civilised and the savage with the 'developed' and the 'underdeveloped' in order to maintain the cohesion of a Westphalian Peace of the Old World order. The discourse of develop-ment offered the Old World a new symbolic order to suppress the threatening narratives of communism and, one might add, democracy, without sacrificing its binary relationship to the New World.

By renaming the New World, the Old World merely sought to re-mould and re-animate the subject-to-be into a field of representation authorised by the Old World.[14] The peoples of the underdeveloped world were made to acknowledge their indebtedness to the market – the God of economic prosperity. In this way the maintenance of an international division of labour within a global market was preserved and expanded in ways similar to the practices of the imperial powers of the eighteenth and nineteenth centur-ies described in the previous chapters. The existing logic of imperialism allowed development aid to penetrate emerging post-colonial nations as if the transfer of resources were an acknowledged burden of the metropolitan powers rather than the colonisation of markets for foreign trade and capital-ist investment. At the commencement of the post-colonial period, France and Britain continually defended the efforts they were making on behalf of

---

12 As Arturo Escobar argues, because 'the essential trait of the Third World was its poverty', 'economic growth and development' were the answers to its salvation (Escobar, 1995).
13 See Chapter Four, above.
14 Lacan, 1993, p 9. See also, Stavrakakis, 1999, p 19.

development 'to realise the potential of the countries under trusteeship'.[15] In 1947 M Laurentine, the French delegate to the Trusteeship Council expressed his satisfaction in seeing his country bring a 'Western mode of reasoning' to the populations of Africa.[16] In 1951 the US delegate to the United Nations General Assembly described the investment of capital and economic and technical aid as a continuation of missionary activities.[17] The flow of commodities and the exploitation of human and natural resources in the 'underdeveloped' world thereby remained accessible to the Old World powers by means of 'poverty eradication' and 'technology transfers', which represented a legitimate means of intervention by the developed world as it undertook to discharge the debt of the underdeveloped regions.[18]

Development's self determination

The ostensible liberation of the New World from its savagery was predominantly constrained by the essential criteria of nationalism – a criteria aimed at maintaining the existing structure in which disciplined subjects defined legally by the concept of national sovereignty remained elementary parts of a greater whole coming together in accordance with humanity's rate of 'progress'. The object-cause of this progress continued to be framed in the promise of self-determination making equal what was new. No stone could be left unturned in that search to overcome the mystery of wholeness – socio-economic globalisation was essential if humanity was to enter a time without space – a time now defined in market terms. The values of nation and the values of development were inseparable.[19] The world continued to be constituted 'not merely to contain resistance and encourage accommodation but to seek to ensure that both could only be defined in relation to the categories and structures of modern political rationalities'.[20]

The modern discourses of development and globalisation did not therefore threaten the nation state; they (re)constituted it. The structure of a Westphalian Peace remained as an assembly of states operating within an international trading space; the globalisation of which was to bring with it the liberalisation of goods and services and the freedom of commoditised peoples. The very nationalism which provided peoples with a sense of 'belonging to a place, a people, a heritage' – 'the home created by a community of language, culture and customs[21] – was thereby bound to a more silent and insidious annihilation of identity. This was Third World repentance; the corresponding subjection of the Third World to the assumed superiority of the First World

---

15 De Senarclens, 1997, p 192.   16 Cited in De Senarclens, 1997, p 192.   17 Ibid.
18 See Orford and Beard, 1998 and Escobar, 1995.
19 Ahluwalia, 2001, p 71. See also, Chatterjee, 1993, p 3.   20 Scott, 1995, p 214.
21 Said, 1993, p 26.

as symbol of a redeemed humanity. Just as Augustine's answer to humanity's redemption had been to return to God by seeking to bring himself into subjection to Him, not in order to become equal with God, but rather to become 'boundlessly free' under His sole domination, so too, the Third World was expected to seek freedom from imperialism by bringing itself under the sole domination of a system of sovereign states operating within an interdependent global system.[22]

Post-colonial nations were allowed to reconstruct the past and present identities of their peoples only in so far as they did not threaten the sense of superiority of First World states. Nationhood was a 'gift' from Europe to 'the rest of the world'.[23] This gift of sovereignty was effectively the same gift of christening given by the Church to its members in order to secure its collective identity, and it was also the same 'gift' of naming employed by European explorers as they sought to bind the New World into a prescribed alliance. As Leela Gandhi argues, nationalism outside the West could only ever be 'premature and partial' and 'symptomatic of a failed or "incomplete" modernity'.[24] This was because the Third World remained at once the origin and cause of Old World lack – the point from which the Old World could see itself as an ideal world, thereby lending authority to its fantasy of its benevolent mission to restore the unredeemed parts of the world to wholeness.

Amin argues that the push toward 'growth with democratisation' in the West benefited many of the national liberation movements in the Third World, as well as promoting economic growth in the South 'in any number of ways'.[25] Yet in many other ways, the very production of a self-determining Third World had been seized by the First World and divested of its potential liberatory meaning. This included the outcomes of the 1955 Conference in Bandung, Indonesia, when the divide between developed and undeveloped nations was taken as an opportunity for the so-called 'emerging nations' to determine themselves. At that conference, the term 'Third World' was adopted by 29 states from Asia and Africa to indicate their independent desire to forge a third way into the world system.[26] In this way, three-quarters of the world's population (the peoples of the Middle East, Africa, the Caribbean, Latin America, Oceania, and most of South, Southeast, and East Asia) were to become known as a world that 'wanted to be something'.[27]

22 Augustine, 1966, Book I, Chapter 12.21.   23 Chatterjee, 1993, p 4.
24 Gandhi, 1998, p 108.   25 Amin, 1997, pp 94–95.   26 Spivak, 1996, p 270.
27 The French demographer Alfred Sauvy coined the expression '*tiers monde*' in French in 1952 by analogy with the 'third estate'. Like the third estate, wrote Sauvy, the Third World is nothing, and it 'wants to be something'. In 1956 a group of social scientists associated with Sauvy's National Institute of Demographic Studies, in Paris, published a book called *Le Tiers-Monde*. Three years later, the French economist Francois Perroux launched a new journal, on problems of 'underdevelopment', with the same title. The term was in common use by the end of the 1950s.

What this 'something' might be has yet to be signified in a way that deconstructs the allure of development discourse. The Third World, despite its own attempt to name itself, and thus its 'development', has continued to operate within the bounds of a Hegelian history that constructs national boundaries in ways that benefits a minority of people in a minority of nation states by exploiting the rest of the world's peoples and resources. According to Kum Kum Sangari, the 'Third World' is 'a term that both signifies and blurs the functioning of an economic, political, and imaginary geography able to unite vast and vastly differentiated areas of the world into a single "underdeveloped" terrain'.[28] From this perspective, underdevelopment has become interchangeable with a number of post-world war references including: 'the South; 'the non-industrialised world'; 'the undeveloped world'; and 'the world of emerging nations'. The New World remains a symptom of what the Old World is attempting to define itself out of. There is little mention of why the international division of worlds remains in place – the colonial past and its ongoing practices have been, and continue to be, erased. Development discourse refuses to re-think the premise of Westphalian Peace and the production of an international division of labour, which erases 'the historical text of imperialist expropriation, the statistics on the flow of resources from the South to the North and the effects on [transnational corporate] capital flight'.[29] While it is true that a reallocation of capital, technology and resources might be wanted and needed, the kind of assistance provided is largely of another kind. It is a form of assistance constrained by a discourse of development that fails to address principles of sovereignty and self-determination that it is ostensibly there to sustain.

The Old World order

To maintain the presence of a Westphalian Peace, the narrative of development was accompanied by the creation of an entirely new institutional framework of international economic and political governance. The United Nations Charter, concluded at the San Francisco Conference from April to June 1945, was meant not only to 'save succeeding generations from the scourge of war' and 'to maintain peace and security', but also 'to develop friendly relations among nations based on the respect for equal rights and self-determination of peoples'.[30] Despite two world wars having emerged in Europe, already in 1946 the Temporary Social Commission on Social Affairs was stating that it was:

28 Sangari, 1990, p 217. See also, Mohanty, 1991, p 5.   29 Guest, 1997, p 86.
30 Article 1 of The Charter of the United Nations, which was signed on 26 June 1945 in San Francisco at the conclusion of the United Nations Conference on International Organization and came into force on 24 October 1945.

[t]he deep gulfs existing between the standards of living of different nations and people are, in the opinion of the Commission, a main source of international discontent, unrest, crisis and, in the last resort, are causes of wars ultimately endangering and devastating countries of high as well as low standards of living. . . .[31]

The threat to peace was located in the poverty of the underdeveloped regions and not in the divisions of the system itself. Indeed, the political system of united nations was strengthened with the Bretton Woods economic organs, which were meant to provide the regulatory framework necessary to address the fear of the Westphalian state structure collapsing back into the economic insecurity of the first half of the twentieth century.[32]

The International Monetary Fund (IMF) and the World Bank were major actors in the management of fear left open by the possibility that the Third World would yield to the temptation of communist or democratic promises.[33] Interestingly, the USA did not support the creation of an international free trade agreement at Bretton Woods. Even today most nations have not entered into the freedom of a global market between all nations. Although membership of international economic organisations such as the World Trade Organisation, the IMF or World Bank agencies might be described as 'global', the politics of weighted voting systems, negotiated agreements or problematic mechanisms of dispute resolution limit the manner in which developing countries manage themselves within that market.[34] Indeed, given the dependence of capitalism on the disciplinary power of the nation state to regulate the bodies of individual labouring subjects, the concept of a borderless global capitalism itself carried and continues to carry with it a certain limit.

Development theories were not limited, of course, to the institutions of capitalist governments. During the Cold War period international development theories and associated aid were used to secure political allies, either in the name of communism or capitalism.[35] Between the end of the Second

---

31 Economic and Social Council First Year, Official Records, Second Session, p 227 cited in De Senarclens, 1997, p 191.
32 The World Bank and the IMF were established at a conference held at Bretton Woods, New Hamphsire in 1944 following decades of negotiations and planning on the part of the USA and Britain. An International Trade Organization was proposed but not established. Instead, international trade was provisionally regulated by reference to a multilateral trade agreement, the General Agreement on Tariff and Trade (GATT). It was not until 1994 that the third limb to the Bretton Woods framework was given institutional form by the creation of the World Trade Organisation (WTO). The World Bank was created to aid post-war reconstruction in Europe and the IMF was designed to maintain the balance of payments between nations.
33 See Pahuja, 2000, p 749.
34 See, for examples, Kurtz, 2004; Cho, 2004; Gerhart and Seema Kella, 2005; Head, 2004; Chimni, 2004.
35 See the work of Escobar, 1995.

World War and the end of the Cold War, the chief criticisms of western development by its socialist adversaries in the Second World were made predominantly from the same 'culturally and intellectually circumscribed perspective' with respect to the Third World.[36] As a consequence, many socialist critiques left unquestioned the traditional view of development as the task of inscribing modernisation onto the 'blank slates' of the Third World – of replacing 'useless traditions' with valuable practices and industry. Socialist development sought, rather, to 'educate' the peoples of the Third World out of its 'false consciousness'. As Kaplan has observed, development must be 'created and engineered. . . . It does not exist in and of itself. Interventions, projects, are designed specifically to "bring" development to those amongst whom it is lacking'.[37]

The celebrated report, produced by the group led by Raul Prebisch for the Economic Commission for Latin America, is illustrative of a socialist critique that takes the deficiency of the New World as its starting point to argue that the unequal relationship between the developed and the developing countries is an outcome of a continuous disadvantage for the latter within international trade.[38] The difficulty faced by all of these critiques, of course, was the challenge of speaking outside the historical dualism of a world already divided by centuries of physical and discursive violence. In most cases the binary nature of worlds was sustained and naturalised, as was the importance of the socialist nation state. While these theories of dependency became essential to a proper understanding of the effects of development theory and practice, they remained within the universalising narratives of a binary global development.[39] That is, they failed to question the construction of development itself and its constitutional narratives of predestination and their inscriptions of nation, race, gender, class, modernity, time, space and lawfulness.[40]

Neither capitalism nor socialism was willing to offer an alternative challenge to progress or the division of worlds as a dichotomy between developed and underdeveloped regions. There was little recognition by either approach that there may be a diversity of approaches to human being and becoming outside the Westphalian system of nation states. The threat of communism had effectively converted the Old World narratives of previous centuries, which had focused on the rule of law and correlated notions of civility, into narratives concerned with economic superiority and the opportunity to exploit one's own labour. Cold War politics, which were framed by the threat of total annihilation, simply did not allow socialist or indeed capitalist theorists to construct alternative forms of governance. Economic interdependence

36 Walker, 1982, p 182.   37 Kaplan, 1999, p 24.
38 Cardoso and Faletto, 1979, p viii. See Baran, 1957; Frank, 1972; Cardoso and Faletto, 1979; Galtung, 1971.
39 Pennycook, 1994, p 56.   40 See Beard, 2001, p 6.

aside, military violence was what was keeping the Peace of Westphalia alive. As a consequence, 'these people' of the 'underdeveloped regions' were unable to dislocate themselves from an origin located in savagery or to cast their future by means other than particularly western-Christian ideas of (unsustainable) progress.

The recession of socialism generally in the 1990s encouraged claims by First World advocates that the end of history had been reached, giving birth to a new era of global capitalism no longer obstructed by socialist nation-building. The task of development since the end of the Cold War has become one of liberal-democratic 'nation-building' and 'good governance', although more recently this has given way to the war against terror.

Even the present war against terror is based on an agenda of development. If one reads carefully the genealogy of development, it is fair to view the 2002 Joint Senate Resolution 46, approved by the Congress, authorising the use of military force, against Iraq as a continued attempt by the First World to eliminate all identities but those recognised by the 'family of nations'. And as Columbus recognised in his discovery of the New World, with the power of naming comes the power to take possession. In a covering statement to the *National Security Strategy* of 20 September 2002, President George W Bush reminded us of the origins of our current identity when he wrote that the 'great struggles of the twentieth century between liberty and totalitarianism ended with a decisive victory for the forces of freedom – and a single model for national success: freedom, democracy, and free enterprise'.[41] Finding 'their prisoners' courage stronger than their torments' the Old World is currently in Iraq repeating the trauma inflicted by the Spanish on the peoples of a newly discovered world.[42] The Peace of Westphalia is alive and well. The First World has been assured by President George W Bush that:

> as we defend peace, we will also take advantage of an historic opportunity to preserve the peace. Today, the international community has the best chance since the rise of the nation-state in the seventeenth century to build a world where great powers compete in peace instead of continually prepare for war. Today, the world's great powers find ourselves on the same side – united by common dangers of terrorist violence and chaos'.[43]

While Osama bin Laden attempts to threaten western identity by constructing a certain Islamic identity that splits the world along changed lines of alterity, the USA and its allies fight to eliminate that threat and maintain instead the transcendental identity of a First World that exists in a space of promise outside time. Columbus's wonder, it would seem, has been burnt

---

41 Bush, 2002.   42 See Montaigne, 1958, Book III, Essay 6, p 697.   43 Bush, 2002.

onto the collective memory of the First World, disabling its peoples from finding their way back to earth's presence. In order to respond to the terror of another world, which seeks recognition, the First World has begun instead to once again re-authorise its myth of origin while the Baconian experiment of nation is being perfected.

Capitalism is left to silently manage a globalised sovereign realm of exchange, which embodies the increasing economic integration (globalisation) of the new world order, while the sovereign lawmakers get on with their own business of savage transformation. The failure to meet the promise of globalisation – in so far as capitalism 'pretends to have resolved what cannot in fact be resolved in terms of the market' is now to be blamed on the terrorism of others.[44]

The global capitalism heralded by modernity will always remain incomplete as long as the debt of its tragic excess survives. Any globalism requires the sacrifice of First World transcendence – until that sacrifice is made, globalisation/totality/development, call it what you will, remains impossible. Needless to say, the perception of a world surviving in the wake of an unfulfilled promise is transferred from the 'transcendent' realm of the First World to the heat of some underdeveloped darkness; an erased memory of historical progress. The implication of development discourse is that it is these hearts of darkness that threaten world peace by preventing capitalism from getting on with business. Capitalism thereby remains mysteriously sacred – a phenomenon that cannot be questioned let alone revealed.[45]

The First World market place

The Old World has renamed itself variously as 'modernity, 'the West', 'the First World', or 'the developed world'. More recently these latter terms have been expanded to include parts of the New World not considered 'western', such as South Korea and Japan, in the same way that 'barbaric' territories were admitted into the family of 'civilised nations' during the nineteenth century once they were able to enter into international trade relations on equal terms. This has not posed a threat to the discursive or geographical 'cohesion' of the First World, however, because these incorporated nation states were offered up either as examples of the spread of peace – of nation-building and development – of a New World redeemed into a New Atlantis, or as economically advanced but lacking in justice.

Still further, there is no freedom in this system of accounting for developing nations to 'be something' other than a First World marketplace. If a state fails to produce a mercantile environment, its functions must be usurped by nation-building organisations, most often the World Bank or the IMF, if not

44 Lazarus, 1999, p 44.   45 Derrida, 1976, p 266. See also, Guest, 1997, p 79.

by the host of non-governmental organisations (NGOs).[46] Government action in the underdeveloped world has become subject to a duty of care to prevent the risks of expropriation, civil unrest, and currency inconvertibility that one would arguably have assumed to rest with private enterprise. Indeed, the insurance market provides the perfect illustration of how development practice and the rule of law work together to hide the tragic excesses of capitalism from their books. In a paper given at the World Bank-sponsored conference, Private Infrastructure for Development: Confronting Political and Regulatory Risks, Nina Bubnova described the historical reasons for political risk insurance:

> The first major shock to the stability of the international regime of private foreign investment appeared with the Russian Socialist Revolution of 1917, which brought about the nationalisation of foreign and domestic investment. Similar events took place decades later, with revolutionary transformations in China, Eastern Europe, Egypt. Classified as 'strategic', natural resource exploration infrastructure was expropriated in Mexico (1938), Iran (1951) and Bolivia (1952). In 1971, assets of the British Petroleum Exploratory Company (Libya) Ltd were expropriated by the Libyan authorities. In the 1980s, Tiananmen Square in China changed what had been considered a safe environment for foreign investment, bringing about US$10 billion in uninsured losses. The drug war in previously stable Columbia had had a similar effect. While most of the 1990s have been characterised by an expansion in private infrastructure investment demand and supply, economic and political crises occurred in Asia, Latin America and Eastern Europe in 1998. The crises involved real losses, dramatically increased investors' perception of market risk, and increased their awareness of the need for adequate political risk management. Political risk is a reality.[47]

Revolution, peoples' resistance to abuses of power, and liberation are all risks that stand in the way of foreign investment in the Third World. The student uprising for greater freedom against the abuse of a sovereign government clinging to 'the false philosophy' of communism is condemned because it ruined a 'safe environment for foreign investment'. The losses of that uprising are not the loss of life, of freedom or democratic processes but US$10 billion in uninsured losses. Money and financial opportunity are the 'real losses' being suffered in the Third World, lending credence to the notion of the Third World as the unredeemed debt of a global world.

The conclusion to be drawn from texts such as these is that the international laws regulating and insuring against financial risk exist first to secure

---

46 Ahluwalia, 2001, pp 53–54.   47 Bubnova, 1999.

the well-being of foreign investors and their agents rather than the ostensible benefactors of development, the citizens of developing nations or the nation state itself. As stated in the abstract of the World Bank-sponsored conference, 'While risks of this kind are not unique to developing countries, perceptions of risk are typically greater in countries that have not yet established long track-records in treating private investors fairly'.[48]

Here, the global market is presumed to be a level playing field ruined by the foul play of those without an established track record in fairness. The continued inequality between the First World and the Third World, the ongoing restrictions on trade, the conditionality of IMF loans, the lack of accountability of global corporations and the refusal by the First World to forgive Third World debt are rarely part of this debate about fairness and volatility in the marketplace.

The 1997 financial crisis (of which Thailand, Indonesia, Malaysia and Korea felt the greatest impact) is a good example of a global crisis that ultimately came to be blamed on a failure by the Third World states to keep up with the promise of development. East Asia had only itself to blame because the 'Asian governments had relied too much on centralised state co-ordination rather than decentralised market incentives to maintain their progress'.[49] As Randy Martin observes, the 'poorly supervised and inadequately regulated' markets are represented as an 'absence of cool reason from Asian globalizers that might have averted the whole mess'.[50] The real failure of 'excessive corporate leverage, financial fragility resulting from poorly designed capital market liberalisation, foreign indebtedness, a slow-down in export markets, worsening terms of trade, and the development of overcapacity in many sectors' remains a secret confined to the corridors of greater powers where the blame for the 'unforeseen' nature of the crisis is placed on the failed governance of the Third World states themselves: 'The flaws were invisible even to the keenest-eyed investor, because financial institutions of the East lack what is called "transparency" '.[51] Based on this premise, 'crony capitalism' and 'relationship-based banking' could only be remedied by greater foreign ownership of national Asian banks to check cultural deficits.[52]

Meanwhile, the hot irons of structural adjustment programmes enforced by international development agencies worked to ensure that inflation would be kept low so that predictions could be made more easily because present and future values could not be greatly distorted. Policies of transparency only ensured that 'estimates for the medium-term budget frameworks become contractual hard-budget constraints for nations seeking international loans, credits and underwriting'.[53] Those were the 'New Arrangements to Borrow' (NAB) provided by the IMF as of 17 November 1998 and the outcome of the

48 Ibid.   49 Clinton, 1999, p 228.   50 Martin, 1999, p 6.   51 Ibid.
52 Ibid.   53 Ibid. See International Monetary Fund, 1998.

panic induced by the 'Asian financial crisis' during the late 1990s: an increase of debt on account of the Third World.

The recovery was no more than the further appropriation of the 'under-developed regions' for 'the preservation and constitution' of the developed world's 'process of the discovery of truth, the establishment of knowledge'.[54] Third World states were thus made to shoulder the blame for the volatility in international finance and investment; the capitalist market itself remained unaccountable.

Development agencies, in a similar fashion, are accountable only to each other in ensuring that governments are made accountable to investors only. In their Common Ground and Common Concerns: Communiqué of the CAPA – World Bank Conference, the churches and the World Bank formed a mutual partnership that recognised that they both have 'limitations and failures in understanding and in carrying out our missions of poverty allevi-ation'. They sought, therefore, 'to improve our mutual understanding and hold each other to mutual accountability'.[55] This fulfils the 'prophetic mis-sion of advocacy' of the Christian Church in support of honesty, integrity and accountability, all of which was important for building confidence among investors, as well as ensuring a just society. Likewise, external failures on a global scale were referred to implicitly in a commitment by the churches and the World Bank to increase the understanding and promotion of fair trade and debt reduction. That these effects might be inevitable consequences of the (Christian) business expertise they promote begs the question.

Where no national government is in a position to be brought to account, NGOs must take that place so that individual subjects of development might enter into communion with development's promise. Non-governmental organisations have infiltrated into the workings of states to fill the void left by their own 'constitutional' failure. 'Where good governance does not exist, new mechanisms should be tried to channel the benefits of debt relief directly to the poor'.[56] The effect is a privatisation of government accountability.[57] Traditional intra-governmental activity becomes a new network of relation-ships of accountability between the non-governmental sector and their fund-ing agencies (usually located in the First World). As Ian Gary observes, 'NGOs in their perceived ability to deliver "development", foster participa-tion, promote civil society, and lessen the social cost of adjustment on "vul-nerable groups" fit in perfectly with the agenda to weaken state governance in the developing world'.[58]

When NGOs become the recipients of foreign aid, they weaken the legit-imacy of national governments, leaving them further reliant on IMF and

54 Spivak, 1976, p xxvi.   55 Belshaw, Calderisi and Sugden, 2001, p 8.
56 Ibid, p 14.   57 Duncanson, 1997.   58 Gary, 1996, p 163.

World Bank lending.[59] Ironically, the governments who take out the loans *are* often corrupt or illegitimate. This does not prevent international development agencies, private banks and the governments of many developed nations making loans to these governments. Such loans are irresponsible and commercially negligent. Yet, very little criticism has been made at an official level of these assistance programmes or their effects. No one is imposing sanctions on these lenders, revoking their authority to lend or requiring them to face the financial consequences of improper lending. Instead, these lenders are 'rescued' while the individuals within the borrower nations, who would have had little or no say about the loans, are brought to account and made to suffer the cost of indebtedness. 'These people', the body politic of the nation state onto which the immutable justice of development discourse inscribes pain through International Monetary Fund and World Bank conditionality, military intervention, economic sanctions and unjust trading conditions.[60] Under these circumstances, the aim of self-determination becomes beside the point. The assumption is that 'these people' who have survived the violent invasion of imperialist aggrandisement still require outside help in order to improve their quality of life.

The people most vulnerable to the interventions of development agencies are those living in so-called 'collapsed states' in the Third World; the formless state that suits well the bio-political disciplinary practices of international development expertise. These are the exceptions to the history of progress. They exist as outlaws – like pirates on the high seas – beyond the right to development, which is based on the assumed existence of the nation state. For the right to development is not made possible as an inherent human right regardless of the state structure but is instead an inscription of value onto human life by the juridico-political discipline of the nation state. People are conscripted into the forces of development out of necessity not right. The strict immigration laws of the developed world serve as one of the more evident reminders of this.[61] In western philosophical terms, the 'collapsed' state, where a sovereign government can no longer perform the basic functions required to politically sustain a community of people, is no more than a state of nature. The failed state is one that has not progressed into modernity. It suffers stunted growth and an unsound capacity to engage in activities normally allowed to a state. It has failed to develop. This is the development discourse within which the World Bank and the IMF have launched and continue to run structural adjustment programmes in response to the failure of Third World states to manage their own 'development' in the 1980s. The idea was to push these states back into some semblance of sanity based on the 'natural workings of the economy' and the mercantile state.

59 Ahluwalia, 2001, p 54.   60 See generally, the work of Orford.
61 See the work of Noll, 2004.

What development discourse fails to admit is that those surviving without the state, place the mythical origins of sovereignty in crisis by revealing the non-original relationship between human survival and national governance. The same logic reduces 'underdeveloped' peoples to their 'lack', to the level of individual 'values', 'attitudes' and 'motivation'. Structural change is thus constructed as a simple matter of form, of 'educating' people, or even just convincing them to change their minds. When communities are not much interested in assimilating into the development of nation, into the Christian civilisation of the Old World, the 'development' of the First World, or if nations themselves are not much interested in assimilating into a hegemonic globalised order, it is easy to arrive at the conclusion that 'the people' are mistaken, that they really are part of the order (even if only as a burden) and that they need only to be convinced of this.[62] How can they exist if not within 'our' understanding, except perhaps as outlaws? This has been particularly evident following the end of the Cold War, when a 'crisis of governance' seemed suddenly to arise in the Third World as the collapse of socialist governments left gaps in the market.

Faith in development

The Old World – the First World – the developed world – thus brings certainty; it provides the particular from which we can intuit a universal totality of place somewhere at the end of history. This is the promise of development as justice, as progress and reason.

The New World, in contrast, remains as the 'world's waste spaces' – a Third World – with no history. As Robert Nisbet has noted:

> By a gigantic act of faith we assume that the Chronology in which we fit (with difficulty and distortion enough!), the events and changes of that tiny part of the earth that is the promontory of Eurasia which we call Western Europe, is also the chronology of [hu]mankind.[63]

Like the word of God, faith in development is something, which is brought, 'to and for some, by others who presumably are more developed'. Development is represented as a signifier of peace such that the sustained efforts of people in post-colonial territories to create for themselves a space within international relations not based on neo-imperial exploitation or a dependence on the Westphalian conception of nation is somehow understood by many in the First World as a form of ignorant or naive ingratitude.[64] The

---

62 Ferguson, 1997, p 227.   63 Nisbet, 1969, p 241.
64 'Peace is essential to economic growth and it depends on justice, social harmony and spiritual fulfilment;' Belshaw, Calderisi and Sugden, 2001, p 14.

development code is a practice of Darwinian proportions: kill or be killed. As Agamben has observed:

> If there is a line in every modern state marking the point at which the decision on life becomes a decision on death, ... this line no longer appears today as a stable border dividing two distinct zones. This line is now in motion and gradually moving into areas other than that of political life, areas in which the sovereign is entering into an ever more intimate symbiosis not only with the jurists but with the doctor, the scientist, the expert, and the priest.[65]

The development practitioner: the jurist, the doctor, the scientist, the expert, and the priest, is constrained to working primarily out of 'the specifications of the world from which he/she has been sent, rather than out of an accurate and sensitive reading of the particular situation with which he/she is actually faced'.[66] Their task is to maintain faith through understanding, an understanding aimed at the possible fulfilment of humanity. Development discourse is therefore concerned with retelling the stories of underdeveloped peoples as subjects who have been lost to the developed world and seek redemption back into a body worthy of salvation. Until that time, the bodies of underdeveloped peoples are separated from a recognised political status 'and abandoned, in a state of exception, to the most extreme misfortunes'.[67]

> In such a space of exception, subjection to experimentation can, like an expiation rite, either return the human body to life (pardon and the remission of a penalty are, it is worth remembering, manifestations of the sovereign power over life and death) or definitively consign it to death to which it already belongs'.[68]

The modern governors of this space are the development experts – those who 'move in the no-man's land into which at one point the sovereign alone could penetrate'.[69] Here the development expert is the law. They descend from a transcendent time of promise into a fallen undeveloped space of their own creation. They work in a 'zone of indistinction between inside and outside, exception and rule, licit and illicit, in which the very concepts of subjective right and juridical protection no longer make any sense'.[70] In this way the work of the development practitioner can be likened to a master confessor who disciplines the actions of Third World subjects and the interactions among them in order to return them to a future-present and the perfect expression of humanity.

65 Agamben, 1998, p 122.   66 Kaplan, 1999.   67 Agamben, 1998, p 159.
68 Ibid.   69 Ibid.   70 Ibid, p 170.

All of them therefore were all renowned and magnified, not through themselves or their own works or the righteous actions which they had wrought, but through his will; and therefore we who by his will have been called in Christ Jesus, *are not made righteous by ourselves, or by our wisdom or understanding or piety or the deeds which we have wrought in holiness of heart, but through faith,* by which Almighty God has justified all men from the beginning of the world; to him be glory for ever and ever. Amen.[71]

Thus, 'submerging the materialist predication that the [practitioner's] *raison d'être* is profiteering for the Northern elite, the [practitioner] can be posited as the saviour of [her] own destructive effects'.[72] Development in this sense is work done for the benefit of a future-perfect humanity by agents, 'who are not made righteous by [them]selves, or by [their] wisdom or understanding or piety or the deeds which [they] have wrought in holiness of heart, but through faith' in development. Development is a discourse of salvation based on practices of repentance, sacrifice and conversion. Each intervention made into the Third World in the name of development necessarily implies a new decision concerning the 'truth' of the subject at hand and its position within a trajectory of progress. Only those subjects that confess in 'words and action' their conversion to capitalist narratives of value remain within development's promise of salvation. As Clement of Alexandria wrote in another context, 'We have learned to call freedom the freedom with which the Lord alone endows us, delivering us from pleasures, lusts and the other passions'.[73] This is the freedom without origin or future. It is the freedom known by a humanity not confined by space, but living in a time of wholeness, of fulfilment, or pure presence corrected by the Second Coming in which the flesh will once again be made whole and in which space will be subsumed by time.[74] This is the promise of development, for which the modern western world continues to yearn. It is the promise underlying the mystery of wholeness. In this, one is expected to have faith.

Faith in Development is the title chosen for a book of essays based on papers given at the Conference on Alleviating Poverty in Africa, held in Nairobi, Kenya, in March 2000 to discuss the principles and practicalities of a partnership between the churches of Africa and the World Bank.[75] The editors of the book and the conference participants agree that 'there is an important area of common ground between faith and development'.[76]

Most of Africa's poor are deeply religious. Those who would serve them,

---

71 Emphasis added. 'The Epistle of St Clement to the Corinthians' in Harmer, 1893.
72 Guest, 1997, p 85.   73 Clement of Alexandria, 1991, Book III, Chapter 44.4, 283.
74 Spence, 1996, p 24.   75 Belshaw, Calderisi and Sugden, 2001.   76 Ibid, p vii.

or would work with them to improve their material condition, must remember that they have spiritual resources to draw on in overcoming their poverty. Why is religion so important to the poor? Why do they value the support of those with religious commitment? Certainly, religion provides consolation in the midst of misery; but typically faith is also part of the poor's personal identity, the foundation of their sense of community, and the basis of their hope.[77]

The intersection of the confessional subject, the Lockean human form, and Darwinian evolution crosses here through the bodies of African peoples with the machinery of the nation state, its scientist-priests and their international development agencies capturing the basis of hope for 'these people'. Whereas the World Bank 'brings a wide and varied experience of dealing with poverty issues and widely researched information on specific aspects of poverty and public policy', as well as 'special access to national and international decision makers' and 'a global perspective and financial and professional resources',[78] the Church brings 'its ability to influence constructively, based on its numbers, its position as the moral conscience of nations, its closeness to the poor, its own accountability to God'.

In a section of the book *Faith in Development* entitled 'Responding to the Voices of the Poor', the World Bank claims it can also speak on behalf of the poor on the basis of its research into 'the voices of the poor', which confirms that the poor also feel powerless and voiceless'.[79] The poor apparently know most about 'the experience of poverty', and their worsening plight 'indicates that they need appropriate partnership with other groups to rise out of poverty'.[80] Furthermore, the Church 'needs to intensify and share with governments, the World Bank and other organisations its own research on the voices of the poor based on the Church's understanding of poverty as also including religious, family, ethical and cultural dimensions'.[81] 'The Church represents the poor and the marginalised and can speak for them truthfully and forcefully'.[82] Although institutions like the World Bank 'are necessarily non-confessional':

they have learned through long experience that economic and social reforms are fruitless if they do not reflect the views of society at large. For that reason, the Bank and its development partners, in cooperation with governments, have intensified their contacts over the last 10 years with

---

77 Ibid, p 3.   78 Kaplan, 1999, p 8.

79 *Voices of the Poor* was a major study undertaken by the World Bank to support the *World Development Report 2000–2001 on Poverty and Development*, World Bank, 2001. The study comprises three reports: see Narayan, 2000a, 2000b and 2002.

80 Belshaw, Calderisi and Sugden, 2001, p 9.   81 Ibid.   82 Kaplan, 1999, pp 8–9.

parliamentarians, private investors, trade unionists, non-governmental organisations and journalists'.[83]

Callisto Madav, the World Bank's Vice President for Africa, underscored the importance of such co-operation:

> If we organise ourselves properly, if we treat people as subjects rather than objects of development, if we consider not just the economic and the social aspects but also the cultural, and yes, even the spiritual, aspects of human aspirations, then we can be a valuable instrument in building a new future for Africa.[84]

A new future, that divides 'these peoples' from their past. A new future – a shared future – a future history of the Old World order. By treating the people as subjects (having conferred upon them their national sovereignty) they must be made able to govern themselves in addition to acknowledging their indebtedness to the market. The continued oppression of Third World peoples through the discourse of development, however, undermines the very possibility of their own subjectivity. Having one's subjectivity bestowed by the developed world merely repeats the dynamic of privilege and domination of a symbolic law not of their own making.[85] The First World is allowed to remain in a space of transcendence that knows no sacrifice save for those development practitioners, who, like the God-man, travel among the peoples of a fallen world to teach them the way of salvation. The Third World, however, knows only sacrifice, confined as it is in the space of unredeemed underdevelopment.

Those who choose another path are not, moreover, loosed from the disciplinary regimes of development practice. Instead, they are subjected to the austerity measures fit for a transgressive, debt-ridden subject; marked by the use of the cruellest juridical and economic mnemontechnics. Like the medieval disciplinary techniques that have shaped the modern West, the concept of development has enabled the creation of practices designed to code 'the flow of desire to accord with that of the collective whole':

> to *breed* man, to mark him in his flesh, to render him capable of alliance, to form him within the debtor-creditor relation, which on both sides turns out to be a matter of memory – a memory straining toward the future.[86]

The effect of attempts by the Christian Church to determine its subjects was to inflict a physical and spiritual objectification on life by reducing it to the limits

---

83 Belshaw, Calderisi and Sugden, 2001, p vii.   84 Madavo, 2001, p 52.
85 Oliver, 2001.   86 Deleuze and Guattari, 1983, p 190 referring to Nietzsche, 1989.

of justice. Such an infliction has been carried through into the austerity measures imposed by international development agencies on developing states. These, too, signify a remarkable sense of subjection, an indenture inscribed onto the body of the subject in order both to bind the subject's own capacity to speak and act within the limitations imposed by development discourse as well as to symbolise publicly its membership within that discourse.

The 'underdeveloped' subject is thereby refused entry into a relationship of negotiation with the 'developed' world but is constituted instead as that debt, which is preventing humanity as a whole from reaching salvation. In as much as this redemptive process is aimed at becoming 'developed' it is represented as an 'inevitable' process – Christ's promise. There is no room for negotiation by the underdeveloped state – the grant of the 'truth' about development is not one of exchange. There is only one form of repayment – one path of redemption. Recall the western rule of law that operates not through mercy but under justice:

> we are speaking of that ultimate mercy by which [God] makes men blessed after this life. . . . that blessedness ought not be given to anyone unless his sins are wholly remitted, and that this remission ought not be done except by the payment of the debt which is owed because of sin [and] according to the magnitude of the sin.[87]

There is only a redeemed life or death for the underdeveloped nation state; being or not being, sovereign embodiment or collapse. The post-colonial subject does not therefore constitute itself but rather it is forced to disappear into the Word of another.

It is within this frame of mind that the participants at the Common Ground and Common Concerns: CAPA – World Bank Conference address their views on the development of Africa. In the introduction to the published papers, John Shao's keynote address is said to summarise the problem of poverty in Africa and emphasises 'human capital formation – that is, educational programs – as a way of promoting investment and industrialisation'.[88] Makonen Getu described how the 'ideal operation of micro-finance credit under Christian non-profit management could help the poor escape from poverty using their own enterprise and effort'.[89] Finally, in his post-conference response, Vinay Samuel argued that it is only through a sense of human dignity and self-worth conferred on the poor through the Christian salvation experience and world view that empowers them to respond pro-actively to opportunities for material improvement. For Samuel, 'the faith of the poor themselves is a significant factor in poverty reduction'.[90]

---

87 Anselm of Canterbury, 1998b Book 1, Chapter 24.   88 Shao, 2001 p 4.
89 Ibid, p 5.   90 Ibid.

The poor are thus governed at the level of their own lives. Capitalism is the only justice to which they are allowed to aspire. In the guise of a productive discourse, development projects seek to 'optimise' the population through orderings of domination and segregation that seek to construct a docile subjectivity that is more efficient and therefore more 'valuable'.[91] In this way development brings the Third World to the 'threshold of modernity'.[92] Development discourse has 'the power to expose a whole population to death' hidden beneath 'the power to guarantee an individual's continued existence'.[93] International law and the international system of nation states play an essential role in this process of assimilating subjects into a particular space of emergence to the extent that 'all the Constitutions framed throughout the world' have made acceptable a particular historical end.[94] The negotiation of a new promise is inconceivable. Justice has already been reasoned out and its promise determined. This is the political economy of desire inherent in the promise of development – of law and ordering in the First World. 'These people' are placed beyond the space of allowable speech, only to be spoken for. And what are the voices of those who are not able to speak out against development intervention saying? They are weakly crying out apparently for further intervention and reform. As Anne Orford and the current author have argued elsewhere, international development agencies, such as the World Bank, do not recognise that people should be able to participate in determining the nature of the political, and thus the economic, system under which they live:

> Popular decision-making about many issues is foreclosed by a model that assumes that much public policy is appropriately developed by economic experts. Development discourse fails to consider, for example, that people might choose to participate in state decision-making by nationalising all private investment, or might want the state to guarantee full public funding for food, health, education or social security. Questions about whether people want to be treated as consumers of privatised or corporatised public services, rather than as the collective owners of those services, do not appear to be open to popular debate. By characterising people in limited economic terms, as stakeholders or consumers, development discourse ignores all the forms of political agency that are ruled out by the economic model [including the inevitability of the state system itself].[95]

---

91 Foucault, 1998b, p 143.   92 Ibid.   93 Ibid, p 137.   94 Ibid, p 144.
95 Orford and Beard, 1998, p 209.

Development as desire

Development practices are not merely an objective and interpretative tool to practise or discuss quality of life, the effectiveness of technology, the improvement in agriculture, the administration of state welfare, the fight against poverty.[96] The discourses of development have become a rational art of governance making knowable the nature and quality of human existence through the integration of individuals into a governable population; a series of practices that lead individuals, peoples, or states to focus their attention on themselves as subjects of development in both the 'First' and the 'Third' Worlds: *Noverim te, noverim me*.

'Africa must reaffirm *in words and action*, that the goal of development is first and foremost the promotion of the well-being of its people'.[97] Is this call to use words and action to affirm a sense of belonging and collective promotion of a people's salvation not a means to convert Third World peoples? Behind this call it is possible to observe the traces of the rationally 'true' subject that seeks recognition through confession – a language that, in this case, is supervised by the supreme truth of development. It is a discourse of development that is defined by the models of development put forward by the First World. The practices of peoples that exist outside this discourse are rejected, just as communism was outlawed as a false truth equivalent to the concept of sin. The premise behind the call to words and action is, therefore, one that encourages those peoples of the Third World who are able to do more than merely survive to 'act out' and to 'confess' the only true form of subjective becoming.[98] In this way, 'these peoples' are converted 'into the larger significance of a story that is not uniquely personal'.[99]

As such, development is as much a story of sacrifice as it is a story about salvation – of one world desperately seeking the totality of peace through a globalised effort to 'develop' the fragmented peoples of the earth into a complete whole. From this perspective, development is a symptom of a hope-producing discourse. The very signification of development as a concept is inevitably one with messianic intent. Development is the performance of the First World promise, the truth of which is deferred to a future-perfect present time outside of space.

Alternatively, development might be understood as the symptom of oppression resulting from a world that has emerged from the development of another world – as the underdeveloped tragic excess of a global capitalism that has captured the Third World in a post-colonial becoming that is not its own. Unable to take the position of their own 'wanting to be', the Third

96 For examples and discussion of development theory or methodology see The World Bank's *World Development Reports*; Booth, 1985; Binder, 1986; Edwards, 1989; Hunt, 1989; Peet and Hartwick, 1999; Hettne, 1990.

97 Emphasis added. Shao, 2001, p 28.   98 Balibar, 1991, p 40.   99 Root, 1997, p 29.

World is coerced through nationalist, military, economic and cultural forces to recuperate an homogenised subjectivity by recognising itself in the First World, thereby identifying with the other's recognition of itself – a recognition embodied in the nation state through international law. As bell hooks argues in a slightly different context, these recognitive dynamics cannot succeed in overcoming oppression. Third World peoples must be able to recognise themselves:

> Fundamental to the process of decentering the oppressive Other and claiming our right to subjectivity is the insistence that we must determine how we will be and not rely on colonising responses to determine our legitimacy. We are not looking to that Other for recognition. We are recognising ourselves and willingly making contact with all who engage us in a constructive manner.[100]

This means that the developed world must cease to see the underdeveloped world as a world where something is missing or indeed to see either world as a separate, fetishised (Other) world at all. This is perhaps an impossible demand, particularly given the material inequalities among and within nations in an integrated world such as the present. The developed world must at least begin to acknowledge that the lack lies within its own identity; that underdevelopment is not 'out there' but everywhere where a promise of development determines our existence. The promise signifying some future globalised redemption is a fantasy; it is nowhere to be found. The promise of development is not, as the current discourse would seem to suggest, the place of salvation. It is a discourse that sustains the image of a developing world within an encompassing, totalising order. Development represents nothing more than the 'lost idea of providence'. Certainly the developed world, wherever it finds itself, does not sit in transcendence over an underdeveloped world where 'the revealed and true reality is present at all times or timelessly'.[101] All peoples and their communities must be allowed to know and live their own histories and experiences rather than having these realities 'confirmed and fulfilled by a deeper meaning' relative to the developed world.[102] The very concept of a developed world is no more than its own fantasy of wholeness not yet completed; a synecdoche.[103]

Those who practise in development discourses should be aware of how this 'deeper meaning' affects their assumed role as keepers of humanity's common future. This future need not be a totalising promise. As Derrida says of the promise:

---

100 bell hooks, 1990, p 22.   101 Auerbach, 1984, pp 72–73.   102 Ibid.
103 McFarland, 1981, p 27.

it is necessary for it to be capable, beyond any program of constraint, of allowing itself to be haunted by the possibility, precisely, of its perversion its conversion into a menace there where a promise can only promise good things, the nonserious commitment of an untenable promise, etc.[104]

At present, development discourse serves western ideas of a universal justice as well as the sovereignty of capitalism. But what is justice when it is shared through 'the use of force or cunning', to make others believe it, 'as they do a miracle, through rhetoric, the school, or the army'.[105] The concept of development has provided the managers of the world market created in the Imperial era with a new global concept of governance to capture the 'emerging nations' of the Third World in peace. The 'underdeveloped peoples' are being left to exist both outside and inside the body of development, as the tragic excess produced by the disciplinary technologies of the modern global economy. Not only are they captured as exceptions to the rule of wealth but also by the existing laws on immigration and asylum that prevent their movement to a better place – laws upheld by those states in which the bodies of labour are subject to some sense of value, thanks to trade union support, government tariffs and other restrictive practices of industrial nations. An exacting Baconian environment indeed.

104   Derrida 1998, p 93, fn 11.   105   Ibid, p 23.

Bibliography

Abbott, DP, *Rhetoric in the New World: Rhetorical Theory and Practice in Colonial Spanish America*, 1996, Columbia SC: University of South Carolina Press

Abelard, P, 'Historia calamitatum' in Radice, B (trans) *The Letters of Abelard and Heloise*, 1974, London: Penguin Books

Aboriginal and Torres Strait Islander Commission, *As a Matter of Fact: Answering Myths and Misconceptions about Indigenous Australians*, 1988, ATSIC

Adas, M, *Machines as the Measure of Men: Science, Technology, and Ideologies*, 1989, Ithaca NY: Cornell University Press

Agamben, G, *Homo Sacer: Sovereign Power and Bare Life*, 1998, Stanford CA: Stanford University Press

Agnew, J, *Worlds Apart: The Market and the Theater in Anglo-American Thought, 1550–1750*, 1986, Cambridge: Cambridge University Press

Ahluwalia, P, *Politics and Post-Colonial Theory*, 2001, London: Routledge

Alan of Lille, *The Art of Preaching*, Evans, GR (trans), 1981, Michigan: Cistercian Publications

Albrecht-Carrie, R, *Britain and France: Adaptations to a Changing Context of Power*, 1970, New York: Doubleday

Alexandrowicz, CH, 'Mogul sovereignty and the law of nations' (1955) 4 Indian Yearbook of International Affairs 318

Amin, S, *Capitalism in the Age of Globalisation: The Management of Contemporary Society*, 1997, London: Zed Books

An Agenda for Development, an Ad Hoc Open-Ended Working Group of the UN General Assembly on 17 June 1997, *A/AC.250/1 (Parts I, II and III)*

Anand, RP, *Confrontation or Cooperation? International Law and Developing Countries*, 1987, Leiden/Boston: Martinus Nijhoff Publishers

Anghie, A, 'Finding the peripheries: sovereignty and colonialism in nineteenth century international law' (1999) 40 Harvard International Law Journal 1

Anselm of Canterbury, 'On truth' in *The Major Works*, 1998a, Oxford: Oxford University Press

Anselm of Canterbury, 'Why God became man' in *The Major Works*, 1998b, Oxford: Oxford University Press

Anselm of Canterbury, 'Monologion' in Hopkins, J, *A New, Interpretative Translation of St. Anselm's Monologion and Proslogion*, 1986a, Minneapolis: Arthur J Banning Press

Anselm of Cantebury, 'Proslogion' in Hopkins, J, *A New, Interpretative Translation of St. Anselm's Monologion and Proslogion*, 1986b, Minneapolis: Arthur J Banning Press

Appadurai, A, *Modernity at Large: Cultural Dimensions of Globalisation*, 1996, Minnesota: University of Minnesota Press

Arendt, H, *The Human Condition*, 2nd edn, 1998, Chicago: University of Chicago Press

Asad, T, *Genealogies of Religion: Discipline and Reasons of Power in Christianity and Islam*, 1993, Baltimore: Johns Hopkins University Press

Asad, T, 'Notes on body pain and truth in medieval Christian ritual' (1983) 12(3) *Economy and Society* 287

Attwood, B, *In the Age of Mabo: History, Aborigines and Australia*, 1996, Sydney: Allen & Unwin

Auerbach, E, *Scenes from the Drama of European Literature*, 1984, Manchester: Manchester University Press

Augustine, Bishop of Hippo, *On the Creed: A Sermon to the Catechumens*, Cornish, CL (trans) Christian Classics Ethereal Library, www.ccel.org/fathers2/NPNF1-03/npnf1-03-30.htm

Augustine, Bishop of Hippo, *On Genesis: Two Books on Genesis Against the Manichees; and On the Literal Interpretation of Genesis, An Unfinished Book*, Teske, RJ (trans), 1990a, Washington, DC: Catholic University of America Press

Augustine, Bishop of Hippo, *Soliloquies and Immortality of the Soul*, Watson, G (trans), 1990b, Warminster: Aris & Phillips

Augustine, Bishop of Hippo, *The Catholic and Manichaean Ways of Life*, Gallagher, DA and Gallagher, II (trans), 1966, Washington: Catholic University of America Press

Augustine, Bishop of Hippo, *Confessions*, Outler, AC (trans), 1955, Philadelphia: Westminster Press

Augustine, Bishop of Hippo, 'The guilt and remission of sins' and 'Infant baptism' in Schaff, P (ed), *A Select Library of the Nicene and Post-Nicene Fathers of the Christian Church. Vol. V: St Augustine: Anti-Pelagian Writings*, 1887, Michigan: Wm B Eerdmans publishing company

Axford, B, *The Global System: Economics, Politics and Culture*, 1995, Oxford: Polity Press

Axtell, JL (ed), *The Educational Writings of John Locke; A Critical Edition with Introduction and Notes*, 1968, Cambridge; Cambridge University Press

Bacon, F, *Sylua syluarum, or, A naturall historie in Ten Centuries*, 1627, London: William Lee

Bacon, F, *The Great Instauration and New Atlantis*, 1980, Illinois: AHM Publishing corp

Bacon, F, *The Advancement of Learning and New Atlantis*, 1974, Oxford: Clarendon Press

Bacon, F, 'De augmentis' in Spedding, J and Ellis, D (eds), *The Works of Francis Bacon: Baron of Verulam, Viscount St Alban, and Lord High Chancellor of England* (14 vols) Vol. IV, [1870], 1968a, New York: Garrett Press

Bacon, F, 'Of tribute: praise of knowledge' in Spedding, J and Ellis, D (eds), *The Works of Francis Bacon: Baron of Verulam, Viscount St. Alban, and Lord High Chancellor of England* (14 vols) Vol. VIII, [1870], 1968b, New York: Garrett Press

Bacon, F, 'Of plantations' in Spedding, J and Ellis, D (eds), *The Works of Francis Bacon: Baron of Verulam, Viscount St. Alban, and Lord High Chancellor of England* (14 vols) Vol. IV, [1870], 1968c, New York: Garrett Press

Bacon, F, 'Novum Organum' in Spedding, J and Ellis, D (eds), *The Works of Francis Bacon: Baron of Verulam, Viscount St. Alban, and Lord High Chancellor of England* (14 vols) Vol. I, [1870], 1968d, New York: Garrett Press

Bacon, F, *The Novum Organon: or A True Guide to the Interpretation of Nature*, Kitchin, GW (trans), 1855, Oxford: Oxford University Press

Balibar, E, 'Subjection and Subjectivation' in Copjec, C (ed), *Supposing the Subject*, 1994, London: Verso.

Balibar, E, 'Citizen subject' in Cadava, E, Connor, P and Nancy, JL (eds), *Who Comes After the Subject?*, 1991, New York: Routledge

Balibar, E and Wallerstein, I, *Race, Nation, Class: Ambiguous Identities*, 1991, London: Verso

Baran, P, *The Political Economy of Growth*, 1957, New York: Monthly Review Press

Barbon, N, *A Discourse of Trade*, 1690, London: Printed by T Milbourn for the author

Bartolovich, C, 'Consumerism, or the cultural logic of late cannibalism' in Barker, F, Hulme, P and Iversen, M (eds), *Cannibalism and the Colonial World*, 1998, Cambridge: Cambridge University Press

Bauman, Z, *Modernity and Ambivalence*, 1991, Oxford: Polity Press

Beale, HK, *Theodore Roosevelt and the Rise of America to World Power*, 1956, Baltimore: Johns Hopkins Press

Beard, J, 'Representations of the liberal state in the art of development' (2001) 10 Griffith Law Review 6

Beard, J and Pahuja, S, *Divining the Source: Law's Foundation and the Question of Authority'*, (2003) 19 Australian Feminist Law Journal 1

Beckett, J, 'Aboriginal history, Aboriginal myths: an introduction' (1994) 65(2) Oceania 97

Beaglehole JC (ed), *The Journals of Captain James Cook on his Voyage of Discovery: Volume 1, The Voyage of the Endeavour 1768–1771*, 1969, Cambridge: Hakluyt Society.

Belshaw, D, Calderisi, R and Sugden, C (eds), *Common Ground and Common Concerns: communiqué of the CAPA* – World Bank Conference' on Faith in Development: Partnership between the World Bank and the Churches of Africa, 2001, Oxford: World Bank and Regnum Books International

Berkeley, G, *The Querist*, 1750, London: Printed for W. Inney and sold by M. Cooper

Berman, HJ, *The Formation of the Western Legal Tradition*, 1983, Cambridge MA: Harvard University Press

Bernheimer, C, 'Fetishism and decadence: Salome's severed heads' in Apter, E and Pietz, W (eds), *Fetishism as Cultural Discourse*, 1993, Ithaca NY: Cornell University Press

Bhabha, HK, 'The other question: difference, discrimination and the discourse of colonialism' in Barker, F, Hulme, P, Iversen, M and Loxley, D (eds), *Literature, Politics and Theory: Papers from the Essex Conference 1976–84*, 1986, Methuen: London

Bhagwati, JN, 'Incentives and disincentives: international migration' (1984) 120(4) Review of World Economics 678

Binder, L, 'The natural history of development theory' (1986) 28 Comparative Studies in Society and History 3

Blackstone, W, *Commentaries on the Laws of England (4 Vols)*, [1783], 1978, New York: Garland Publishing

Blainey, G, 'Land that bypassed a revolution', *The Age – Saturday Extra*, 21 August 1993

Bloch, E and Adorno, T, 'Something's missing: a discussion between Ernst Bloch and Theodor Adorno on the contradictions of utopian longing' in Bloch, E, *The Utopian Function of Art and Literature: Selected Essays*, Zipes, J and Mecklenburg, F (trans), 1988, Cambridge MA, MIT Press

Bodin, J, *Method for the Easy Comprehension of History*, Reynolds, B (trans), 1966, New York: Octogon Books

Boehmer, E, *Empire, the National, and the Postcolonial, 1890–1920: Resistance in Interaction*, 2002, Oxford: Oxford University Press

Boesky, A, 'Bacon's new Atlantis and the laboratory of prose' in Fowler, E and Greene, R (eds), *The Project of Prose in Early Modern Europe and the New World*, 1997, Cambridge: Cambridge University Press

Booth, D, 'Marxism and development sociology: interpreting the impasse' (1985) 13 World Development 761

Bordo, S, *The Flight of Objectivity: Essays on Cartesianism and Culture*, 1987, New York:, State University of New York Press

Bowie, M, *Freud, Proust, and Lacan: Theory as Fiction*, 1987, Cambridge: Cambridge University Press

Boyle, WJ, 'The summa for confessors as a genre, and its religious intent' in Trinkaus, C and Oberman, HA (eds), *The Pursuit of Holiness in Late Medieval and Renaissance Religion: Papers from the University of Michigan Conference*, 1974, Leiden: EJ Brill

Braswell, MF, *The Medieval Sinner: Characterization and Confession in the Literature of the English Middle Ages*, 1983, London: Associated University Presses

Brown, CB, 'Somnambulism. A Fragment' in A Weber (ed), *Somnambulism and Other Stories*, 1987, Frankfurt am Main: Peter Lang

Brown, P, *Augustine of Hippo: A Biography*, 1969, London: Faber

Bubnova, N, 'Guarantees and insurance for re-allocating and mitigating political and regulatory risks in infrastructure investment: market analysis', Paper presented at a World Bank-sponsored conference, 1999, on Private Infrastructure for Development: Confronting Political and Regulatory Risks

Buchanan, R and Pahuja, S, 'Legal imperialism: empire's invisible hand?' in Passavant, P and Dean J (eds) *The Empire's New Clothes: Reading Hardt and Negri*, 2003, London: Routledge

Buchanan, R, 'Global civil society and cosmopolitan legality at the WTO: perpetual peace or perpetual process?' 16 (2003) Leiden Journal of International Law 673

Budick, S and Iser, W (eds), *Languages of the Unsayable: The Play of Negativity in Literature and Literary Theory*, 1989, New York: Columbia University Press

Burchell, G, 'Liberal government and techniques of the self' in Barry, A, Osborne, T and Rose, N (eds), *Foucault and Political Reason*, 1996, Chicago: University of Chicago Press

Burke, K, *The Rhetoric of Religion; Studies in Logology*, 1970, Berkeley: University of California Press

Bush, G, *The National Security Strategy of the United States of America*, September 2002, Washington DC: The White House

Calderisi, R, 'The World Bank and Africa' in Belshaw, D, Calderisi, R and Sugden, C (eds), *Faith in Development: Partnership between the World Bank and the Churches of Africa*, 2001, Oxford: World Bank and Regnum Books International

Cardoso, FH and Faletto, E, *Dependency and Development in Latin America*, 1979, Berkley: University of California Press

Chakrabarty, D, 'Postcoloniality and the artifice of history: who speaks for "Indian" pasts?' (1992) 37 Representations 1

Charter of the United Nations, June 26, 1945, 59 Stat. 1031, T.S. 993, 3 Bevans 1153 and www.un.org/aboutun/charter

Chatterjee, P, *The Politics of the Governed: Reflections on Popular Politics in Most of the World*, 2004, New York: Columbia University Press

Chatterjee, P, *The Nation and its Fragments*, 1993, Princeton: Princeton University Press

Cheyfitz, E, *The Poetics of Imperialism: Translation and Colonization from The Tempest to Tarzan*, 1997, Philadelphia: University of Pennsylvania Press

Chimni, 'International Institutions Today: An Imperial Global State in the Making' (2004) 15 European Journal of International Law 1

Cho, S, 'The WTO's Gemeinschaft' (2004) 56 Alabama Law Review 483

Clement of Alexandria, *Stromateis*, Ferguson, J (trans), 1991, Washington DC: Catholic University of America Press

Clinton, WJ, *Economic Report of the President Together with the Annual Report of the Council of Economic Advisors*, 1999, Washington DC: GPO

Cohen, JM (ed), 'Digest of Columbus's log-book on his first voyage made by Bartolome de las Casas', Cohen, JM (trans), in Cohen, JM (ed), *The Four Voyages of Christopher Columbus*, 1969, London: Penguin Books

Cohen, T, *The Fires of Tongues: Antonio Vieira and the Missionary Church in Brazil and Portugal*, 1998, Stanford CA: Stanford University Press

Coleman, J, *Ancient and Medieval Memories*, 1992, Cambridge: Cambridge University Press

Colish, M, *The Mirror of Language: A Study in the Medieval Theory of Knowledge*, 1968, New Haven: Yale University Press

Connolly, W, *Identity/Difference: Democratic Negotiations of Political Paradox*, 2002, Minneapolis: University of Minnesota Press

Connolly, H, *The Irish Penitentials and their Significance for the Sacrament of Penance Today*, 1995, Dublin: Four Courts Press

Corbridge, S, *Capitalist World Development: A Critique of Radical Development Geography*, 1990, London: Macmillan

Covenant of the League of Nations, embodying an amendment of Article 6, in force from August 13, 1924, and amendments of Articles 12, 13 and 15, in force from September 26, 1924, 1925, London, H. M. Stationery Office (now TSO)

Cover, R, 'Violence and the word' (1986) 95 Yale Law Journal 1601

Crush, J (ed), *Power of Development*, 1995, London: Routledge

Cyprian, 'The epistles' in *A Library of the Fathers of the Holy Catholic Church Vol. 75*, 1844, Oxford: Parker

Daniels, WM, *The Four Point Program*, 1951, New York: H.W. Wilson, p 10

Davenant, C, *Essay Upon the Balance of Trade*, 1699, London: Printed for J Knapton

de Nebrija, A, *Gramatica de la lengua castellana*, 1980, Madrid: Editora Nacional

de Senarclens, P, 'La crise des Nations Unies' in Rahnema, M and Bawtree, V (eds), *The Post-Development Reader*, 1997, London: Zed Books

de Vattel, E, *The Law of Nations or Principles of Natural Law*, [1758], Fenwick, C (trans), 1916, Washington DC: Carnegie Institution

de Vitoria, F, *De indis et de jure belli relectiones*, 1917, Oxford: Clarendon Press

Dean, M, 'Foucault, government and the enfolding of authority' in Barry, A et al. (eds), *Foucault and Political Reason*, 1996, Chicago: University of Chicago Press

Debray, R, *God: An Itinerary* (trans J Mehlman), 2004, London: Verso

Defoe, D, *A General History of Trade, and especially Consider'd as it Respects British Commerce (4 Vols)*, 1713, London: printed for J Baker

Deleuze, G and Guattari, F, *Anti-Oedipus: Capitalism and Schizophrenia*, (trans Hurley, R, Seem, M and Lane, HR), 1983, Minneapolis: University of Minnesota Press

Derrida, J, *Monolingualism of the Other; or, The Prosthesis of Origin* (trans P Mensah), 1998, Stanford CA: Stanford University Press

Derrida, J, 'Remarks on deconstruction and pragmatism' in Mouffe, C (ed), *Deconstruction and Pragmatism*, 1996, London: Routledge

Derrida, J, *On the Name*, 1995, Stanford CA: Stanford University Press

Derrida, J, *Specters of Marx: The State of the Debt, the Work of Mourning, and the New International* (trans P Kamuf), 1994, New York: Routledge

Derrida, J, *Aporias: Dying – Awaiting (One Another at) the 'Limits of Truth'* Dutoit, T (trans) 1993, Stanford CA: Stanford University Press

Derrida, J, 'Force of Law: The Mystical Foundation of Authority', in D Cornell and M Rosenfeld (eds), *Deconstruction and the Possibility of Justice*, 1992, New York: Routledge

Derrida, J, 'How to avoid speaking: denials' in Budick, S and Iser, W (eds), *Languages of the Unsayable: The Play of Negativity in Literature and Literary Theory*, 1989, New York: Columbia University Press

Derrida, J, *Limited Inc.* Weber, S (trans), 1988 Evanston, IL: Northwestern University Press.

Derrida, J, *Of Grammatology*, Spivak, GC (trans), 1976, Baltimore: Johns Hopkins University Press

Descartes, R, *The Philosophical Works of Descartes Vol 1*, Haldane, E and Ross, GRT (trans), 1911, Cambridge: Cambridge University Press

Devlin, DS, *Corpus Christi: A Study in Medieval Eucharistic Theory, Devotion, and Practice*, A Dissertation submitted to the Faculty of the Division of Social Sciences of the University of Chicago in Candidacy for the Degree of Doctor of Philosophy, Chicago, Illinois, August 1975

Donne, J, *The Anniversaries* 1963, Baltimore: Johns Hopkins Press

Dooley, K, 'From penance to confession: the Celtic contribution' (1982) XLIII Tijdschrift voor Filosofie en Teologie 390

Doty, RL, *Imperial Encounters: The Politics of Representation in North-South Relations*, 1996, Minneapolis: University of Minnesota Press

Duncanson, I, 'Unchartered lands in an age of accountability' (1997) 3(1) Res Publica 3

Ebert, TL, *Ludic Feminism and After: Postmodernism, Desire and Labor in Late Capitalism*, 1996, Ann Arbor: University of Michigan Press

Edwards, M, 'The irrelevance of development studies' (1989) 11 Third World Quarterly 116

Eliade, M, *The Myth of the Eternal Return: or, Cosmos and History*, Trask, WR (trans), 1965, Princeton: Princeton University Press

Escobar, A, *Encountering Development: The Making and Unmaking of the Third World*, 1995, Princeton: Princeton University Press

Evans, GR, *Anselm and Talking About God*, 1980, Oxford: Oxford University Press

Fanon, F, *Black Skin, White Masks*, Markmann, CL (trans), 1967, New York: Grove Press

Ferguson, A, *The Articulate Citizen and the English Renaissance*, 1965, Durham NC: Duke University Press

Ferguson, J, 'Development and bureaucratic power in Lesotho' in Rahnemam, M and Bawtree, V (eds), *The Post-Development Reader*, 1997, London: Zed Books

Fink, B, *The Lacanian Subject Between Language and Jouissance*, 1995, Princeton: Princeton University Press

Fischer, S, *On the Need for an International Lender of Last Resort*, 1999, www.imf.org/external/hp/speeches/1999/010399/htm, 1999

Fitzpatrick, P, *Modernism and the Grounds of Law*, 2001, Cambridge: Cambridge University Press

Foster, D, *Confession and Complicity in Narrative*, 1987, Cambridge: Cambridge University Press

Foucault, M, 'A preface to transgression' in Carrette, JR (ed), *Religion and Culture*, 1999a, New York: Routledge

Foucault, M, 'On the government of living' in Carrette, JR (ed), *Religion and Culture: Michel Foucault*, 1999b, New York: Routledge

Foucault, M, *Power/Knowledge: Selected Interviews and Other Writings, 1972–1977*, Gordon, C (trans), 1998a, Sussex: Harvester Press

Foucault, M, *History of Sexuality Vol. I*, Hurley, R (trans), 1998b, London: Penguin Books

Foucault, M, 'Difendera la societa' in Stoler, AL, *Race and the Education of Desire: Foucault's History of Sexuality and the Colonial Order of Things*, 1995, Durham NC: Duke University Press

Foucault, M, *La Volonté de Savoir*, 1994a, Paris: Gallimard

Foucault, M, *The Order of Things: An Archaeology of the Human Sciences*, 1994b, New York: Vintage Books

Foucault, M, 'Faire vivre et laisser mourir: la naissance du racisme' (1991) 46 (535) Les Temps Modernes 37

Foucault, M, *The Archaeology of Knowledge*, 1989, New York: Routledge

Foucault, M, 'Technologies of the Self' in Martin, LH, Gutman, H, and Hutton PH (eds), *Technologies of the Self: A Seminar with Michel Foucault*, 1988, Amherst: University of Massachusetts Press 16–49

Foucault, M, 'Nietzsche, genealogy, history' in Rabinow P (ed), Bouchard DF and Simon S (Trans), *The Foucault Reader*, 1984, New York: Pantheon

Foucault, M, *Discipline and Punish: The Birth of the Prison*, Sheridan, A (trans), 1979, New York: Vintage Books

Franck, TM, 'Editorial comments: terrorism and the right of self-defense' (2001) 95 American Journal of International Law 839

Frank, AG, 'The development of underdevelopment' in Cockcroft, JD, Frank, AG and Johnson, DL (eds), *Dependence and Underdevelopment: Latin America's Political Economy*, 1972, Garden City, NY: Anchor Books

Freud, S, 'The uncanny', Strachey, A (trans) in Nelson, B (ed), *On Creativity and the Unconscious: Papers on the Psychology of Art, Literature, Love, Religion*, 1958, New York: Harper Colophon Books, Harper Row

Freud, S, 'Moses and monotheism' in Strachey, J (ed), *Standard Edition of the Complete Psychological Works of Sigmund Freud Vol 18*, 1953, London: Hogarth Press

Fukuyama, F, *The End of History and the Last Man*, 1992, New York: Free Press

Furniss, ES, *The Position of the Labourer in a System of Nationalism: A Study in the Labor Theories of the Later English Mercantilists*, 1965, New York: Augustus M Kelley

Gallagher, J and Robinson, R, 'The imperialism of free trade' (1953) 6 Economic History Review 1

Galtung, J, 'A structural theory of imperialism' (1971) 8(2) Journal of Peace Research 81

Gandhi, L, *Postcolonial Theory: A Critical Introduction*, 1998, Edinburgh: Edinburgh University Press

Gary, I, 'Confrontation, co-operation or co-optation: NGOs and the Ghanaian state during structural adjustment' (1996) 23(68) Review of Political Economy 149

Gellrich, J, *The Idea of the Book in the Middle Ages: Language Theory, Mythology, and Fiction*, 1985, Ithaca NY: Cornell University Press

Geoffrey, H, *The Ascetic Imperative in Culture and Criticism* 1987, Chicago: University of Chicago Press

Gerhart, P and Seema Kella, A, 'Power and preferences: developing countries and the role of the WTO appellate body' (2005) 30 North Carolina Journal of International Law and Commercial Regulation 515

Gibson-Graham, GK, *The End of Capitalism (As We Knew It): A Feminist Critique of Political Economy*, 1996, Oxford: Blackwell

Gordon, C, 'Governmental rationality: an introduction' in Burchell, G, Gordon, C and Miller, P (eds), *The Foucault Effect: Studies in Governmentality: with Two Lectures by and an Interview with Michel Foucault*, 1991, London: Harvester Wheatsheaf

Grafton, A, Shelford, A and Siraisi, N, *New Worlds, Ancients Texts: The Power of Tradition and the Shock of Discovery*, 1992, Harvard: The Belknap Press

Grbich, J, 'Tracing the figure of the native in postcolonial theory and native title law: enlightenment, aesthetics and Charles Harpur' (2005) 22 Australian Feminist Law Journal 127.

Grbich, J, 'Law and semiotics down-under – aesthetics in Christian juridico-theological tracts: the wanderings of faith and nomos' (1999) 12(4) International Journal for the Semiotics of Law 351

Grbich, J, 'The taxpayer's body: genealogies of exertion' in Cheah, P, Fraser, D and Grbich, J (eds), *Thinking Through the Body of the Law*, 1996a, Sydney: Allen & Unwin

Grbich, J, 'The form of the tax reform story: Marshall, ordinary meanings and the city men' (1996b) 5 Griffith Law Review 40

Green, LC, 'Claims to territory in colonial America' in Green, LC and Dickason, OP (eds), *The Law of Nations and the New World*, 1989, Edmonton: University of Alberta Press

Greenblatt, S, *Marvellous Possessions: The Wonder of the New World*, 1991, Oxford: Clarendon Press

Greenblatt, S, 'Psychoanalysis and Renaissance culture' in Parker, P and Quint, D (eds), *Literary Theory/Renaissance Texts*, 1986, Baltimore: John Hopkins University Press

Griffiths, B, 'John Cassian' in Walsh, J (ed), *Spirituality through the Centuries*, 1964, New York: Kennedy & Sons

Grosz, E, 'Lesbian fetishism?' in Apter, E and Pietz, W (eds), *Fetishism as Cultural Discourse*, 1993, Ithaca NY: Cornell University Press

Grosz, E, *Jacques Lacan: A Feminist Introduction*, 1990, London: Routledge

Grotius, H, *On the Origin of the Native Races of America: A Dissertation*, Goldsmid, E (trans), 1884, Edinburgh: [sn]

Grotius, H, *The Rights of War and Peace: Including the Law of Nature and of Nations*, 1814, Campbell, AC (trans), Pontefract: B Boothroyd

Guest, K, 'Exploitation under erasure: economic, social and cultural rights engage economic globalisation' (1997) 19(1) Adelaide Law Review 73

Guillaumin, C, 'The idea of race and its elevation to autonomous scientific and legal status' in Guillaumin, C, *Racism, Sexism, Power, and Ideology*, 1995, London: Routledge

Hakluyt, R, 'Pamphlet for the Virginia Enterprise by Richard Hakluyt, Lawyer, 1585' in Taylor, EGR (ed), *The Original Writings & Correspondence of the Two Richard Hakluyts with an Introduction and Notes by EGR Taylor*, (Vol 2) 1935, London: Printed for the Hakluyt Society

Hakluyt, R, *Voyages*, 1907, New York: Dutton

Hakluyt, R, *The Principal Navigations Voyages Traffiques and Discoveries of the English Nation*, Volume VIII, 1904, Glasgow: James MacLehose and Sons

Hakluyt, R, *Divers Voyages Touching the Discovery of America and the Islands Adjacent*, 1850, London: Hakluyt Society

Hall, WE, *A Treatise on International Law*, 2nd edn, 1884, Oxford: Clarendon Press

Hamelman, S, 'Psychic fragmentation and ego defense in Charles Brockden Brown's "Somnambulism. A fragment" ' (2001) 7 PsyArt: A Hyperlink Journal for Psychological Study of the Arts, Article number 010907, www.clas.ufl.edu/ipsa/journal/2001_hamelman01.shtml

Hanning, RW, *The Individual in Twelfth-Century Romance*, 1977, New Haven: Yale University Press

Haraway, D, 'Deanimations: maps and portraits of life itself' in Brah, A and Coombes, AE (eds), *Hybridity and its Discontents: Politics, Science, Culture*, 2000, London: Routledge

Haraway, D, *Simians, Cyborgs and Women: The Reinvention of Nature*, 1991, London: Free Association

Haraway, D, *Primate Visions: Gender, Race, and Nature in the World of Modern Science*, 1989, New York: Routledge

Harmer JR (ed), *The Apostolic Fathers: comprising the Epistles (genuine and spurious) of Clement of Rome, the Epistles of S. Ignatius, the Epistle of S. Polycarp, the Martyrdom of S. Polycarp, the Teaching of the Apostles, the Epistle of Barnabas, the Shepherd of Hermas, the Epistle to Diognetus, the Fragments of Papias [and] the Reliques of the Elders Preserved in Irenus*, Lightfoot, JB (trans), 1893, London: Macmillan

Harper, L, *The English Navigation Laws: a Seventeenth Century Experiment in Social Engineering*, 1939, New York: Columbia University Press

Harpham, G, *The Ascetic Imperative in Culture and Criticism*, 1987, Chicago: University of Chicago Press

Hay, W, *Remarks on the Laws Relating to the Poor*, 1751, London: Printed for R. Dodsley, and sold by M. Cooper

Head, J, 'Seven Deadly Sins: an assessment of criticisms directed at the International Monetary Fund' (2004) 52 University of Kansas Law Review 521

Hegel, GWF, *The Philosophy of History*, Sibree, J (trans), 1956, New York: Dover Publications

Hegel, GWF, *The Phenomenology of Mind*, Baillie, JB (trans), 1910, London: S Sonnenschein & Co. Ltd

Henkin, L, Pugh, R, Schachter, O and Smit, H. *International Law: Cases and Materials*, 1993, St Paul, MN: West Publishing Co

Hettne, B, *Development Theory and the Three Worlds*, 1990, London: Methuen

Hirschman, AO, *Essays in Trespassing: Economics to Politics and Beyond*, 1981, Cambridge: Cambridge University Press

Hobbes, T, *Leviathan*, 1991, Cambridge: Cambridge University Press

Hobbes, T, *De Cive*, 1983, Oxford: Clarendon Press

hooks, b, *Yearning: Race, Gender, and Cultural Politics*, 1990, Cambridge MA: South End Press

Hörisch, J, *Heads or Tails: The Poetics of Money*, Horning, A (trans), 2000, Detroit: Wayne State University Press

Hulme, P, 'The spontaneous hand of nature: savagery, colonialism, and the enlightenment' in Hulme, P and Jordanova, L (eds), *The Enlightenment and its Shadows*, 1990, London: Routledge

Hunt, D, *Economic Theories of Development: An Analysis of Competing Paradigms*, 1989, New York: Simon and Schuster

Ignatieff, M, 'Nationalism and narcissism of minor differences' (1995) 102(1) Queens Quarterly 14

International Monetary Fund, *World Economic Outlook and International Capital Markets: Interim Assessment*, 1998, www.imf.org/external/np/fad/trans/manual, 1998

'Introductory', (1896) 1(1) The Australasian Anthropological Journal 3

Iorns, CJ, 'Indigenous peoples and self-determination' (1992) 24 Case Western Reserve J. International Law 199

Janowitz, A, 'Coleridge's 1816 Volume: Fragment as Rubric' (1985) 24(1) Studies in Romanticism 21

Jentleson, BW and Paterson, TG (eds), *Encyclopedia of U.S. Foreign Relations*, 1997, Oxford: Oxford University Press

Jewish Agency for Palestine, *Documents Relating to the Balfour Declaration and the Palestine Mandate*, 1939, London: Jewish Agency for Palestine

Jones, W, *The Tudor Commonwealth 1529–1559*, 1970, London: Athlone Press

Judovitz, D, *Subjectivity and Representation in Descartes: The Origins of Modernity*, (1988) Cambridge: Cambridge University Press

Jungmann, JA, *The Mass of the Roman Rite: Its Origins and Development*, Brunner, FA (trans), revised Riepe, CK (revised), 1959, New York: Benziger Brothers

Juteau-Lee, D, 'Introduction: (re)constructing the categories of "race" and "sex": the work of a precursor' in Guillaumin, C, *Racism, Sexism, Power and Ideology*, 1995, London: Routledge

Kaplan, A, *The Developing Of Capacity*, 1999, Cape Town: Community Development Resource Association:

Keenan, T, 'The point is to (ex)change it: reading capital rhetorically' in Apter, E and Pietz, W (eds), *Fetishism as Cultural Discourse*, 1993, Ithaca NY: Cornell University Press

Kleinschmidt, H, *Understanding the Middle Ages: The Transformation of Ideas and Attitudes in the Medieval World*, 2000, Woodbridge, Suffolk: Boydell Press

Korhonen, O, 'Liberalism and international law: a centre projecting a periphery' (1996) 65 Nordic Journal of International Law 481

Koskenniemi, M, 'Whose intolerance, which democracy?' in Fox, GH and Roth, BR (eds), *Democratic Governance and International Law*, 2000, Cambridge: Cambridge University Press

Kurtz, J, 'Developing countries and their engagement in the World Trade Organization', (2004) 5 Melbourne Journal of International Law 282

Lacan, J, *The Seminar Book III: The Psychoses, 1955–6*, Grigg, R (trans), 1993, London: Routledge

Lacan, J, *The Seminar Book VII: The Ethics of Psychoanalysis, 1959–60*, Porter, D (trans), 1992, New York: WW Norton & Company

Lacan, J, 'Seminar II, Book 1, Freud's papers on technique, 1953–1954', Forrester, J (trans), in Miller, J (ed), *The Seminar of Jacques Lacan*, 1988, Cambridge: Cambridge University Press

Lacan, J, *The Four Fundamental Concepts of Psychoanalysis*, Sheridan, A (trans), 1978, New York: Norton

Lacan, J, *Ecrits, A Selection*, Sheridan, A (trans), 1977, New York: Norton

Lacan, J, *The Language of the Self: The Function of Language in Psychoanalysis*, Wilden, A (trans), 1968, Baltimore: Johns Hopkins Press

Laclau, E, 'Preface' in Zizek, S, *The Sublime Object of Ideology*, 1989, London: Verso

Lafitau, JF, *Histoire des decouvertes et conquestes des Portugais dans le nouveau monde*, 1734, Paris: Se trouve a Amsterdam chez J. Wetstein, & G. Smith

Larmore, C, 'The concept of the constitutive subject' in MacCabe, C (ed), *The Talking Cure: Essays in Psychoanalysis and Language*, 1981, London: Macmillan Press

Lawrence, T, *The Principles of International Law*, 1895, London: Macmillan

Lazarus, N, *Nationalism and Cultural Practice in the Postcolonial World*, 1999, Cambridge: University Press

Le Goff, J, 'Merchant's time and Church's time in the Middle Ages' in Le Goff, J, *Time, Work and Culture in the Middle Ages*, 1980, Chicago: University of Chicago Press

Lea, HC, *A History of Auricular Confession and Indulgences in the Latin Church*, 1896, Philadelphia: Lea Brothers & Co

Lefort, C, *Democracy and Political Theory*, Macey, D (trans), 1988, Cambridge: Polity Press

Lefort, C, *The Political Forms of Modern Society: Bureaucracy, Democracy Totalitarianism*, 1986, Cambridge: Polity Press

Levinas, E, *Totality and Infinity: An Essay on Exteriority*, Lingis, A (trans), 1969, Pittsburgh: Duquesne University Press

Lewis, CS, *The Discarded Image*, 1964, Cambridge: Cambridge University Press

Locke, J, *Some Thoughts Concerning Education*, 1996, Indianapolis: Hackett Publishing Company

Locke, J, *Questions Concerning the Law of Nature*, Horwitz, R, Strauss Clay, J and Clay, D (trans), 1990, Ithaca NY: Cornell University Press

Locke, J, *An Essay Concerning Human Understanding*, 1975, Oxford: Clarendon Press

Locke, J, 'The second treatise' in *Two Treatises of Government*, 1960, Cambridge: Cambridge University Press

Locke, J, 'A discourse of miracles' in Ramsey, IT (ed), *The Reasonableness of Christianity: With a Discourse of Miracles and Part of a Third Letter Concerning Toleration*, 1958a, London: Black

Locke, J, 'The reasonableness of Christianity' in Ramsey, IT (ed), *The Reasonableness of Christianity: With a Discourse of Miracles and Part of a Third Letter Concerning Toleration*, 1958b, London: Black

Lorimer, J, *The Institutes of the Law of Nations: A Treatise of the Jural Relations of Separate Political Communities (Vol. I)*, 1883, London: W. Blackwood and sons

Louis, M, *Utopics: The Semiological Play of Textual Spaces*, Vollrath, RA (trans), 1990, Atlantic Highlands, NJ: Humanities Press International

Louis, M, *Portrait of the King*, Houle, MM (trans), 1988, Minneapolis: University of Minnesota Press

Lowe, L, *Immigrant Acts: On Asian American Cultural Politics*, 1996, Durham NC: Duke University Press

Luscombe, D (ed), *Peter Abelard's Ethics: An Edition with Introduction*, Luscombe, D (trans), 1971, Oxford: Clarendon Press

Mackinnon, C, 'Feminism, Marxism, method and the state: toward feminist jurisprudence' (1983) 8 Signs: A Journal Of Women in Culture and Society 635

Macquarie Dictionary (2nd edn), 1989, Victoria NSW: Macquarie University, The Macquarie Library Pty Ltd

Madavo, C, 'Serving the poor in Africa' in Belshaw, D, Calderisi, R and Sugden, C (eds), *Faith in Development: Partnership between the World Bank and the Churches of Africa*, 2001, Oxford: World Bank and Regnum Books International

Markus, A, 'Between Mabo and a hard place: race and the contradictions of Conservatism' in Attwood, B, *In the Age of Mabo: History, Aborigines and Australia*, 1996, Sydney: Allen & Unwin, p. 88

Marin, L, *Portrait of the King*, Houle, M (trans), 1988, Minneapolis: University of Minnosota Press

Martin, J, *Francis Bacon, the State and the Reform of Natural Philosophy*, 1992, Cambridge: Cambridge University Press

Martin, R, 'Globalisation? The dependencies of a question' (1999) 60(17(3)) Social Text 1

Marx, K, *Capital: A Critique of Political Economy Vol. 1*, Fowkes, B (trans), 1976–81, Harmondsworth: Penguin

Marx, K, *Grundrisse: Foundations of the Critique of Political Economy*, Nicolaus, M (trans), 1973, Harmondsworth: Penguin Books

Marx, K, *Theories of Surplus Value, Part 3*, 1971, Moscow: Progress Publishers

Marx, K, *Capital: A Critique of Political Economy Vol. 1*, Eden & Cedar Paul (trans from the 4th German edition), 1930, London: JM Dent

McFarland, T, *Romanticism and the Forms of Ruin*, 1981, Princeton: Princeton University Press

McIntyre, J, *St. Anselm and His Critics: A Reinterpretation of the Cur Deus Homo*, 1954, Edinburgh: Oliver and Boyd

McNeil, JT, *Medieval Handbooks of Penance*, 1938, New York: Columbia University Press

McVeigh, S, Rush, P and Young, A, *A Judgement Dwelling in Law: Violence and the Relations of Legal Thought*, 2002, Princeton: University of Princeton Press

Meens, R, 'The frequency and nature of early medieval penance' in Biller, P and Minnis, AJ (eds), *Handling Sin: Confession in the Middle Ages*, 1998, The University of York Centre for Medieval Studies: Woodbridge Suffolk: Boydell & Brewer, York Medieval Press

Merchant, C, *The Death of Nature: Women, Ecology and the Scientific Revolution*, 1980, New York: Harper & Row

Milton, J, *The Complete Poems of John Milton*, Eliot, CW (ed), 1909, New York: P. F. Collier & Son

Mohanty, CT, 'Introduction' and 'Under Western eyes' in Mohanty, CT, Russo, A and Torres, L (eds), *Third World Women and the Politics of Feminism*, 1991, Bloomington: Indiana University Press

Montaigne, M, *Complete Essays*, Frame, DM (trans), 1958, Stanford CA: Stanford University Press

Morgan, H, 'Transcript: Opening Address to Returned Services League of Australia', Victorian Branch, Annual Conference, 30 June 1993

Moon, TP, *Imperialism and World Politics*, 1927, New York: Macmillan

Morris, C, *The Discovery of the Individual 1050–1200*, 1972, London: Society for Promoting Christian Knowledge

Muchembled, R, *Popular Culture and Elite Culture in France 1400–1750*, Cochrane, L (trans), 1985, Baton Rouge LA: Louisiana State University Press

Mun, T, *England's Treasure by Forraign Trade, or, The Ballance of our Forraign Trade is the Rule of our Treasure*, [1664], 1989, Dusseldorf: Verlag Wirtschaft und Finanzen

Murray, A, 'Confession as a historical source in the thirteenth century' in Davis, RHC and Wallace-Hadrill, JM (eds), *The Writing of History in the Middle Ages: Essays Presented to Richard William Southern*, 1981, Oxford: Clarendon Press

Mykitiuk, R, 'Fragmenting the body' (1994) 2 Australian Feminist Law Journal 63

Nairn, T, *The Break-Up of Britain: Crisis and Neo-nationalism*, 1977, London: NLB

Narayan, D, et al., *From many lands*, 2002, New York: Oxford University Press

Narayan, D, et al., *Can anyone hear us?*, 2000a, New York: Oxford University Press

Narayan, D, et al., *Crying out for change*, 2000b, New York: Oxford University Press

Nancy, J and Lacoue-Labarthe, P, *The Title of the Letter: A Reading of Lacan*, Raffoul, F and Pettigrew, D (trans), 1992, Albany: State University of New York Press

Nandy, A, *The Intimate Enemy: Loss and Recovery of Self under Colonialism*, 1983, Delhi: Oxford University Press

Nietzsche, F, *On the Genealogy of Morals*, Kaufmann, W and Hollingdale, RJ (trans), 1989, New York: Vintage Books

Nietzsche, F, *The Gay Science*, Kaufmann, W (trans), 1974, London: Vintage Books

Nietzsche, F, *Will to Power*, Haufman, W (trans), 1968, London: Vintage Books

Nisbet, R, *Social Change and History: Aspects of the Western Theory of Development*, 1969, Oxford: Oxford University Press

Noll, G 'Salvation by the Grace of the state? Explaining credibility assessment in the asylum procedure,' in Noll, G (ed), *Proof, Evidentiary Assessment and Credibility in Asylum Law*, 2005, Leiden/Boston: Martinus Nijhoff publishers, p 197

O'Donnell, JJ, *Augustine: Confessions*, 1992, Oxford: Clarendon Press

Oliver, K, *Witnessing Beyond Recognition*, 2001, Minneapolis: University of Minnesota

Oppenheim, L, *International Law* (2 vols), 2nd edn, 1912, London: Longmans, Green

Oppenheim, L, 'The science of international law: its task and method' (1908) 2 American Journal of International Law 313

Oppenheim, L, *International law: a Treatise*, 1905, London: Longmans

Orford, A, 'Beyond harmonization: trade, human rights and the economy of sacrifice' (2005) Leiden Journal of International Law 179.

Orford, A, *Narrating Humanitarian Intervention*, 2003, Cambridge: Cambridge University Press

Orford, A, 'Globalisation and the right to development' in Alston, P (ed), *Peoples' Rights*, 2001, Oxford: Oxford University Press

Orford, A, 'Contesting globalization: a feminist perspective on the future of human rights' (1998) 8 Transnational Law and Contemporary Problems 171

Orford, A, 'Locating the international: military and monetary interventions after the Cold War' (1997) 38 Harvard International Law Journal 443

Orford, A, 'The politics of collective security' (1996a) 17 Michigan Journal of International Law 373

Orford, A, 'The uses of sovereignty in the New Imperial Order' (1996b) 6 Australian Feminist Law Journal 63

Orford, A and Beard, J 'Making the state safe for the market: the World Bank's World Development Report 1997' (1998) 22 Melbourne University Law Review 195

Paden, WE, 'Theaters of humility and suspicion' in Martin, LH, Gutman, H, and Hutton, PH (eds), *Technologies of the Self: A Seminar with Michel Foucault*, 1988, Amherst: University of Massachusetts Press

Pahuja, S 'The postcoloniality of international law' (2005) 46:2 Harvard journal of International Law, 459–69

Pahuja, S, 'Technologies of empire: IMF conditionality and the reinscription of the North/South divide' (2000) 13 Leiden Journal of International Law 749

Palmer, RR and Colton, J, *A History of the Modern World*, 3rd edn, 1965, New York: Knopf

Panikkar, KM, *Asia and Western Dominance; a Survey of the Vasco Da Gama Epoch of Asian History, 1498–1945*, 1954, London: Allen & Unwin

Peet, R and Hartwick, E, *Theories of Development*, 1999, New York: Guildford Press

Pennycook, A, *The Cultural Politics of English as an International Language*, 1994, London/New York: Longman

Perry, M, 'When We Landed in Japan', [1854], in Internet Modern History sourcebook created 1997: last revised 9/22/2001, Fordham University: www.fordham.edu/halsall/mod/1854Perry-japan1.html

Pettus, J, *Volatiles from the History of Adam and Eve*, 1674, London: Printed for T. Bassett

Petyt, W, *Britannia Languens, or, A Discourse of Trade*, 1680, London: Printed for T Dring and S Crouch

Phillips, R, *Society, State and Nation in Twentieth Century Europe*, 1996, New Jersey: Prentice Hall

Pietz, W, 'Fetishism and materialism: the limits of theory in Marx' in Apter, E and

Pietz, W (eds), *Fetishism as Cultural Discourse*, 1993, Ithaca NY: Cornell University Press

Plato, 'Phaedrus', Cooper, L et al. (trans), in Hamilton, E and Cairns, H (eds), *The Collected Dialogues of Plato, including the Letters*, 1961, New York: Pantheon Books

Pocock, J, 'Modes of political and historical time in early eighteenth-century England' (1976) 5 Studies in Eighteenth-Century Culture 97

Pollexfen, H, *Of Trade*, 1700, London: Printed for John Baker

Pomian, K, *Collectors and Curiosities: Paris and Venice, 1500–1800*, 1990, Cambridge: Polity Press

Pye, C, *The Vanishing: Shakespeare, the Subject, and Early Modern Culture*, 2000, Durham NC: Duke University Press

Reiss, T, 'Montaigne and the subject of polity' in Parker, P and Quint, D (eds), *Literary Theory/Renaissance Texts*, 1986, Baltimore: John Hopkins University Press

Roling, BVA, *International Law in an Expanded World*, 1960, Amsterdam: Djambatan

Roosevelt, T, 'Backward races must be trained for civilization' [1905] in Hagedorn, H (ed), *Memorial Edition: Works of Theodore Roosevelt, Vol. XVIII*, 1923–1926a, New York: Charles Scribner's sons

Roosevelt, T, 'Forum' [April 1894a] in Hagedorn, H (ed), *Memorial Edition: Works of Theodore Roosevelt, Vol XV*, 1923–1926b, New York: Charles Scribner's sons

Roosevelt, T, 'New world heritage for white civilization' [1894b] in Hagedorn, H (ed), *Memorial Edition: Works of Theodore Roosevelt*, Vol XIV, 1923–1926c, New York: Charles Scribner's sons

Root, J, *Space to Speke: The Confessional Subject in Medieval Literature*, 1997, New York: Peter Lang Publishing

Rose, J, 'The imaginary' in MacCabe, C (ed), *The Talking Cure: Essays in Psychoanalysis and Language*, 1981, London: Macmillan Press

Rosemann, PW, *Understanding Scholastic Thought with Foucault*, 1999, New York: St. Martin's Press

Rushdie, S, *Midnight's Children*, 1995, London: Vintage

Russel, B, *History of Western Philosophy*, 2nd edn, 1961, London: Allen & Unwin

Sachs, W (ed), *The Development Dictionary: A Guide to Knowledge and Power*, 1992, London: Zed Books

Said, E, *Culture and Imperialism*, 1993, London: Chatto & Windus

Said, E, *Orientalism*, 1978, New York: Pantheon Books

Saint Benedict's Rule for Monasteries, Doyle, LJ (trans), 1948, Collegeville, MN: St. John's Abbey Press

Sangari, K, 'The politics of the possible' in JanMohamed, A and Lloyd, D (eds), *The Nature and Context of Minority Discourse*, 1990, New York: Oxford University Press

Santos, B, *Toward a New Legal Common Sense* (2nd edn), 2002, London: LexisNexis/Butterworths

Sawday, J, *The Body Emblazoned: Dissection and the Human Body in Renaissance Culture*, 1995, London: Routledge

Scarry, E, *The Body in Pain: The Making and Unmaking of the World*, 1985, New York: Oxford University Press

Schaff, P, *History of the Christian Church*, 1910, Grand Rapids: Eerdmans

Schmitt, C, *Politische Theologie, Vier Kapitel zur Lehre von der Souveranitat*, 1992, Munich/Leipzig: Duncker & Humbolt

Schmitt, C, *Das Nomos von der Erde*, 1974, Berlin: Duncker & Humbolt

Schroeder, PW, *Metternich's Diplomacy at its Zenith, 1820–1823*, 1962, Austin: University of Texas Press

Schwarzenberger, G, 'The standard of civilisation in international law' (1955) 8 Current Legal Problems 220

Scott, D, 'Colonial governmentality' (1995) 43 Social Text 191

Sennett, R, *The Uses of Disorder*, 1970, New York: Alfred A Knopf

Sessions, WA, *Francis Bacon Revisited*, 1996, New York: Twayne Publishers

Shao, J, 'Alleviating poverty in Africa' in Belshaw, D Calderisi, R and Sugden, C (eds), *Faith in Development: Partnership between the World Bank and the Churches of Africa*, 2001, Oxford: World Bank and Regnum Books International

Shennan, JH, *The Origins of the Modern European State 1450–1725*, 1974, London: Hutchinson's University Library

Sherman, WH, 'Anatomizing the Commonwealth: language, politics, and the Elizabethan social order' in Fowler, E and Greene, R (eds), *The Project of Prose in Early Modern Europe and the New World*, 1997, Cambridge: Cambridge University Press

Shiva, V, *Stolen Harvest: The Hijacking of the Global Food Supply*, 2000, Cambridge, MA: South End Press

Slater, T, 'Moral Aspect of Divine Law' *The Catholic Encyclopædia Vol. IX*, 1999, Online Edition, www.newadvent.org/cathen/09071a.htm

Smith, A, *An Inquiry into the Nature and Causes of the Wealth of Nations* 1993, Oxford: Oxford University Press

Smith, P, *Millennial Dreams: Contemporary Culture and Capital in the North*, 1997, London: Verso

Southern, RW, *Scholastic Humanism and the Unification of Europe*, 1995, Oxford: Blackwell

Southern, RW, *Medieval Humanism and Other Studies*, 1970, Oxford: Blackwell

Southern, RW, *Saint Anselm and His Biographer: A Study of Monastic Life and Thought 1059–1130*, 1963, Cambridge: Cambridge University Press

Southern, RW, *The Making of the Middle Ages*, 1954, London: Hutchinson's University Library

Spence, S, *Texts and the Self in the Twelfth Century*, 1996, Cambridge: Cambridge University Press

Spivak, GC, 'Scattered speculations on the question of value', pp 107–40, and 'Translator's preface and afterword to Mahaseta Devi's "Imaginary Maps", pp 267–86 in Landry, D and MacLean, G (eds) *The Spivak Reader* 1996, London: Routledge

Spivak, GC, *Outside in the Teaching Machine*, 1993, New York: Routledge

Spivak, GC, *The Post-Colonial Critic: Interviews, Strategies, Dialogues*, 1990, New York: Routledge

Spivak, GC, *In Other Worlds: Essays in Cultural Politics*, 1988, New York: Methuen

Spivak, GC, 'Translator's Preface' in Derrida, J, *Of Grammatology*, Spivak, GC (trans), 1976, Baltimore: Johns Hopkins University Press

Stavrakakis, Y, *Lacan and the Political*, 1999, London: Routledge

Stavrianos, LS, *The World Since 1500: A Global History*, 1966, Englewood Cliffs, NJ: Prentice-Hall

Stoler, AL, 'Sexual affronts and racial frontiers: European identities and the cultural politics of exclusion in colonial Southeast Asia' in Brah, A and Coombes, AE (ed), *Hybridity and Its Discontents: Politics, Science, Culture*, 2000, London: Routledge

Stoler, AL, *Race and the Education of Desire: Foucault's History of Sexuality and the Colonial Order of Things*, 1995, Durham NC/London: Duke University Press

Tellenbach, G, *Church, State and Christian Society at the Time of the Investiture Contest*, 1940, Oxford: Blackwell

Tentler, T, *Sin and Confession on the Eve of the Reformation*, 1977, Princeton: Princeton University Press

Tentler, T, 'The summa for confessors as an instrument of social control' in Trinkaus, C and Oberman, HA (eds), *The Pursuit of Holiness in Late Medieval and Renaissance Religion: Papers from the University of Michigan Conference*, 1974, Leiden: EJ Brill

Tertullian, *De paenitentia*, Le Saint, WP (trans), 1959, New York: Newman Press

Tertullian, 'Of baptism' in A Roberts and J Donaldson (eds), *Ante-Nicene Christian Library: Translations of the Writings of the Fathers Down to 325AD, Vol XI: The Writings of Tertullian, Vol I*, 1867–1897, Edinburgh: T and T Clark

Thurston, H, *The Catholic Encyclopedia Vol X*, 1911, New York: Robert Appleton Company

Torpey, J, *The Invention of the Passport: Surveillance, Citizenship and the State*, 2000, Cambridge: Cambridge University Press

Treaty of Westphlia, 24 October, 1648 at www.yale.edu/lawweb/avalon/westphal.htm

Truman, H, 'Inaugural Address' January 20, 1949, www.trumanlibrary.org/calendar/viewpapers.php?pid=1030 administered by the *National Archives and Records Administration*, Harry S. Truman Library & Museum

Tully, J, *An Approach to Political Philosophy: Locke in Contexts*, 1993, Cambridge: Cambridge University Press

Ullmann, W, *The Individual and Society in the Middle Ages*, 1967, London: Methuen & Co Ltd

United Nations Economic and Social Council, First Year, Official Records, Second Session

van der Veer, P, 'The foreign hand: orientalist discourse in sociology and communalism' in Breckenridge, C and van der Veer, P (eds), *Orientalism and the Postcolonial Predicament: Perspectives on South Asia*, 1993, Philadelphia: University of Pennsylvania Press

Verhaeghe, P 'Causation and destitution of a pre-ontological non-entity: on the Lacanian subject' in Nobus, D, 1998, *Key Concepts of Lacanian Psychoanalysis*, London, Rebus Press

Verhaeghe, P, 'Social bond and authority: everyone is the same in front of the law of difference' (2000) 5 Journal for the Psychoanalysis of Culture and Society 91

Voltaire, *Philosophical Letters*, Dilworth, E (trans), 1961, Indianapolis: Bobbs-Merrill

Walker, B, *The Annals of Tacticus: A Study in the Writing of History*, 1952, Manchester: Manchester University Press

Walker, RBJ, 'Foreword' in Edkins, J, Persram, N and Pin-Fat, V (eds), *Sovereignty and Subjectivity*, 1999, London: Lynne Rienner Publishers

Walker, RBJ, 'World politics and western reason: universalism, pluralism, hegemony' in Walker, RBJ (ed), *Culture, Ideology and World Order*, 1982, Colorado: Westview Press

Wallace-Hadrill, M (ed), *The Writing of History in the Middle Ages: Essays presented to Richard William Southern*, 1981, Oxford: Clarendon Press

Warren, ML 'Griselda's "unnatural restraint" as a technology of the self', *ORB Online Encyclopedia*, 1998 at www.the-rb.net/encyclop/culture/lit/griselda.html

Webb, J and Enstice, A, *Aliens and Savages, Fiction, Politics and Prejudice in Australia*, 1988, Sydney: Harper Collins

Webster, C, *The Great Instauration: Science, Medicine, and Reform, 1626–1660*, 1975, London: Duckworth

West, J, *The History of Tasmania* [1852], Shaw, AGL (ed), 1971, Sydney: Angus & Robertson

Westlake, J, *Chapters on the Principles of International Law*, 1894, Cambridge: Cambridge University Press

Wheaton, H, *Elements of International Law: with a Sketch of the History of Science*, 1836, Philadelphia: Carey, Lea & Blanchard

Widder, N, *Genealogies of Difference*, 2002, Urbana-Champaign: University of Illinois Press

Williams, R, *Keywords: A Vocabulary of Culture and Society*, 1988, London: Fontana Press

Wood, I, 'The Vita Columbani and Merovingian hagiography', (1982) 1 Peritia 63

Woodhead, L, *Christianity: A Very Short Introduction*, 2004, Oxford: Oxford University Press

World Bank, *World Development Report 2000–2001: Attacking Poverty*, 2000, Oxford: Oxford University Press

Zepp LaRouche, H, '*Keynote Speech, Alternatives to War and Depression: The LaRouche Doctrine*', delivered to an Executive Intelligence Review seminar in Washington, DC, May 5, 1999 www.schillerinstitute.org/strategic/hzl_t_of_w_0599.html

Zizek, S, *Tarrying With the Negative: Kant, Hegel, and the Critique of Ideology*, 1993, Durham NC: Duke University Press

Zizek, S, *For They Know Not What They Do: Enjoyment as a Political Factor*, 1991, London: Verso

Zizek, S, 'Beyond discourse-analysis' in Laclau, E (ed), *New Reflections on The Revolution of Our Time*, 1990, London: Verso

Zizek, S, *The Sublime Object of Ideology*, 1989, New York: Verso

Index